Pottersfield Press

THE MASKED RIDER

Cycling in West Africa

by Neil Peart

Pottersfield Press
Lawrencetown Beach
Nova Scotia, Canada

Canadian Cataloguing in Publication Data

Peart, Neil.
     Masked rider
     ISBN 1-895900-02-6

1. Peart, Neil — Journeys — Africa, West. 2. Africa, West — Description and
travel. 3. Bicycle touring — Africa, West. I. Title

DT472.P42 1996   966.03'29   C96-950140-4

Acknowledgement is made for use of quoted material from the following:
Aristotle. *Ethics*. London: Penguin, 1953.
Van Gogh, Vincent. *Dear Theo*. Edited by Irving Stone. New York: Doubleday, 1937.
Crowther, Geoff. *Africa on a Shoestring*. South Yarra, Australia: Lonely Planet, 1986.

Cover design by Hugh Syme
Back cover photograph: "Checking the map with the Chief of Tchevi" by
                        David Mozer
Inset by Elenora Alberto
All other photographs by the author

Pottersfield Press gratefully acknowledges the ongoing support of the Nova
Scotia Department of Education, Cultural Affairs Division, as well as the
Canada Council and Department of Canadian Heritage.

Pottersfield Press
Lawrencetown Beach
RR 2 Porters Lake
Nova Scotia, Canada B0J 2S0

Printed in Canada

To my mother and father
Who brought me up to know better...

Continuing thanks to Mark Riebling and Danny Peart
for criticism and advice
And to Jackie and Selena
for allowing the time

MOROCCO

TUNISIA

ALGERIA

LIBYA

EGYPT

MAURITANIA

MALI

NIGER

CHAD

SUDAN

DJIBOUTI

SENEGAL

GAMBIA

GUINEA-BISSAU

BURKINA FASO

GUINEA

2

NIGERIA

ETHIOPIA

SIERRA LEONE

IVORY COAST

1

CENTRAL AFRICAN REPUBLIC

SOMALIA

LIBERIA

GHANA

3

EQ. GUINEA

ZAIRE

UGANDA

KENYA

GABON

RWANDA

CONGO

BURUNDI

TANZANIA

1- TOGO

2-BENIN

3-CAMEROON

ANGOLA

MALAWI

ZAMBIA

MOZAMBIQUE

ZIMBABWE

NAMIBIA

BOTSWANA

SWAZILAND

SOUTH AFRICA

LESOTHO

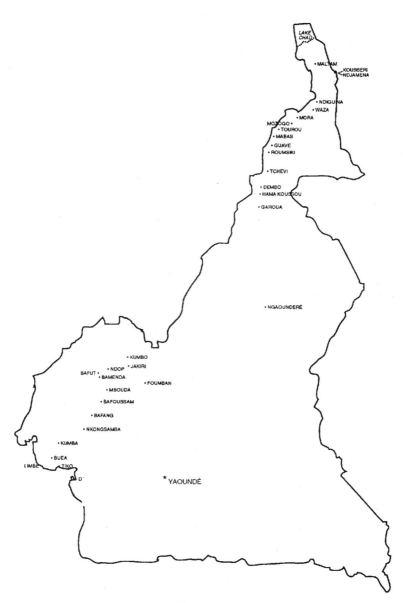

LAKE
CHAD

• MALTAM
KOUSSERI
NDJAMENA

• NDIGUINA
• WAZA
• MORA
MOZOGO •
• TOUROU
• MABAS
• GUAVE
• ROUMSIKI

• TCHEVI

• DEMBO
• HAMA KOUSSOU

• GAROUA

• NGAOUNDERÉ

• KUMBO
• JAKIRI
BAFUT • • NDOP
• BAMENDA
• FOUMBAN
• MBOUDA
• BAFOUSSAM
• BAFANG
• NKONGSAMBA
• KUMBA
• BUEA
LIMBE TIKO
D.

* YAOUNDÉ

Cameroon

It is said that one travels to East Africa for the animals, and to West Africa for the people. My first dream of Africa was a siren-call from the East African savanna ... great herds of wildlife shimmering in the heat haze of the Serengeti, the Rift Valley lakes swarming with birds, the icy summit of Kilimanjaro. So I went there, and I loved it. The following year I went looking for an interesting way to visit West Africa, to learn more about the African *people* — the animals drew me to Africa, but the people brought me back.

After much searching I found a name: Bicycle Africa, and signed up for a month-long tour of "Cameroon: Country of Contrasts." At the end of it I swore I'd never do anything like *that* again — but the following year I forgot my vow, and returned to bicycle through Togo, Ghana, and the Ivory Coast.

Cycling is a good way to travel anywhere, but especially in Africa; you are independent and mobile, and yet travel at "people speed" — fast enough to move on to another town in the cooler morning hours, but slow enough to meet the people: the old farmer at the roadside who raises his hand and says "You are welcome," the tireless woman who offers a shy smile to a passing cyclist, the children whose laughter transcends the humblest home. The unconditional welcome to tired travelers is part of the charm, but it is also what is simply African: the villages and markets, the way people live and work, their cheerful (or at least stoic) acceptance of adversity, and their rich culture: the music, the magic, the carvings — the masks of Africa.

Africa is such a network of illusions, a double-faced mask. It is as difficult to see into it as it is to see out of it. To those who've never been there it is an utter mystery, a continent veiled in myths and mistaken impressions, but it is equally obscure to those who have never been anywhere else. It used to be said that electronic media would bring the world closer together, but too often the focus on the sensational only distorts the reality — drives us farther apart. That is why in Ghana the children followed me down the street chanting "Rambo! Rambo!" and that is why Canadians look at me as if I were a lunatic when I tell them I've been cycling in Africa — they can only picture it from wildlife documentaries, TV images of starvation camps, and old Tarzan movies.

Africa fascinates me — in the true sense, I suppose, as a snake is said to transfix its prey. And the more times I return, the more countries I visit, the more the place perplexes me. Africa has so much magic, but so much madness. Yet I keep returning, and surely will again. This attraction is compelling and seems to grow stronger, but, like any lasting relationship, it is no longer blind.

And maybe that's always true. After the first infatuation we're always most critical of what we *feel* the strongest about. It's too often the case in relationships, and certainly regarding one's own family or country. You can criticize your own, but don't let anyone *else* try it. That's when love shows its teeth.

If my attraction to Africa is no longer blind, it is still blurry. From within and without, Africa is as much the "Dark Continent" as it was two hundred years ago — hard to see into, hard to see out of. The mask obscures a face which is so complex and contradictory; it takes a lot of traveling even to get a sense of it. And traveling in Africa is, by necessity, adventure travel.

Some people travel for pleasure, and sometimes find adventure; others travel for adventure, and sometimes find pleasure. The best part of adventure travel, it seems to me, is *thinking* about it. A journey to a remote place is exciting to look forward to, certainly rewarding to look back upon, but not always pleasurable to live minute by minute. Reality has a tendency to be so uncomfortably *real*.

But that's the price of admission — you have to do it. One reason for making such a journey is to experience the mystery of unknown places, but another, perhaps more important, reason is to take yourself out of your "context" — home, job, and friends. Travel is its own reward, but traveling among strangers can show you as much about yourself as it does about them. To your companions and the people you encounter *you* are the stranger; to them you are a brand-new person.

That's something to think about, and if you try you might glimpse yourself that way, without a past, without a context, without a mask. That can be a little scary, no question, but you may get a look behind someone else's mask as well, and that can be even scarier.

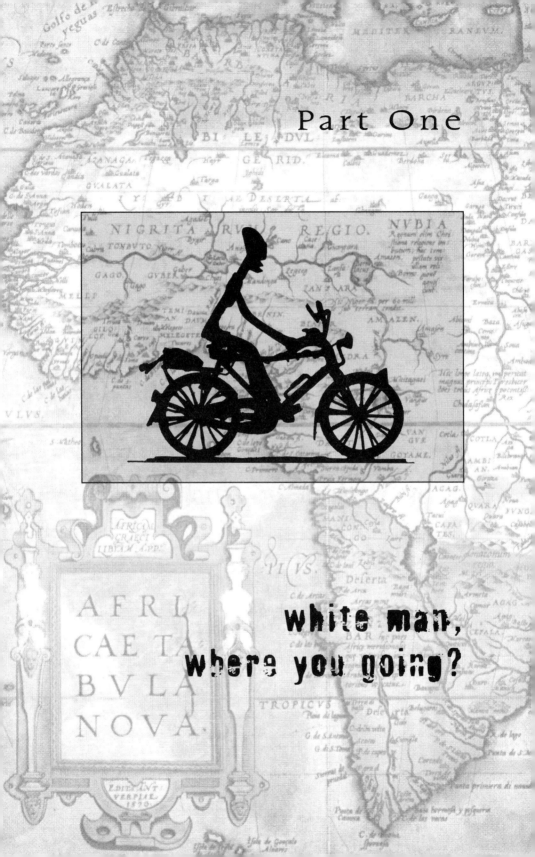

Part One

white man, where you going?

Northern Cameroon — Country estate in picturesque village. Spectacular view. Traditional design in stone, Old World charm, room for the whole family. Open fireplace, rooftop pantry, close to fields and market. Only one mile to modern CARE well, easy commute to Roumsiki, scenic three-day walk to telephone. Mexican hats included. MAKE AN OFFER!

inferno

The first traveler's tale of Cameroon reaches us from the fifth century B.C., when the Phoenician explorer Hanno led an expedition around the west coast of Africa. His fleet of sixty ships reached present-day Senegal, and Hanno attempted to land there, but was soon driven back by the local warriors. He sailed on past forested mountains and wide rivers, afraid to go ashore because of the hippopotamuses and crocodiles (it would appear Hanno wasn't the most stalwart of explorers). He came upon an island which looked safe at first, but when he tried to land he was frightened off again, this time by "fires and strange music." And once more, he ran away, stating,

> Sailing quickly away thence, we passed by a country burning with fires and perfumes and streams of fire supplied then fell into the sea. The country was impassable on account of the great heat. We sailed quickly thence being much terrified and passing on for four days we discovered at night a country full of fire. In the middle was a lofty fire which seemed to touch the stars.

Next morning, just before Hanno "sailed quickly away" again, this time for home, he saw a mountain of fire which he named *Theon Ochema*: the Chariot of the Gods. Being "much terrified," Hanno was no doubt given to exaggeration, but Mount Cameroon, the only live volcano in West Africa, is said to be that great mountain of fire which kept the tourists out of Cameroon for another two thousand years.

Then, in the sixteenth century, the Portuguese navigator Vasco da Gama cruised by and dropped anchor in the Wouri River. He stood at the rail and admired the small crustaceans in the water, and decided to name the river after them: Rio-des-Cameroes, "River of Prawns." Thus the Portuguese called their "discovery" Cameroes, until 1887 when the Germans claimed the land and called it Kamerun. After World War I it was taken from Germany and divided between the French, who called it Cameroun, and the English, who called it The Cameroons. What the people who lived there called it is not recorded, but no doubt it had nothing to do with small crustaceans.

• • •

By the time I got to Cameroon, in November 1988, the country was once again in the hands of the people who lived there. I saw no mountain of fire, and I saw no prawns, but my first impression of Cameroon was not unlike Hanno's: heat and darkness and fires, a strange inferno which *did* seem to suggest "sailing quickly away thence." The air was heavy, even at sunset, and the exertion of assembling my bicycle outside the airport left me dripping. Among a confusion of upended frames, wheels, bike-bags, and tools, a crowd of boys gathered around to watch me and a few other North Americans struggle with our handlebar stems and seat posts. I kept an uneasy watch on my possessions, and thought about cycling around Cameroon for a month in that kind of heat. A month can be a long time.

We pedaled away from the airport into the sudden equatorial night, following the broken shoulder of the highway into the city. A few dim streetlamps lit the skeletons of abandoned cars and uneven rows of gray plank and cinder-block houses. Corrugated-metal roofs gleamed among the looming, ivy-hung trees. Scattered oil-drum fires flickered on dark faces, flashing eyes, and teeth bared in demonic laughter that was drowned by the music which raged out from everywhere. Indecipherable wailing chants and pulsing rhythms chugged out of straining loudspeakers as I tried to find a path through the crowds. People turned to stare, evidently surprised to see a white man in a funny hat riding a bicycle.

One of the oil-drum fires lighted a member of our group at the roadside, where he had stopped to ask directions. The light flickered on his curly dark hair and beard, framing close-set eyes and vaguely Middle-Eastern features. That was David, our guide from Bicycle Africa — also, we learned, its founder, director, and secretary. "My office looks suspiciously like my bedroom," he confessed with a laugh.

Only later did David tell us that "Cameroon: Country of Contrasts" was "the most difficult bicycle tour on the market." He had been advertising it for two years and could only attract four customers. Us. He had led a tour of Cameroon just once before, two years earlier, with only three clients, one of whom, like Hanno, had turned around and gone home in less than a week. Had I known these things as I followed David's white helmet through the shadowy crowds, my excitement might have been tempered. But that's the good part about the future: it doesn't have to contain any flaws until it becomes the present.

I had enough to worry about in the dark here-and-now of crowded streets, sudden taxis, motorcycles, and crater-sized potholes. Everything seemed to blare like car horns: the music, the smells, the faces, the headlights, all in dizzy confusion. I tried to concentrate on my riding and keep an eye on David up ahead. I didn't want to miss a turn and get lost in the gauntlet of madness which seemed to comprise Douala, the largest city in Cameroon.

We made our way to the Hôtel Kontchupé, a chain of low buildings on a narrow street above the waterfront, where I could see the lights in the rigging of a small freighter. We parked our bicycles on a terrace fenced with black wrought iron. A mural decorated one mustard-colored wall, a montage of musical instruments, masks, and a pre-Cubist angular figure raising what looked like a martini glass.

Three of us moved along the terrace to the Café des Sports while David spoke with the manager in "survival French," the same kind I possessed. Still too early in the evening for nightlife; the bar was empty and smelled of stale beer and cigarette smoke. The young bartender was just putting on a record, and West African rhythms pumped out of the speakers. The walls were decorated with lurid black-light posters of skeletal bikers and voluptuous leather-clad females. After a long look around, the three of us took a seat at the bar.

Usually when I begin a trip like that, the hardest thing is learning everybody's name. You meet ten or twenty people at one time and their names float right through your head, or, as often happens, your brain assigns them names which suit them, but aren't necessarily *theirs*. You put on an open-friendly face, try to make neutral conversation, and wait for someone else to address them by name. This time, though, it would be easy — only five people on the tour, and I knew two of their names already: David's and my own.

I helped my two companions order drinks, as they were from California, where French is normally limited to Chardonnay and Perrier. I was getting their names now. Leonard was the tall black guy with the thick rimless glasses, and Elsa was the older woman, slender, with short pale hair and sharp features. No problem. Then a commotion outside intruded, even over the loud music, and the three of us moved to the door. A Japanese taxi was pulled up in front of the hotel, and David was helping the driver lift a boxed bicycle out of the trunk. Our fifth rider had arrived, and she stood looking on, her hands moving as if she wanted to help but didn't know what to do. I couldn't remember her name from the roster, but David came to my rescue. "This is Annie." While I shook her hand I tried to stamp it into my memory. Okay, Annie. Leonard is the tall black guy; Elsa is the older woman, and Annie is the long dark hair with the open-mouth smile.

Annie joined us in the bar, still smiling, her hands still tending to move as if she wanted to help but didn't know what to do. Someone asked about her job, described on the roster as systems analyst.

"The ultimate post-modern job description," I said with a laugh.

"Um, well ... heh heh ... it's the best definition I could think of for a kind of ... um ... *everything* job," Annie said, and we nodded and smiled and made small talk with the conscious politeness of strangers who know they are going to be living together for a month. A month can be a long time.

David returned to lead us to our rooms, back into the hotel side of the building and through a maze of stairs and corridors, something M.C. Escher might have drawn. One room for the men, one for the women, and all of us sharing a dingy toilet which crouched in a closet along the zigzag hall. An arched doorway led into our room: green linoleum floor, dark ceiling of peeling wood, and walls of grimy white stucco decorated with an incongruous Afro—Arabian-gypsy-disco kind of hanging. Naked bulbs in the corners spread feeble light down over two drooping beds. The bar downstairs was warming up for the night, and the music vibrated up through the walls.

Having inspected the room, we decided to go out for something to eat. Just as we stepped off the terrace of the Hôtel Kontchupé, one of a group of men standing there called out to us. It appeared to be a warning, but the rudimentary French which David and I possessed could not decipher it. Then I realized he was pointing at my leather beltpack, and telling me to be careful against thieves.

Now I had just finished reading a section in *Africa On A Shoestring* on Douala:

> "It isn't a particularly pleasant place: mosquitoes and muggings are both problems at night, so watch out. Even during the day you may well find suspicious-looking people following you around waiting for the right opportunity."

So although my bag was firmly attached around my waist, I closed one hand around it and put on what I hoped was a menacing face. As we turned the corner into the main street, David suggested that in a place like Douala he made it a point to walk down the *middle* of the street at night. It seemed like an excellent idea.

Unlike the part of town we had ridden through earlier, this was not an area of nightlife. No inferno here; in the humid half-light it wore the air of a decadent avenue after midnight. Lone cars whisked by at intervals. The sparse streetlights were further attenuated by thick trees, ferns growing between the limbs and vines along the branches. Most of the store windows were protected by iron grilles, guarding displays of cheap furniture, appliances, stereo equipment, and even a croissant shop.

A row of trestle-tables along the sidewalk offered the only life and the only visible commerce, a kind of on-the-street convenience store selling food, drinks, and cigarettes. David spoke to a threadbare man who tended a glowing brazier, and we sat down on a rough wooden bench while he cracked eggs into a pan.

The dark boulevard was called the Boulevard du Président Ahmadou Ahidjo, and I'd learned something about that name. Ahidjo had been the president of Cameroon from independence in 1961 until 1982, when he stepped down in favor of his chosen successor, the current president Paul Biya. For some reason Ahidjo changed his mind, and in 1984 attempted a coup from outside the country. Though unsuccessful, there was bloody fighting in the streets of Yaoundé, the capital city, and the aftermath was sweeping. Ahidjo had represented the Islamic northerners, many of whom were purged from the government. Strikes were banned, the national press became a propaganda puppet, foreign journalists came under continual harassment, and the government adopted unlimited powers to suppress dissidence. Amnesty International claims that Cameroon keeps hundreds of political prisoners imprisoned without trial. The most visible effect to us would be that, because the coup had been engineered from outside Cameroon, a deep suspicion of foreigners was forged. For the next month we would travel under the shadow of that xenophobia.

The omelette man delivered his wares one at a time, lifting the fried circles of smashed eggs onto plastic plates, then passing us a boxful of cutlery. The omelette was excellent, spiced with sausage and pimento. By the glow of a kerosene lamp, small talk flickered among our group, and I smiled to be alone among strangers once again, in a place I'd barely heard of just a few months before.

We strolled a little farther along the quiet street, everything indistinct and a little spooky in the shadow of the trees, and reached a corner where a closed gas station served as a gathering place for a crowd of lounging youths. When they turned toward us and began to mutter among themselves, David suggested it might be prudent to retrace our steps to the hotel.

The walls of our room still rocked with the exuberant music from the downstairs bar, which had modulated into a series of American '50s rock. But I had no trouble falling into a deep sleep, even to the throbbing lullaby of "Rock Around The Clock."

• • •

Though the Hôtel Kontchupé was in the heart of the city, I awoke to the sound of roosters, as I would nearly every morning in Cameroon. We packed our belongings into our panniers and hung them on the bikes, then pedaled a short way down Boulevard de Président Ahidjo to the croissant shop. The morning was already hot, though the sky was white with overcast, as we lined our bikes together against a tree and took a table by the street.

People hurried past along the sidewalk, the men wearing western-style trousers and light-colored shirts, though a few wore the long Islamic robes of white cotton. Some women dressed in blouses and modest skirts, but most seemed to be clad in the colorful print wraps called *pagnes*, which covered them from the waist to the ankles, with a matching headscarf and a plain blouse. They were handsome people, strong well-formed bodies walking proudly, and their features were often arrayed in a nearly circular symmetry of mouth and eyebrows, sometimes suggesting a moon-face. We looked raw and pink and conspicuous, except for Leonard, and men and women alike turned to look at us. But these were sophisticated urbanites. They never broke stride.

After strong coffee and rolls, we climbed back on the bicycles and rode out into the traffic. Concrete buildings of two or three storeys were painted in pale colors, but stained by mold and smoke, their walls hung with crumbling balconies and weathered shutters. Slender palms curved overhead, while giant ferns and exotic shrubs crowded over the walls like clusters of green swords. I moved in behind Leonard, and as we pedaled through town I watched his gray T-shirt darken with sweat.

We covered the last-minute errands: changing money, buying the postcards and stamps which would not be available where we were going. During a quick tour of the artisan's market we were urged by the voices and gestures of the merchants to spend some time and money with them, but we only scanned the carvings, spears, masks, drums, and brass figurines. As David pointed out, "If you're thinking seriously about buying anything, you'd better think seriously about carrying it around for a thousand miles."

By mid-morning the heat had become an electric blanket, and even the trees appeared to droop over the roadway, wilting in the humid swelter. It was already apparent that Elsa was going to have trouble, as we waited for her at every intersection and stop. (Basic rule of bike touring: Always wait for the next rider at a turn, and the last rider should never be left alone.) But, at sixty years old, Elsa was entitled to allowances, and a slower rider is not necessarily a problem among a faster group. You see more by stopping occasionally to wait for them than you would by pedaling steadily along, and it can be more relaxing to hang back and take it easy. I made a mental resolution to try to be more relaxed in my own pace, not be so driven and urgent to reach the destination every day. I would take time to enjoy it; I would stay back with Elsa.

At last we were on our way out of town. A long, crumbling causeway traversed the Wouri River (the one Vasco da Gama had named the River of Prawns) wide and shallow near its delta, then led us into a low-lying coastal region. Heavy waving reeds and grasses on either side of the road gave way to tall palms and opaque deciduous trees. Occasional patches of pond and swamp opened among the greenery, and made a home for water birds like the Hamerkop, a peculiar bird I'd come to know in East Africa.

The Hamerkop is a small brown heron, named for its ice-axe-shaped head. It is known as "The Lightning Bird," or "The King of Birds" to Africans, and is enshrined in myth and legend. East Africans call it the King of Birds because of its palatial taste in residences, for each year a pair of Hamerkops selects a tree overhanging the water, then spends three months (a long time in birdland) building a roughly spherical mass of sticks up to six feet in diameter, with a small side entrance. Once the family has been raised and the home abandoned, it will be replaced by a new palace every year, and the huge nest will provide tenement living for other creatures: snakes, rodents, insects, owls, and penthouse-dwelling hawks.

Just after I passed a third Hamerkop stalking a choked waterway, I had to pull over and stop on the shoulder while a herd of longhorn cattle plodded across, tended by a stick-wielding farmer. Straddling the bike, I reached down for my plastic bottle and squeezed the warm water into my mouth. The farmer waved and smiled as he passed me, but his features were strangely twisted. His mouth smiled, but his brows were knit in dubious wonder.

High noon in Africa is an expressive enough description of the heat. An hour's cycling had taken me about twelve miles, an average cruising speed, but I felt as if I'd been *racing*. My whole body streamed with sweat, and I was already working on my second water bottle. Spying the burned-out hulk of a car at the roadside, I wheeled in beside it and rested one foot on its rust-blotched fender. I was surprised to see how much of a car can burn, and how much can melt; the rear view mirrors had drooped down the side like a Dali painting.

Leonard pulled up behind me, taking the red bandana from around his neck and wiping his face and trim beard, cleaning the rimless glasses, then swallowing a draft of water. Another bandana, a blue one, covered his head (he was the only one of us who didn't wear a helmet) and he was sweating furiously. I was astonished to see him pull off his T-shirt and actually *wring it out* between his hands, a stream of water dripping to the ground. "Elsa's just a bit behind me," he said. "She's having a rough time, I've had to wait for her a lot."

I agreed to stay back with her for awhile, and he was gone down the road. I noticed for the first time what a relaxed and confident riding style he had, strong runner's legs spinning slowly, and his long body centered easily in the saddle. The previous night Leonard had told me he did a lot of running, and I'd also learned that he was a Vietnam veteran — days he referred to as "when I worked for the government." Now he worked for IBM as an electrical engineer, and his favorite thing, he told me, was flying gliders, "when I can afford it."

I baked by the burned-out car for twenty minutes until Elsa coasted to a stop behind me, gasping and slumping over the handlebars. "Doesn't David ever *stop*?" she said, with petulance on her sharp features and a hint of despair in her voice. "This heat..."

"We're going to stop soon. He knows a place at the crossroads up ahead where we can buy some drinks."

"How *far* up ahead? I feel all light-headed."

"Not far," I lied, thinking that if twelve miles of flat road was giving her such a rough time, she could be in for worse. At sixty years old, it was her first bicycle tour, though the previous night she'd made a point of telling us she'd been training for three months, swimming every day, and had once done a seventy-five-mile bike ride. (Uh ... *once?*) But she seemed to be fit enough; more worrisome was her "externalizing." Blaming David, the heat, the distance. Her face was a mask of bitterness, and I tried to cheer her up.

"Yeah, the first day, with the jet lag and everything, sometimes it hits you that way. It happened to me on the first day of a bike tour once, in Spain, when I suddenly conked out in the afternoon. Same thing, I went all light-headed. It was a horrible feeling."

Finally she pushed off down the road and I fell in behind her, pedaling slowly to match her unsteady pace and pulling up at her frequent stops. Elsa hadn't learned how to drink from her water bottle while riding, and so had to stop each time she wanted a drink. Maybe she just wanted to stop. I could imagine the dark cloud in her brain and didn't say anything more.

When the crossroads finally came into view, I saw three bicycles leaning against the porch of a small brown building, and three riders sitting on benches in the shade with bottles of soda. Signs on the wall behind them advertised Guinness beer: "It's Good For You," Canada Dry: *"C'est Cool,"* and other drinks and cigarettes in a mixture of French and English.

Elsa and I leaned our bikes beside the others, and she stumbled across the porch and lay back on one of the benches, both arms raised over her face. I bought another bottle of spring water for myself, and then brought out a Fanta orange for Elsa. She half-rose enough to drink it down, then collapsed back again. But when I stepped away to take a photo of her "in repose," she suddenly leaped up, dashed to her bicycle, pulled out her camera and handed it to me, then hopped back to the bench and resumed her state of supine exhaustion. I took her picture.

We turned west at the crossroads, onto a quiet road bordered by shoulder-high grass and dense rainforest. The roar of passing diesels was replaced by the ceaseless whirr of insects — *big*-sounding insects. David and I rode together at the back of the pack, pedaling easily along the paved road. The keychain thermometer on my handlebar bag showed ninety degrees. A flattened reptile lay pressed into the pavement, a dry and stiff length of skin.

I began to notice brown lumps on the road, scattered like crushed seedpods. Looking closer as my wheels passed over one, I saw that it resembled a giant worm, with a segmented carapace and macerated insides. But, I mean a *giant* worm, about six inches long and two inches thick, and I remarked to David that these were even more revolting than the slugs of his native Pacific Northwest.

"Nah," he grinned, "just everyday old millipedes."

I asked David when he'd started bicycle touring, and he told me he'd first crossed the United States nearly twenty years before. I was impressed by his story of back-to-back touring days of two hundred miles, a punishing distance even to do *once*, on an unladen bicycle, let alone for days on end with a loaded touring bike. After college David had signed up as a Peace Corps volunteer in Liberia, and had brought his bike with him to that small West African country. When his two-year teaching stint was up, he'd set out to explore more of the continent, eventually traveling through more than half of the countries in Africa.

From those experiences had come the International Bicycling Fund, which he established to lobby for cyclists, and especially to promote cycling as transportation for the Third World. Then came Bicycle Africa, to introduce westerners to East and West Africa by this friendly and efficient mode of transport, and also to introduce Africans to the sight of white people in funny hats riding bicycles. He was a good guide too, even knew the names of birds.

A black and white crow flapped across the road ahead of us, and David raised a hand from the bars to indicate it. "Pied Crow, probably the most common bird in West Africa." I saw that its name derived from the white "T-shirt" over its chest and wings. Higher up a dark bird of prey circled above the forest, wings held out motionless and its wedge-shaped tail acting as rudder, angling sharply to one side and the other.

"Some kind of kite," offered David, not very scientifically.

Although most of Cameroon is poor agricultural land, much of it dry grasslands, and eighty per cent of the people survive on subsistence farming, in this coastal area near Mount Cameroon the soil was rich, and the rainfall plentiful. Rainforests and plantations of rubber trees, banana, and oil palms crowded up to the road, and above all rose the silk-cotton trees, towering two hundred feet and more. They stood in solitary grandeur, smooth elephant-gray trunks rising way up to graceful fans of leaves.

Elsa had fallen behind again, and David stopped to wait for her while I pedaled on ahead to catch Leonard and Annie. Together we stopped in the shade of a mango tree. A small house stood nearby, its walls of gray planks decorated with a few beer and soft-drink signs. A design of bottle caps had been pressed into the clean-swept earth in front. There was no sign of anyone. Goats, chickens, and pigs wandered freely around the house, scratching and rooting for food as we rested in the shade and drank from our water bottles. I started a chorus of "Underneath The Mango Tree," and Leonard laughed me into silence just as David and Elsa came riding up. Elsa was grateful for another break.

"I like it here," I said to no one in particular.

"Yeah, it's a nice spot," said David. "When we get to the north, where it's *really* hot," (Elsa's eyes flashed at this) "it's nice to find a place like this in the late morning, and take a siesta for a couple of hours. Otherwise the midday heat just sucks the strength right out of you."

Another cyclist rolled by, an African man in his forties wearing a straw hat and riding a battered old Chinese bike with two large baskets sagging to either side. I remarked that this was the root of the name "panniers" — French for baskets — which we gave to our saddlebags, and this cyclist's *true* panniers were weighed down with a five-gallon plastic container on each side, both of which seemed to be full. That would be twice the weight that any of us was carrying, with the exception of David, whose mountain bike was loaded with panniers over the front *and* rear wheels, carrying a selection of arcane tools, bike parts, books, maps, water filter, waterbags, and items he had brought as presents, like calendars, T-shirts, and International Bicycle Fund newsletters, in addition to his clothes and bedroll.

When I finally rose from the comfortable mango tree and pushed my bike back to the road, I noticed a home-made sign, posted where a trail led away between the ragged palms:

D A N G E R
KOKE BRIDGE IS VERY-UN SAFE
YOU ARE CROSSING IT
AT A VERY BIG RISK

But we weren't going that way.

Another two hours of paved road brought us to the Airport Hotel near Tiko. No airport appeared on the map, and none was visible from the road, but as we stood before the wrought-iron gates of the hotel a sudden roar burst into the air, and a big airplane banked steeply just above the trees. Leonard identified it as an American C4-B, a four-engine military cargo plane ("working for the government" had educated him well in the machines of war). No one could imagine what it might be doing in the tiny village of Tiko, as we shaded our eyes and watched it drone into the distance, disappearing into the clouds toward the long shadow of Mount Cameroon.

That mountain was a looming presence in our future, as we knew that in two days we would be cycling up to the highest town on its shoulder. Mount Cameroon is a broad-shouldered old volcano (*Theon Ochema*, the Chariot Of The Gods) and it is the tallest mountain in West Africa. Its seaward slopes attract the abundant rain; the coastal town of Debundscha is said to be the second-wettest place in the world, drenched by over a thousand centimeters of rain annually. In contrast, the dry north of Cameroon, where we would end our travels, receives only *fifty-four* centimeters a year.

The Airport Hotel was surrounded by high walls of concrete and spiked wrought-iron, its name printed on a billboard showing Mickey Mouse, Donald Duck, and a large bottle of orange pop, with the slogan "My Friend Fanta." Behind the sliding iron gate was a wide terrace roofed in sheets of corrugated metal, and behind it the two-storey concrete building. For all its fortifications, the place seemed deserted, but David eventually found a sleepy young guy who sold us cold drinks from the bar, and told us it would take a while for the rooms to be ready.

David and Elsa took the benches and quickly fell asleep, while I sat with Leonard and Annie, talking quietly. A curious poster was pasted to the wall, just under a "Guinness Is Good For You" sign:

DON'T HELP IN THE TRANSMISSION OF AIDS
with a cartoon of a young couple cuddling on a bench.
"You and me," *says the boy, in blue trousers and shirt, and penny loafers.*
"Until death," *replies the corn-rolled and modestly dressed girl.*
**STICK TO ONE PARTNER OR SAME
PARTNERS IN CASE OF POLYGAMY**

It was nearly dark before we finally hauled our bikes up the stairs, once again divided by gender into two rooms. Ours was large, though furnished with a single small bed, and the plastered walls were grubby and scarred by smashed insects and the afterthought of electrical wiring. An antiquated air conditioner chugged ineffectually beneath the glass-louvered window, and the linoleum was crusted with grime like the floor of a gas station.

We did have the unexpected luxury of an "en suite" bathroom, a cube of raw concrete with stained fixtures and a shower-head which spilled unheated water onto the floor. But even a cold shower was welcome, and with clean clothes on I felt revived and ready for the walk into Tiko in search of food.

I had noticed all day that no one wore shorts, except very small children, no matter how warm it was. David told us it was a matter of modesty, but it was acceptable for us to wear shorts while on the bikes, being *"sportifs."* He had already advised the women to wear long pants or a skirt whenever they were off their bikes, and suggested that Leonard and I would feel more comfortable if we dressed according to local customs. I don't know if "comfortable" is the word, as it was often damned unpleasant pulling on long trousers in ninety degree heat, but we agreed that we didn't want to offend anyone.

You had to blame the missionaries. The West Africans had once gone about comfortably and suitably naked, or nearly so, and it had been the prudish missionaries, so often the emissaries of western civilization, who had convinced the Africans that God wanted them to wear trousers, shirts, and dresses. Though Africa has finally thrown off the white man's rule, some things, though alien to the African world-view, had been planted too deep — commerce, politics, real estate, colonial borders, and prudery. When Cameroon gained its independence in 1961, the new government even issued a directive that women were to dress "decently and modestly," meaning no more naked breasts.

The road into town was unlighted, and Leonard and I tried to pick out a path with our flashlights. An occasional passing car blinded us, and with the night sky shrouded in black clouds it was as if we moved through a tunnel. Small groups of people, all but invisible, appeared suddenly before us, then passed on, talk and laughter carrying on the air.

The road ended suddenly, and we stumbled through the ruts of the village streets. David led us to the market, where a few oil-drum fires flickered on people carrying boxes and baskets from the kiosks to a cluster of cars, gleams of glass and metal in the darkness. The market appeared to be closing, though music still blared from every direction, each speaker trying to outdo the other in volume, if not in fidelity. Again the Inferno image came to mind as I walked apprehensively through this purgatory of people, fires, mysterious darkness, and loud, sensual music. Just like Hanno, scared by "fires and strange music."

David asked a passing man where we might find some food. He stared at us for a moment, then waved toward a passageway which led inside the market. The four of us followed David in dumb procession. I kept a hand on my beltpack. We stopped at a few kiosks while David asked if there was any food available. They all shook their heads, so we turned back and wandered down a narrow rutted street, a single weak streetlamp making it seem all the darker.

At the Park Hotel, another seedy-looking building of cinder-block and wrought-iron, we were sent up an outside stairway to a small empty dining room. We sat around an oilcloth-covered table and admired the peacock-blue walls decorated with posters of body-builders, "WORLD SUPERSTARS '89." (In 1988!) Naturally, banal comments were made about grotesquely overdeveloped bodies.

Another poster drew my attention: a cartoon figure of a woman in profile, with her lips padlocked shut. But it *wasn't* a joke!

Keep Our Secrets Tight
There would be the greatest peace on earth
When on every bad mouth a padlock is hung
Do you want a long, good life, then watch
your tongue and keep your lips from gossips
and lies.

On another wall, a chalkboard listed the menu, but chicken and rice were the only recognizable offerings among the unknown names. I wondered about *fufu*, *ugali*, and *ndole*, and Leonard wondered about a beer. Elsa brought out some photographs of her grandchildren and passed them around, while Annie made a sketch of the girl with the padlocked lips. Our voices reverberated in the bright room. No one appeared to take our order.

Finally a round-faced young fellow in a white shirt pushed through the beaded curtain and came up to the table, and David asked him in French if there was any food.

Non.

David nodded, unsurprised, and asked if we might get some omelettes. The sober-faced young man turned and left.

"Are we going to get fed?" asked Elsa.

"I *think* so," David said, "maybe he's gone to buy some eggs."

The adjacent kitchen suddenly came alive, and in a few minutes the round-faced waiter brought us spicy omelettes, bread, and hot water for tea, chocolate, or Nescafé. A plain but satisfying meal, and now it was tme to head back to the Airport Hotel for the next big event: sleep.

Our "air conditioner" chugged all night like a diesel, but had no effect on the temperature, though it *almost* overwhelmed the bass drum throbbing through the walls from the bar downstairs. The room contained only one droopy little bed, and David and I ceded it to Leonard, spreading our sleeping bags on the grimy floor. David said "I often find the floors in Africa are more comfortable than the beds anyway."

I lay in the humid dark holding that thought, a symbol for the conflicting responses I had felt that day. On one level I was painfully aware of lying on a dirty floor; but on another level I realized that I was lying on a dirty floor in *Africa*. On that level I was excited, looking forward to a whole month of adventures to come.

But deep down I realized that a month can be a long time.

A loyal supporter of President Biya.

dance party

By 6:30 a.m. we were back on the bicycles, climbing with the sun up a long hill. Sometimes it is just as well to go directly from sleep to a struggle like that, as a sleep-dulled brain seems less impressed by effort. The world was green and the sky translucent in the haze. Moon-faced people turned to stare as I pedaled by them; children walked in groups on their way to school, carrying satchels and books, and serious-faced women walked with erect carriage and easy grace, a posture endowed by the large baskets and bundles many of them bore on their heads. Men sauntered along the roadside, strolled across between the speeding minibuses and taxis to greet each other, or simply stood around, proving what is said about women doing eighty per cent of the work in Africa.

The minibuses and taxis were crammed so full that the passengers' shoulders flattened against the windows as they sped by, and all the buses carried signboards on their roofs, slogans painted in circus red and yellow: "Take Care Men," "Say What You Like, God Loves Me," "James Bond 007," "A Disappointment Is A Blessing."

After two steep miles the village of Mutengene sprawled over the crown of the hill in rows of wood and corrugated-metal houses. Leaning our bikes against a yellow building decorated with signs advertising Delta cigarettes, we took stools at the lunch counter outside. In the swept yard beside us a woman sat on a stool by a fire, dropping balls of dough into hot oil to make *beignets*, dumplings of deep-fried bread. Two small children played in the dirt beside her, the older girl sometimes glancing over at us, then turning away. Once I caught her eye and smiled, and she laughed and hid her face.

"I was arrested here once," David said. "You remember back there we saw a building called the 'ETS MEN'S WORK?' Then just after it the 'WOMEN'S OWN CLUB?' Well, I stopped to take a photograph of that, and a policeman came and arrested me and took me to the station. He said there was a bare-breasted woman in the background of the picture, but I sure never saw her!"

Leonard laughed: "Not likely to miss a thing like that, hmm?"
Elsa and Annie gave him an eloquent look, while I turned to David:
"Touchy about that sort of thing, are they?"

"I guess. They kept me there for about two hours, and finally
took the film out before I got my camera back."

Leonard's eyes crinkled behind his glasses as he turned to
David. "Yeah, remember last year in Kenya when that girl Denise
took a photo of the Kenyan flag and got arrested." He turned to the
rest of us. "They kept her for hours too, and took the film away. She
tried to tell them she would get it developed and send them the
negative, but they kept saying 'No, no, *we* will develop,' and then
they phoned Nairobi to find out what 'develop' was." Leonard shook
his head slowly and laughed.

"You've got to be really careful with your camera," David went
on, "Many people here don't like to have their pictures taken by foreigners, and they often think you only take pictures that will *embar-
rass* them, show them at their worst and sensationalize their poverty. I remember in Liberia once, I wanted to take a photo of a family, but they waved me to '*wait, wait,*' then ran off and dressed up
the children, and returned to pose for me, each of them with a hand
on their *radio!*"

"So it's not so much a religious thing here," I said, "not like those
people who think you're stealing their souls?"

"No, more of a cultural thing. They just don't trust cameras."

"Hear hear," I agreed.

After omelettes and Nescafé we moved down to the bikes, which
were stacked against each other so that none could be reached until
Annie's was out of the way. Yet she stood to the side, pushing her
thick hair under her helmet and looking expectant, then moving her
hands as if she wanted to help but didn't know what to do: "So ... um
... should we get going?"

David spoke up: "Well, no one's going anywhere until you move
your bike!"

"Oh yeah ... um ... right ... heh-heh," and she took hold of the
handlebars and pushed it away. David turned to me, smiling and
shaking his head. "It amazes me how many times I go through this
on tours. Sometimes it takes people *weeks* to figure that out."

It was to be our shortest day of cycling for a month, a mere
twelve miles to the coastal town of Limbe, so we set a relaxed pace

through the lush plantations and Hawaiian-postcard hills. Pied crows flapped lazily over the road, while the kites soared in high circles. Mount Cameroon was a constant shadow on the right, its great bulk veiled by haze and clouds. A few villages sprouted among the trees, but they seemed to grow *into* the forest rather than out of it. Wooden structures were under constant attrition from dampness, insects, and mossy growths; the planked walls were weathered gray, the corners disintegrating, and even the metal roofs were dull brown under a patina of lichen and rust.

We continued along the coastal plateau, Annie out front and one of us always staying back to ride "sweep" with Elsa. We had such a short distance to travel that I felt no pressure to arrive, which on longer journeys always weighs heavily on me, and I pedaled along with a light heart. Sometimes I even sang a little, when no one was close enough to hear. My singing is best kept to myself.

We coasted in a line down a two-mile hill, feet motionless on the pedals and bodies bent into the wind, drifting around sweeping bends between the trees and unable now to wave at the faces calling out from the roadside. Snatches of distorted music from radios and tape players blared suddenly, then fell behind. We passed under a yellow railway bridge with "WELCOME TO LIMBE" painted across it, as the road leveled out and we began pedaling again, past rows of houses. Straight ahead was the Atlantic Ocean, a swath of ultramarine glittering in the morning sun. Though it was still only 9:00, the heat was already a dense curtain; no fresh breeze blew from the sea.

We circled a roundabout and turned into a side street, then wove through the narrow, neat streets of Limbe. David stopped in front of an official-looking two-storey white building, and we parked our bikes against the wall. A sign read: *"Mairie"* — town hall.

"Just wait here a minute," David said, "I'm going to see if we can meet the mayor."

He pulled a pair of plastic warm-up pants over his shorts, then spoke to one of the policemen standing by the doorway, asking for the mayor's office. One of them pointed inside.

I noticed that the policemen spoke English, and realized that we were now in the English-speaking part of the country. At independence some of Britain's slice of Cameroon went to Nigeria, but a narrow corridor remained, a remnant of British colonial rule with a few token Briticisms like language, school system, and sliced white bread. True, no *baguettes* here, and as we traveled around Cameroon the bread would always be the clearest sign of what language the local people might speak.

The mayor agreed to see us, so the girls wrapped their skirts over their shorts, while Leonard and I dug out our long pants. We mounted the stairs to a small meeting room, chairs placed in rows around the walls.

The mayor emerged from another door, a short, round man dressed in a close-fitting outfit of shirt-jacket and pants in a matching light brown polyester, the classic leisure-suit uniform of the West African functionary. He stepped forward to greet us with a friendly smile and a firm handshake, then motioned us to take a chair. He remained standing, his bulk rocking a little from side to side as David described where we'd been and where we were going, and he nodded and smiled with interest. When he learned that most of the group was American, the mayor mentioned that he had gone to school in the U.S. at, of all places, the University of Wisconsin. David asked about an ambulance which was being presented to Limbe by its sister city, David's home town of Seattle. The mayor told him that he expected it to arrive in a month or so, and that he would be meeting the American delegation at that time. David wanted to know where he would have them stay.

"At the Atlantic Beach Hotel I think. It is the best in Limbe. You will stay there?"

David looked uneasy: "Well, maybe."

And there the conversation faltered, as everyone nodded and smiled in the sudden silence, the mayor still swaying from side to side uncomfortably. "I am just taken aback at your visit. I am taken aback."

The four of us smiled and nodded some more, the smiles becoming frozen and the nods becoming vacuous, then David finally rose to say goodbye. The rest of us were on our feet in a second, as the mayor smiled with renewed vigor and shook our hands again. "Perhaps I may see you at the Atlantic Beach Hotel later for a drink?"

"Yes, certainly," said David, "that would be nice," and we smiled some more and thanked the mayor for his time as we headed down the stairs. As we put away long pants and skirts and remounted the bikes, David gave a short laugh, "Well, I guess I'm trapped into the Atlantic Beach Hotel now. I wish he hadn't said that."

"Why, what's the problem?" I asked, "Isn't it any good?"

"Oh no, it's a nice hotel all right," he trailed off, and I understood. It might be a bit rich for our budget. The Bicycle Africa tours were designed to operate with a minimum of about eight people, so our little group was a strain on David's finances — as he put it, "not to lose *too* much."

We pedaled slowly along the sun-baked streets toward the water, then turned along the seawall and stopped at a life-size statue of a man. ALFRED SAKER, said the inscription, and I had read that he was the English missionary who founded Limbe. In the 1850s he arrived on the island of Fernando Po, a Spanish territory just off Cameroon's coast, where he worked with a group of Jamaican priests among freed slaves who had taken refuge there. The local Jesuits, appalled at the presence of Protestants on "their" island, forced the governor to expel these hard-working heretics, and Saker moved his people to the mainland. There he proved himself to be one *good* missionary. He bought a stretch of waterfront property from the chief of the local Douala tribe — didn't take it, *bought* it — cleared the land, built a school, and taught the local boys carpentry, printing, brick-making, and medicine. He learned the Douala language and translated grammar books and the Bible, built a sugar mill, and introduced breadfruit, pomegranates, avocados, and mangos. The next day, one presumes, he rested. Saker's mission grew into the town of Victoria, named by this loyal Brit for his sovereign, but was renamed Limbe in the 1970s under the continent-wide movement for Africanization. Limbe has become a busy seaside market town and a popular weekend escape from Douala, but unfortunately its future as a resort is threatened by the presence of one of the largest oil refineries in West Africa, which pours its waste directly into the sea to come washing up on the beaches.

At the edge of town we crossed a bridge over a small river, just where it emptied into the ocean, and I smiled at the shouts and laughter of a crowd of children playing in the water, escaping the heat in time-honored, international style. On the other side of the bridge, upriver, a herd of long-horned cattle browsed on the tender grasses in the shallows. We parked our bikes at the Atlantic Beach Hotel, a low white building with blue-trimmed windows and terraces amid coconut palms and bushes of frangipani and hibiscus. A swimming pool and a pair of blue gazebos faced the sea, where a row of tiny islands poked up from the blue Atlantic like rocky fingertips.

Everyone was soon occupied with washing, resting, or doing laundry, so I cycled alone back along the shore, where a beach curved around the wide bay, and stopped to admire the view. A few tall wooden fishing boats, with outboard motors set into square holes in the stern, nodded lazily on the waves. A man worked on his motor, bent over it above the water, his dark sinewy arms shining in the sun. A long skeleton of twisted iron gridwork ran out from shore, the remnants of a pier from colonial days now useless and rusting. Dugout rowboats were pulled high on the beach, up to the pavement where I had stopped, and men carried baskets of fish from the boats to a line of brightly-clothed women who sat along the curb, bending forward as their hands stirred through the baskets, sorting brown crabs and trout-sized silver fish. Sharks and barracudas were carried one at a time over to a small white ice-house.

I was determined to take a photograph of this colorful scene, but I knew I had to be careful. I didn't want to *cause* a colorful scene. I stood casually by the ruins of the pier, looking everywhere but at the "fishwives." My camera dangled carelessly at my side as I pretended to watch children playing in a schoolyard across the road. I whistled a tuneless tune. When the moment came, and the women all seemed to be looking the other way, I brought the camera up, quickly pushed the shutter, then turned away to my bike.

But I was caught. An irate voice called out: "Why you snap people dem?"

And I looked back to see an angry woman facing me, and a murmur of unrest sweeping through the others. Then again, "Why you snap people dem?"

Like Hanno, I ran away, climbed on my bike and pedaled swiftly down the road, feeling embarrassed and ashamed. The picture didn't come out either. I'd brought the camera up so quickly that the wrist-strap flew in front of the lens. Justice was served.

I took shelter in the crowds at the open-air market, pushing my bike along the rows of metal-roofed tables and kiosks selling fruits, vegetables, meats, rice, and fish, and then an outside perimeter of stalls which sold tools, dishes, buckets, and shoes. Hundreds of rolls of cloth stood on end, the bright-colored prints which were the raw material for the long skirts, *pagnes,* and headscarves which the women wore. I stood by and watched the bargaining, counting the money changing hands to see how much the locals were paying, then stepped in and made a deal for a nice crimson and dark green pattern. It would serve me well as a bedsheet, dressing gown, a mat for siestas, and a useful souvenir.

Two conspicuously pale figures appeared in the crowd, Annie and Elsa, who were also shopping for *pagnes*, as a solution for the modesty problem. Since they were expected to cover their legs whenever they were off the bikes, a *pagne* could simply be wrapped around their shamefully exposed nether limbs, rather than pulling on skirts or long pants.

We regrouped for lunch on the hotel terrace, overlooking the palms and rocky shoreline. Crab claws, an excellent salad, fresh fish, pineapple, good strong coffee. We couldn't know that it was the last taste of luxury and ease we would enjoy for many days, but I had experienced enough cycle touring to know that when you're finished pedaling by 9:30 in the morning, with the rest of the day free and a nice hotel by the ocean, you should enjoy it. We brought our books to the row of chairs by the water, where low tide exposed the sharp volcanic rocks. A paved walkway led into the warmest sea I've ever felt, protected from waves and currents by a low seawall. Didn't know then about the oil refinery.

David had admired my close-shaven haircut, and asked if I'd cut my hair off for this trip, or "Is it just a crazy rock n' roll hairstyle?" I laughed and told him I always cut my hair short before a bike tour — one less thing to worry about. He decided that was a good idea, and convinced Leonard to give him a trim. While Leonard stood behind David's chair, clipping away at his curly mass of hair, Annie, Elsa, and I sat beneath a blue gazebo, our faces buried in our books. I had packed only two books for this trip, as I seldom do much reading on a cycling tour, but they proved to be good choices. One was Aristotle's *Ethics*, and the other *Dear Theo*, the letters of Vincent van Gogh to his brother.

Aristotle was perfect in the daytime, his clear and rational discussions of virtuous behavior and the "golden mean" a welcome diversion while I lay in the shade of a tree during a midday siesta. Vincent's more romantic flights of artistic struggle suited the warm nights, as I lay back in my sleeping bag with a flashlight on my shoulder. That afternoon by the sea, while Annie began a sketch of Mister Leonard's waterfront beauty salon, I decided I wasn't ready for Aristotle yet, and between dips in the water I waded into the unpromising first chapters of *Dear Theo*.

Poor Vincent. An impoverished and confused young man, he gives up a position with his uncle the art dealer, with no regrets on either side, and then wanders destitute around London for a time. I happen to know, autobiographically, that if there *is* a good place to be destitute, it is not London.

Then Vincent tumbles into a morass of religion, and his letters begin to peal with the tiresome piety of a new believer. Deciding that evangelism is his true calling, but unable to get himself ordained, he retreats to a sad little mining town in Belgium and stews there for a while, dejected, rejected, and supremely miserable.

I, on the other hand, was supremely happy. I put down the book and lay back on a chaise longue, looking up at the sky. So many levels of movement: swallows and crows arrowing over the water, low clouds bulging swiftly across the sky, and above them the high, thin clouds riding a slow jetstream. In between, the frigate birds stretched their boomerang-shaped wings and soared on the thermal updrafts; the gentle wind blended flowers and salt water. A freighter moved slowly across the horizon, out beyond the chain of tiny islands, the rocky fingertips. Fishing boats bobbed on the waves closer in, or motored across the bay in distant silence. I lay back in the late afternoon sun, its healing warmth on my face.

After the swift performance of sunset over the Atlantic, which I appreciated in the proper fashion, from the bar's terrace, with a Scotch on the rocks, and the lazy rhythm of the surf, we went in search of a dinner that would be a little less expensive, and a little more "cultural," than the Atlantic Beach Hotel. We walked tentatively down unlighted streets, Leonard and I trying to cover everyone's path with our flashlights. Fugitive washes of light from the low buildings caught moving silhouettes, or played on faces and ghostly clothes. The five of us were equally masked in darkness, and for once attracted little attention.

David led us to a "chophouse," as he called it, and we passed through a lacy curtain into a low, dimly-lighted room and seated ourselves around a plank table. A massive woman emerged from a back room to ask us what we wanted. David asked her what she had, but the answer made no sense to the rest of us, so we agreed to let him order a "special meal" for us.

I had read about a West African dish called *fufu* and was eager to try it. I didn't know what it *was*, but I liked the name. It turned out to be lumps of pounded maize, a cold, doughy mass reminiscent of Play-doh. We broke off pieces with our fingers and dipped them into a spicy meat broth with chunks of beef (I think). This sauce could also be ladled over the bowls of white rice, a combination we would encounter many times, and which I christened "rice with junk on it." In Third World countries, poverty is the mother of invention.

• • •

The next day's ride took us up to Buea, a small town perched high on the shoulder of Mount Cameroon. Because of its pleasant highland climate, Buea had been the capital of the German colony, and it remained a favored spot for missionaries to ply their trade. David told us there were more churches around Buea than he'd seen in any other place in West Africa. I wouldn't have thought missionaries chose their missions according to climatic comfort, but I did notice that low-lying swampy villages had been deemed less in need of "saving" than were the pleasant highland locations. To be fair, though, the early missionaries had often perished from yellow fever and malaria, diseases of the tropical lowlands.

Our route from Limbe and the sea took us back up the long hill and through the Hawaiian-postcard landscape. Children waved and smiled at us on their way to school, and three young girls shyly allowed me to take their picture. All of them had their hair trimmed very short, and wore cotton dresses and rubber flip-flops. One girl's dress was printed with an almost life-size black-and-white portrait of President Paul Biya. I was to see quite a few of these patriotic dresses, and even some that portrayed Pope John Paul. I tried without success to visualize a Canadian woman wearing Brian Mulroney.

A sloppy-looking youth leaned out into the road and shouted at David, "Hey, give me something from your pack!"

David replied, reasonably enough, "Well, what do you need?"

"Whatever you have!" We laughed and rode away.

As we pedaled by five little boys, one of them held up a big crawfish, greenish-brown, shiny, and very alive. The boys all started yelling at us in a confusion of shouts, each one of them now waving a slowly gyrating crustacean. 'Voodoo,' I thought to myself.

Another group of children stood at the side of the road clapping their hands in rhythm and chanting, *"Bicycle rider try your best! Bi-*

cycle rider try your best!" and jumping up and down in excitement as we wheeled by. David explained this as another legacy left by the French, the popularity of bicycle racing. The children were used to cheering for the racers.

As if in proof of this, a pair of local racers came charging up to Mutengene, where we sat resting at the side of the road. In answer to our wave of greeting, the two cyclists pulled up beside us, and David and I spoke with them as well as our limited French allowed. One of them was unmistakably the leader, not only because he did all the talking, but because he rode a sophisticated racing machine with all the latest gear: aerodynamic brake levers, cables routed through the frame, clip-in pedals, and he wore colorful lycra cycling clothes. His partner's bike was less state-of-the art, and his clothes were plain old cotton. He would be what is called a *domestique*, one of the members of a racing team who is responsible for helping the team's strongest rider to win by engaging in tactical duels with other racers, or letting the number one rider take it easy in his draft, to conserve his strength for a sprint at the finish. These two were training for a stage race up in Algeria, and their morning's training ride had taken them over the same route we had followed, though they covered in a few hours what had taken us three days.

We turned straight up the side of the mountain; it would be a ten-mile climb to Buea. I was grateful for the overcast, but the heat was rising in my muscles and my face. I blew out hard to spray the tickles of sweat off my nose. Just behind me Elsa groaned out loud, muttering, "Doesn't he know anything but *hills*?"

Guessing she meant David and not God, I laughed over my shoulder, "Well, I don't think he made it this way!" but she was silent. On a climb like that there was no question of riding at "anyone *Elsa's*" pace. It's just as difficult to ride *slower* than your own rhythm as it is to ride *faster*, so everyone spread out. I was out of the saddle with my hands over the brake hoods, rocking the bike from side to side and using my weight on the pedal strokes. I noticed that David up ahead was more of a "spinner," sitting down and pedaling at a higher cadence in a lower gear. Better for him, I knew, and more aerobic, but I'd become comfortable doing it the "wrong" way.

A few buses sped by, with names like "Air Chariot" and "Justice," and as usual on a long climb, there was time to look around. Everything was greener and more lush in the shadow of the mountain.

Royal palms speared up to the sky amid cedar-like evergreens with the pretty name of casuarina. Even the power lines were hung with garlands of mauve and white flowers. Framed among the leaves at the roadside, a man hacked at a tree with his machete. In another yard a man worked under the hood of an ancient Peugeot, which looked as if it had been parked in front of his house for a long time. As I slowly climbed past him, he sang out: *"I want to be a white man!"* then chuckled without malice. What could I do but laugh?

A little higher up the mountain, I noticed a sign in front of a tumble-down house:

PROFESSOR JEROME **NGWA**
SPIRITUAL HEALING HOME
Specialist in —
MADNESS, GASTRIC PAIN, HEART PAIN, STOMACH ACHE,
PILE, STERILITY, WITCHCRAFT, POISON,
YELLOW FEVER, EPILEPSY, RHEUMATISM, ETC.

And these claims of Professor Ngwa's were modest. Some of the other "herbalists" promised to cure more than madness and witchcraft — even cancer and AIDS. On a later trip to Ghana, I saw this sign at the roadside:

OHEAKOH HERBAL TREATMENT
CLINIC AT NUNGUA
IMPOTENCE
Are you
IMPOTENT?
You will recover from
IMPOTENCE
Within 5 to 10 minutes
a) IF your PENIS is lacking sufficient
STRENGTH in SEXUAL
b) IF your PENIS is WHOLLY
lacking in SEXUAL POWER

VENEREAL DISEASES
If you feel WAIST PAINS and there is LIQUID
Coming from your PENIS or VAGINA
If you feel PAINS and there is BLOOD
Coming from your PENIS or VAGINA
INFERTILITY
WAIST PAINS   LUMBAGO   BLINDNESS
ASTHMA   NERVOURSNESS   PILES
HYPERTENSION   STROKE   FITS
RHEUMATIC PAINS   GOUT
SICKLE CELLS   ABDOMINAL PAINS
DIABETES   MADNESS
CANCER   SKIN DISEASES
URINAL TROUBLES

GOOD TREATMENT ASSURED→ **AIDS** DISEASES
And lots and lots of SICKNESS You can consult me for HELP

Though it is hard not to smile at these claims, some of the traditional African cures, like those in China, have proved effective, though perhaps not against cancer or AIDS. The power of faith in healing is undeniable as well, and it is partly for this reason that the missionary doctors dislike these "fetish doctors." The conflict of faiths. Science and superstition alike are aided by the patient's faith in them, and the opposing practitioners are jealous of that faith.

In Togo I once visited an American doctor, a Baptist missionary, who had constructed a remarkable hospital in the West African bush. With good old missionary zeal and hard work, backed by churches in Michigan and Indiana, he had assembled two operating rooms, twenty-five beds, an air-conditioned dispensary, and even an old M*A*S*H* X-ray machine, all powered by generator. The doctor told us that when the local people thought their relatives were about to die in the hospital, they hurried to get the patient home because the taxi fare for a corpse was ten times that for a live person, but when we discussed the fetish doctors, his face hardened. He told us he had just witnessed the funeral of an evil fetish priest, and the villagers had carried the body along in a stretcher, beating it with sticks, then dumped it into a grave of thorns, so the priest would have to sleep in pain forever. When asked if he allowed the village doctors to visit his patients in the hospital, the doctor's response was surprisingly vehement, "No, we don't. They do the work of Satan, and we're trying to do the work of God."

Africans tend to be pragmatic, and are still likely to consult *both* kinds of doctor, and magician, like a businessman I know who remains open to all religions, "just in case they're right." And, like elsewhere in the world, there seems to be a relationship between faith and the difficulty of life. For example, independence has been tougher on Ghana than Cameroon. The Ghanaian people have suffered radical governments, regular coups, and the corresponding economic chaos, while faith seems stronger and more serious there. Judging by the roadside signs, many more traditional doctors practise in Ghana; there are definitely more churches, and even the minibus signs reflect the harsher life. You see no frivolous ones in Ghana, no "Air Chariot" or "James Bond 007." All the Ghanaian buses have devotional names like "Blessed Assurance" or "Good Father." No sense of humor — just like faith. You could sometimes say reason is a luxury everywhere in the world. It works fine as long as *life* is reasonable, but when guns, poverty, and drought start pushing people around, they often retire into faith.

And if you're going to retire into faith, go to Buea. Missionaries may be crazy but they're not stupid. When David and I panted up the mountainside to the cool and healthful air of Buea, the road was lined with one church after another: Baptist, Catholic, Lutheran, Methodist, I don't know *what* all. Sweating and breathless, we finally stopped at a crossroads, and I sat on a bench to wait for the others while David went off in search of a hotel.

Leonard and Annie hauled themselves slowly up to me, and wilted into the shade. Then came a vision: Elsa being *pushed* up the hill by a young guy who trotted behind her. We laughed and ran for our cameras as Elsa coasted up saying, "I didn't mind that a bit!"

Her "pusher" stopped to talk with us, and we soon discovered that he could be pushy in more ways than one. Chifor Ignatius was his name, a skinny young man in baggy white shirt and dark trousers. His eyes were sharp and guarded, and did not inspire trust in me.

He started right in on Elsa. "Will you give me your address so I may write to you? I meet many people who say they will write, but nobody is ever writing back to me."

A common syndrome in Africa, especially in countries like Ghana where every second person wants your address. Bad feelings are often caused by foreigners who promise to send photographs and letters to friends made in the glory days of a vacation, but then return home to the work-a-day world and forget all about it. I'm sure many would rationalize it, "Well I just wanted to be friendly. Maybe I'll get to it sometime." But of course to the people they disappoint, it's just another broken promise. Then again, offering your address can be an invitation to requests for money, a television set, an airline ticket, or one day you may find your forgotten African friend at your door.

Once in Ghana I had stopped at a roadside bar for a Coke, and a young man came up to me, pushing through the children who had gathered around to stare. He sat down in front of me and immediately demanded my address and wanted me to write to him. He explained that he was ambitious, and as proof he pointed around at my bicycle and my camera. "Someday I will have one of those. And one of those." He was very plain about what he wanted with me; he pushed his baseball cap back on his head and leaned forward to say, "All I need is a white man to help me."

I could only laugh, but I have found this approach and this attitude to be all too common among Africans, especially the youth. They see a white man as a *ticket* to something; they think every white man holds the power to make things happen. Sometimes you tell an African that you're bicycling around his country, and at first he's amazed; but then he thinks again, waves his hand and says, "Well, it's easy for a white man."

Many young Africans have discussed their ambitions with me, and not one of them has ever talked about *doing* things, but only *having* things. They never spoke of wanting to be a doctor or an architect, they just wanted to go to America and get rich. The limited view, unfortunately, of too many westerners as well — the idea that the goal of life is to *get* things, like on a game show. When life-support is on the line, money is everything, but beyond that threshold of survival life ought to get *bigger*. Or am I too idealistic? Perhaps. But thus have many young Africans inherited the western curse of acquisitiveness, without the accompanying drive for *accomplishment*. They dream of having, not doing. And a white man can help them.

Elsa moved away from Chifor Ignatius, and the four of us had a quick, whispered huddle. We agreed that we didn't really want to take the responsibility of saying we would write to people like Chifor Ignatius who barely crossed our path, but we wanted to be diplomatic as well. Elsa finally gave him a few coins for pushing her, took down his address, and promised to send him a postcard.

Then he approached me. "You were snapping a photograph of me pushing the lady."

I knew he wanted either a copy of the picture, or to be *paid* for being in it, so I put him off firmly. "It wasn't a picture of you, it was a picture of her. You were behind her."

He looked doubtful. "I am not in the photograph?"

"It was of her." This careful response was true, if equivocal, and ended the discussion. When the photograph was developed, he did appear, sort of, as a white-shirted shadow in the background.

David returned and led us to a three-storey tenement of white-washed concrete, the Parliamentarian Flats Hotel. I had to learn the impressive name from a giant fob on the room key, as there was no sign at all in front of the building. The man at the desk told us he was waiting for a new sign, which had been promised to him by a *brasserie* — brewery.

Africa On A Shoestring says the Parliamentarian Flats Hotel "looks as pretentious as it sounds," which I can only attribute to its being three storeys tall. The Lonely Planet researchers also describe it as "clean, quiet and comfortable," which I can only attribute to guesswork. Our room was a grubby pink plaster cell with filthy white doors and trim, a linoleum floor encrusted with dirt, and a single light fixture full of dead bugs. The toilet had no seat, the tub had no shower, and the sink drained straight onto the floor.

We went for a walk. Outside the perfume of montane forests carried on the air, and Mount Cameroon loomed high behind the hotel, an enormous darkness wrapped in clouds.

Buea's small market was still open, a square of beaten earth, a network of mismatched stalls of wood and corrugated metal. Women chatted and laughed, sometimes selling a handful of rice, yams, plantains, palm nuts, or dried fish. The traditional West African approach to free enterprise is well represented by the market women. There may be five or six of them in a row behind their tables, and each of them will be selling the same thing, say oranges, for the same price. No price-cutting, no real competition; they sit together all day talking and waiting, trusting that they will *all* sell their oranges, eventually.

Leonard was delighted with a common West African snack. A woman sat paring oranges until the skins were thin and white, then stacking them in little pyramids. When Leonard handed over a few francs to buy one, she sliced the top off the orange, like a little lid, to make a convenient serving of fresh orange juice. Easy to squeeze, and no sticky fingers. "Gotta get the franchise for this idea," he said. "Make a *fortune* in California!"

Following David, we ducked through a curtain into a stall of wood and corrugated metal, where a single table sat on a floor of swept dirt. In the itinerary, Buea's dinner was listed as "café." I guess David felt "chophouse" didn't have the same ring. He asked what we wanted, and I suggested "rice with junk on it?" Not that there was much choice. A very large woman began ladling bowls of rice from a tall metal pot, then a tasty sauce of cassava greens, and another spicier sauce with a hunk of meat in it. A single, *big* hunk of meat.

While we ate, we razzed David about the morning's adventure. On the way out of Limbe he had wanted to lead us through the Botanical Garden, a park created by the Germans at the turn of the century to test the plants which they wanted to introduce to Cameroon. David had thought there was a road that would take us there, and stopped at a small, steep sideroad. "I think this is it. Anyone want to try it?"

Elsa had taken one look at the steep little lane and decided she didn't want to start her day with a vertical detour. She said she'd meet us at the roundabout. David's wheels were already pointed up the hill and the rest of us followed him, straining and sweating in our lowest gears. At the top we found ourselves between two small houses, and at the end of a *driveway*.

David scouted around the yard, found a footpath leading down between the trees, and looked a question at us as he pointed at the path. "Well, I know it's in that direction."

In this way David and I were alike. If lost, I'd rather go around the *world* than turn back the way I'd come. So I said "sure" and Leonard and Annie nodded. The dirt path was too steep and narrow to ride on, so we walked our bikes down into the trees. An Eden closed around us; the path became a lush tunnel winding beneath a canopy of palm fronds and ancient trees. The earth was soft underfoot, and water gleamed on vines and brilliant flowers.

So we told Elsa about the little expedition she'd missed by waiting at the roundabout. Leonard needled David: "Some guide. Right outside the hotel he gets us lost in the jungle!"

David just repeated what I'd said to him when we realized we were lost. "Hey, we didn't come here to know where we're going!" I would later regret those words.

We strolled back down the main street of Buea, where a few shops blared the usual distorted music. We began to notice many soldiers in khaki or camouflage fatigues, and David had warned us not to even *show* our cameras in Buea. The town remained an important government center (missionaries may be crazy but they're not stupid, and politicians may be stupid but they're not crazy — both appreciate a good climate). Photography would be considered an act of espionage. The white walls and gilded cupolas of the old governor's mansion stood above the trees, and we walked toward it, passing more soldiers then metal sheds full of jeeps, tankers, and transporters, all in camouflage paint. All around were barracks, offices, and hundreds of soldiers standing guard, lounging around the buildings, or strolling along the road staring at us.

Since we didn't dare photograph the governor's mansion, we thought we'd at least like a closer look, and found a ridge on the mountainside about a hundred yards away from it. As we looked across the steep chasm to the landscaped grounds and red-tiled roof, a soldier appeared on the wall and called out sternly, "What are you doing?"

David called back, "Just looking!"

The soldier held up his rifle and waved it at us. "You must not. Go away!"

We heeded his words, and his gun, and went off shaking our heads. Drums and singing carried up the hill from the main road, and we followed the echoes to a large concrete-block gymnasium with a paved basketball court outside. David asked someone what was happening.

"It is a competition with some of the other villages. They are practising inside, then they will perform here," and he indicated the basketball court. We sat on the grass and watched the crowds gather and fill the bleachers on one side of the court. The people were handsome, men muscular and women walking with that upright head-carrying posture, their features seemingly rounded by the arc of their eyebrows. Many of the women wore their hair in thin braids looping out from their heads and back again, creating dark, filigreed haloes around their faces that were oddly attractive.

Elsa's "pusher," Chifor Ignatius, appeared and attached himself to us with the effusiveness of a long-lost friend. I asked him if I would be able to take pictures of the dancing, but he made a worried face. "It would be dangerous. You do not have authorization." I left the camera in its case on my belt.

A row of chairs was placed at courtside for the mayor in his leisure suit and the local chiefs in pale robes and embroidered caps. A procession of musicians carried out their different kinds of drums and began to play them. Some were tall, slender wooden cylinders with protruding pegs to tension the animal-skin membranes, and were played as hand-drums, with a sound that could be varied by how they were struck, from a dark pulse-beat to a bongo-like *tok*. Slit drums, made of long hollow logs with a notch carved lengthwise along the middle, were played with pieces of tree-branch, and gave a loud, hollow resonance with a distinct note. The powerful slit drums had once carried messages between villages, they were the original "talking drums."

Two more drummers sat on the ground playing giant marimbas, called balofons, each of which consisted of several lengths of heavy wood. The wooden beams, or "keys," were struck by heavy sticks with padded ends, and the sound too was like a giant marimba, a percussive attack with a clean, sharp note. These players supplied the melodic and rhythmic foundation for the other drummers, laying down steady interweaving rolls which meshed like gears, and were propelled by the momentum of rattling shakers.

Then came a leaping procession of agile young men in colorful pajamas, and another troupe dressed in flower-print *pagnes*. The lead dancer, in black with red trim, conducted the company into lines and shifting patterns around the basketball court as the drummers played a circular rhythm, pulsing and sensual. A story was being told in that dance, though we could not follow it. It certainly seemed to be a *rude* story. At certain points the pajama-men fell to the ground and stretched out flat on their faces with their bodies undulating and hips pumping. This set the women in the audience shrieking with pleasure, while the children laughed at how *silly* it looked.

The dancers left the stage to cheering applause. After a short break in the drumming, the mood suddenly changed. The drummers began a darker, hypnotic rhythm with a menacing undertone. Chifor Ignatius whispered that the *juju* dancers were coming now.

Two dancers crept out wearing long black robes, their faces bandaged in white gauze and crowned by large wooden masks, one a leering humanoid, the other a cow's head with a sheaf of grass stuck in its mouth. More dancers came slinking out in bright blue *pagnes*, and they were also masked, one a chicken, one a goat, and one a distorted human face.

Only the leader's face could be seen. He skipped among the other dancers carrying a wooden bucket with a serpent-shaped branch in it. In his other hand he wielded a cluster of dark green leaves, which he used to sprinkle palm wine on the ground and the other dancers. The crowd swayed in respectful silence. I sat cross-legged on the grass beside the drummers, my whole being resonating to the drums and balofons.

And the masks. There is something disturbingly inhuman about a moving body whose face you cannot see, even if it's under a cartoon head. But how much more disturbing to watch a dancing figure, genderless in a black robe, whose features are replaced by a fixed, malevolent leer.

Suddenly the air was empty. The drumming stopped. Time descended and Space closed in around the masked dancers on the basketball court, and they were gone. A wave of polite applause washed over the crowd, and I joined in, but there was no boisterous cheering or whistling. The bleachers quickly emptied as people slipped away into the evening shadows, hurrying to get home before dark.

"Drums along the sidewalk."
Sultan's Palace, Foumban.

hell hole

The rising sun shadowed the ridges of Mount Cameroon, unclouded for the first time and etched against the sky. The sun's rays had not yet begun to move down the mountain, so the air retained the freshness of night. I crouched into the wind, arms tucked in close to my body against the chill. The country was awake as early as we were, even on a Sunday. Smoke drifted up from the houses, and the earliest minibuses began to pass in both directions. The first one I saw bore the portentous name of "White Man," a phrase I would hear a *lot* that day, as our fifty-mile ride took us around the shoulder of the mountain to the north, and into the interior, to Kumba. This was where the *adventure* would begin.

"White Man! White Man!" called a voice from somewhere, and I shook my head, then smiled grimly to imagine an African cycling through Canada to cries of "Black Man! Black Man!" But there was no doubt of it; we caused a sensation. "White Man!" assailed me from houses, fields, and passing buses. I learned later that it's not so much a *racial* term as cultural, a generic name for Europeans and North Americans. Annie and Elsa were constantly called "white man" too, and even *Leonard* was considered a "white-man-black-man." But at the time I didn't know all that, and took to protesting these cries with a more exact description, calling out: "I'm not white — I'm beige!" which at least seemed to confuse them.

Already Mount Cameroon was disappearing into cloud, and even in the shade of dense trees, the heat began to grow oppressive. In the tiny village of Muea we stopped for breakfast at a tin-roof shack, painted yellow with purple shutters. We drew a large audience as we sat outside on benches to enjoy the usual omelettes. Children pushed as near as they dared to stare at us, and especially at our bicycles, while scattered cries from the crowd continued to lump us all together as "male caucasians." Leonard laughed at this, but Elsa and Annie were not impressed. Dervla Murphy related in her book,

Cameroon With Egbert, that when she grew tired of being called a man by the people of Cameroon, she took to opening her shirt to silence the doubters.

As we started off again we left the crowds behind, and wheeled easily down the paved road, bordered by high grasses, trees, and stands of delicate bamboo. A stream bubbled beneath a mango tree, and a tulip-tree flamed with orange flowers. A few little houses appeared in the trees, and boys and women walked along the roadside with cutlasses in one hand and long bamboo stalks balanced on their heads. The mountain air was fresh and I felt a swelling in my chest, a sensation of freedom and joy that only cycling gives me.

The people made me happy too. An old man raised his hand in greeting and called out "Welcome!" When I wished a "Good Morning!" to an old woman as I pedaled by, she turned in surprise and answered, "You are welcome!" A wonderful way to greet a stranger, especially a strange-looking stranger. Even the police were friendly that morning. As I approached a checkpoint the officer made as if to flag me down, then laughed warmly and waved me on.

In the little village of Banga Bakundu I received a riotous reception, a crowd of little children so excited, jumping up and down, running and frolicking as they chanted, *"Bicycle Ride! Bicycle Ride! Bicycle Ride!"*

And an unseen voice sang me a little song from the trees: "White ma-a-an, where you go-o-o-ing?"

A good question. I sang my answer back: "Kum-ba-a-a!"

In each village twelve or fifteen little houses lined the road, built of plank and corrugated metal, with the occasional old-fashioned roof of woven palm fronds. The yards were swept clean, for bare dirt is preferred to grass, where snakes might hide. Scattered plots had been cleared from the forest where the villagers cultivated maize, yams, plantains, or cocoa. Many of the houses advertised produce for sale, by way of a bunch of plantains placed at the roadside, or an occasional heap of lumpy dirt-brown yams. Poverty, yes, but not squalor, and I made the distinction in my mind: "poverty with industry."

The same industry was demonstrated by the birds. Hundreds of yellow and black weavers gathered in noisy colonies dotted with their nests of woven grass. Each pair of birds built as many as six nests, and the empty ones were left as decoys to distract snakes and larger birds. Whenever I passed a tree or line of bushes that served as "weaver village," the air was suddenly alive with the sound of a thousand squeaky wheels.

Yet on the whole the birdlife seemed meager. I had noticed it the first day out of Douala, but had thought perhaps the birds were quiet in the heat of the day. Only the bright red flicker of the occasional fire-finch moved in the leaves. Even at dawn the trees seemed strangely silent, and as the days went on I would see the pied crows, the kites soaring up high, but very few songbirds compared with the avian variety that had overwhelmed me in East Africa. I asked David about it, and he agreed it was true, but couldn't explain it either. "You see a lot of the LBJs here," he said.

"LBJs?"

"Yeah. Little brown jobs!"

Then the road dropped away in front of me, the sky suddenly wide at the edge of the mountain. "Here we go!" David said, and I stopped pedaling and coasted, tires humming as we gathered speed. At first David's heavy load pulled him ahead of me, but my narrower tires and lower riding position gave me the aerodynamic advantage, and I quickly gained on him, then sped by with a whoop. Crouched over the handlebars, leaning into the wind, I felt my pulse accelerate. A momentary fear triggered a mental image of crashing, but I pushed it aside, resisting the impulse to reach for the brakes. My eyes were fixed on the road rushing toward me, and I heard only the wind, so strong that it lifted my helmet and pulled against the chinstrap. When that happened I knew I'd reached fifty miles an hour (from previous experiments with a speedometer) and I felt myself grimace, eyes wide in a mask of melodramatic fear. When the hill flared and I finally slowed down, I had to laugh at myself; amused at my foolishness, relieved at my survival, and disappointed that the hill was over.

As I began to pedal again I noticed small flocks of church-goers, mostly women arrayed in their Sunday-best *pagnes*, kerchiefs, and clean white blouses, walking along the road together with prayer books tucked under their arms. Choir music wafted through the open churches, and in the village of Yoke a boy stood outside the church, calling the faithful to worship by banging a stick against an old truck rim hanging from a tree. I stopped for a moment to watch a procession of women all in yellow *pagnes* and kerchiefs, then another group all in white, and a third group all in black with white collars and kerchiefs. Men in black suits walked alongside them, tapping out a marching cadence on small hand-drums. The parade filed into a palm-thatched pavilion in a field, where a speaker played recorded drum music from the altar at one end. The preacher stood waiting for his flock to assemble, but I waited no more. Leonard wheeled by and I rode off after him.

A third cyclist fell in behind us, a boy riding a one-speed bike with a big plastic cooler on the back. As the three of us passed through the villages in a line, he honked a bulbhorn like Harpo Marx, and I soon saw that he was a "pedaling-pedlar," stopping to sell plastic-wrapped sticks of red ice from the big cooler. Once the sale was made, he'd be after us again, making up in determination — and probably practice — what he lacked in equipment. Leonard and I smiled at each other to see that as we coasted down the short hills, he pedaled his old bike like mad to stay with us, even downhill. He would fall back on the climbs, not having the gears we did, but he always came up behind us once more. I heard another call from the side of the road. "White Man!" Or perhaps it was "Ice Man!" a call for the freezie-man, as he stopped there and we didn't see him again.

Neither did we see any more villages as we entered an uninhabited area called the Mungo Forest. Impenetrable growth closed over the road, trees, undergrowth, and vines winding together in green profusion. The silk-cotton trees towered overhead, gray columns rising to canopies of small leaves. The odd dead one rose stark and leafless, but every branch was intact and silhouetted against the sky. An ancient, primitive kind of palm raised its fronds upward in fans. All that was missing was a diplodocus, maybe a couple of pterodactyls.

Midday was approaching, and Leonard and I began to look for a suitable siesta spot. We figured we'd covered half of the fifty miles to Kumba, agreed that a break would be nice, and had no doubt the others would concur, particularly Elsa. An oasis of grass and shade at the side of the road invited us in, and we parked our bikes beneath a row of oil palms. I put down my foam sleeping-pad, spread my brand-new *pagne* over it, and used my rolled-up sleeping bag for a pillow. Everything was set. Leonard had made his own little nest and was nearly asleep already. I pulled out the *Ethics* and lay back under the tree. Having finished the lengthy introduction, I was now ready for the real thing.

I read the opening sentence. "Every rational activity aims at some end or good."

Well.

I might as well have stopped right there. That statement alone could give me enough to think about for the whole trip. If not for a whole *life*.

Every rational activity aims at some end or good. Okay, what is "good"? *Define your terms*, for a start. Well, I knew that Aristotle considered the highest good to be happiness. That helps. So every rational activity should aim at happiness. That makes sense. Let's try the second sentence.

But wait — is it always true? Reading Aristotle, for example, certainly one of the most rational of activities, does that really aim at *happiness*? Enlightenment; stimulation; distraction; hopefully education — are these happiness?

Ah, no. But they *aim* at happiness. Every word counts.

And what about a thing like *this*? What about bicycling around Cameroon?

Oh, of course! Every word counts. He said *rational activity*. No one would call *this* a rational activity.

I saw that Elsa definitely wouldn't, as she rode up with David and Annie. Annie smiled, David smiled. Elsa glowered. The heat was getting to her again. As she groaned and stretched herself on the ground, she asked if anyone knew the temperature. I got up to check the little thermometer on my handlebar bag. "Ninety."

She groaned again as she lay down and rested the back of her hand over her eyes.

Leonard lifted the bandana from his face for a moment, his eyes flickering open. "Hey white man!"

I turned on my radio DJ voice for him. "Hey-y-y, it's a balmy ninety degrees here in the Mungo Forest, and it's time to go look at the white folks!" Leonard laughed and pulled the bandana back over his face, and Annie remarked that she was tired of telling people she was a white woman.

I turned to David. "Not many white people come here, huh?"

He shook his head. "A few European tourists come to Cameroon, but they only visit the coast for the beaches. Or they fly to the north for the scenery, or Waza, the game park. Not many would travel around here."

"I wonder why that is," I said, "it seems so beautiful."

Elsa opened her eyes, "I can think of *ninety* good reasons," she said, "Fahrenheit."

I opened the *Ethics* once again, working my way through "The science that studies the supreme Good for man is politics," which would no doubt raise a few modern eyebrows, though the next, "Politics is not an exact science," would set a few modern heads nodding in agreement. Then my mind rested comfortably on one that most everyone could deal with. "The end is no doubt happiness, but views of happiness differ." Indeed.

Then I got to the quote from some guy called Hesiod:

> "That man is best who sees the truth himself;
> Good too is he who listens to wise counsel.
> But who is neither wise himself nor willing
> To ponder wisdom is not worth a straw"

By that point I was dizzy enough, and lay the open book over my face with a sigh, wondering if I *wanted* to be worth a straw. *White man, where you going?*

As everyone lay quietly beneath the oil palms, dozing in the welcome shade, once again I was struck by the silence of the forest. We were surrounded by trees, vines, and undergrowth, with plenty of food for *anything* to live on, and yet the chirp of a bird was so rare as to be almost startling. I couldn't figure it out. Maybe away from the road I might find some birds.

I rose quietly and followed a faint trail back into the trees, where cocoa and coffee plants were scattered among the wild bushes. A few fruits lay on the ground near the cocoa shrubs, mushy yellow oblongs split open to reveal the brown seeds, from which my beloved chocolate was derived. I picked up a seed to smell it, but detected no perfume of Cadbury's.

As I went deeper into the forest, still following the winding little path, I became a bit uneasy, wondering where it might lead, and to whom it might belong. The path wasn't well-tracked enough to be walked on every *day*, so perhaps it was only used by the farmer. His coffee and cocoa plants were so casually located among the trees and bushes that they could almost have grown there naturally.

When the path split into three even fainter tracks, I decided I'd gone far enough and would turn back. But just then I heard a rustling from the bushes ahead. An old man was standing before me, short and very thin, with wrinkled skin draped over his bones as loosely as the ragged trousers that were his only clothing. His splayed teeth were yellow, like the· whites of his eyes, but his smile was unmistakably warm. He seemed remarkably unsurprised to find me there, certainly less so than I'd been to come upon him. In slow, considered English he asked me where I was from, and I told him. He nodded. "Aah, Canada." Still smiling, he asked me if I was coming from Douala.

"Yes, I am traveling around Cameroon by bicycle, with my friends back at the road, and so far we have been to Douala, Tiko, Limbe, and Buea."

He nodded and smiled, contemplating. "You are proceeding to Kumba now." He extended his hand, wished me a pleasant journey, and turned and walked back into the bushes. Through the leaves I saw him lay down on the ground to continue his siesta.

White man, where you going?

I am proceeding to Kumba.

• • •

When we set off again Leonard and I stayed back with Elsa, and let David go ahead with Annie. The rolling hills continued, a series of short, steep ups and downs. As I sweltered past an old woman laboring up the hill with a load on her head, she turned to me and said: *"Ashea."* Spoken in a soft friendly voice, I took it to be a local greeting, and began repeating it to others who said it to me: a sweet little girl with a basket as big as herself on her head, a boy startled by my sudden appearance beside him.

Later I learned that this beautiful-sounding word *ashea* meant "sorry," or "sympathy," and these wonderful people were expressing their sympathy for me. I was touched by that thought. What a contrast it made to all the cries of "White man!" In the midst of their difficult lives, these people could actually feel sorry for my labors. *Ashea.* Yeah.

Poor Elsa was falling behind again, and Leonard and I had to stop at the bottom of nearly every hill to wait for her. Once when I'd lost sight of both of them behind me, I stopped in a valley and straddled my bike for a few minutes, only to see Leonard come cruising slowly up the road, steering with one hand while the other held a black *umbrella* over his head.

At the top of the next long climb we saw a pavilion with a thatched, pointed roof. The small building beside it was decorated with metal signs advertising beer and sodas, so we pulled in to see if we might buy some drinks and give Elsa a rest. When she arrived we moved into the shade of the pavilion, sprawling on the benches with bottles of orange and grapefruit soda. Five or six children followed us inside, crowding over to the other side and staring at us silently. The patriarch, a spare old man with graying hair, came into the pavilion and greeted us cordially, though he spoke no English or French. A man in his forties, the patriarch's son, spoke a little English, and introduced himself as Albert Assante. He shook hands with us in the two-handed way: left hand supporting his own right wrist in an especially nice gesture, which symbolised that his hand was so heavy with respect that it took two hands to hold it up.

An enormously fat woman sat across from us, her great bulk draped in a flowered tent-sized dress, and a wide smile on her wide face. She sat immobile, buddha-like; only a pudgy hand occasionally pulled the neck of her dress up to wipe the perspiration from her face. She seemed to speak no English, but she laughed frequently at *something*, her deep, booming voice so natural, so unrestrained, that it was almost frightening.

"Voodoo mama," I whispered to Leonard, and he chuckled, nodding in agreement. Albert Assante introduced her as his sister.

Albert asked about our journey, and our homes, but he was particularly entranced by Leonard. "I don't wish to be impolite," Albert said to him, "but I am wondering something."

"What's that?" Leonard said.

"Well, I am wondering how it is that you are American, and yet—" he pointed to his own arm, "you are the same color as we are."

We laughed at that one, and Leonard tried to explain. "There are many black people in the United States," and Elsa and I nodded in corroboration. Elsa added, "America is a country of many different peoples."

Albert Assante looked from one to the other of us in disbelief, completely mystified, while the rest of his family waited for his explanation. The Voodoo Mama wiped her face with her dress. The three of us looked at each other, uncertain where to begin. Was it possible that these people, living in West Africa in the twentieth century, had never heard of *slavery*? Didn't they know of the thousands of Africans who had been taken from their homes and shipped off to America? Or the millions of black people, the descendants of the slaves, who lived there now?

Yes, it was possible, and no, they didn't. We were — what? *aghast*, I suppose. It seemed inconceivable that the survivors would not even be aware of one of the greatest crimes of the ages, a scourge that had been the most virulent right in *this* part of Africa.

But their tribal histories would have told the *local* stories, of the wars, the raids, the kidnappings by neighboring tribes, the individual tragedies that had robbed them of their people. The fate of the victims — being sold by their African captors to the Arab or European slavers — would never have been told. Their own ancestors wouldn't have known about it, as of course they hadn't been taken.

What little education these people might have received, perhaps from the missionaries, would never have included this sorry history. Their Christian teachers would not feel it necessary to tell them what *other* Christians (and *other* Africans, it must be stressed) had done to their people. Still, it was incredible.

I made an attempt. "Hundreds of years ago, many Africans were taken away as slaves, and a lot of them ended up in America. Then they were freed, and millions of their descendants live there now."

It seemed strange to say, such an oversimplification. But how can you *not* oversimplify a saga like that? As the Assante family continued to stare at us, uncomprehending, I even felt a vicarious guilt, like a German meeting Jewish people in Poland who had never heard of the Holocaust, or that there were Jews in America, and trying to explain it to them. *Ashea*, I wished I could say. *Ashea*.

Elsa pulled out some little cards, the same as the ones I'd seen her give to the mayor of Limbe, and handed them around. Curious, I asked for one too. "Beyond War" said the front of the folded card, and the attached lapel pin was a green and blue globe. I read on:

We live on one planet, with one life-support system. The survival of all humanity, all life, is totally interdependent. I believe that the development of nuclear weapons has forever changed our world. **War is now obsolete**.

> I have decided to work together with others to build a world beyond war.

And on the inside:

> I believe conflict can be resolved only with a sincere search for truth and a spirit of good will. Therefore, I will not pre-occupy myself with an enemy. Instead, I will accept the responsibility to work for creative solutions that will benefit everyone.
>
> I will wear this pin each day to express my commitment to these beliefs.

Continuing on the back:

> This pin symbolizes the earth we all share, surrounded by a spirit of good will. When you wear this pin, remember, pray or meditate on this thought until it becomes a reality.

I don't know what the Assante family made of all this New Age praying and meditating for world peace, but they were glad to receive the pins and cards anyway, and waved and smiled as we set off again.

At the sign for Kumba the paved road came to an abrupt end, along with the trees and grass — and any notion of earthly beauty. We entered a desolate place of brown dirt and stark, dilapidated buildings of crumbling earth and blotched corrugated metal. The streets were rippled and heaved like an unmade bed, so rough that David warned us, "Don't even bother riding on the road, it's a mess. Just stick to the sides." We rode slowly amid the reek of open drains and garbage piled outside the rows of hovels. Smoke twisted up from half-burned heaps of refuse, and people squatted in the doorways, silent and dour, squinting up at us with hooded eyes. A few buses and taxis crawled along the street, squeezing between the bumps, potholes, and sleepy-looking pedestrians. Abandoned cars and vans, rusting hulks left to rot where they died, had sunk to their hubs in the dirt.

"What a horrible place," I said to David, "a real hell-hole."

"Yes, it's not very nice. Sometimes people get upset when I bring them to towns like this."

"Well, no, I'm glad in a way. It's important to know a place like this exists. But it's one of the worst things I've ever seen."

"Yeah, I know what you mean."

The Queen's Hotel was an anonymous gateway, a walled-in compound of cinder blocks along an alley of neglected shacks. Across the street a rooster chased a squawking hen between the old car doors and mysterious rusty castings which leaned against a wall. A feral brown dog trotted down the alley, tongue dragging as he sniffed at the living scum in the ditches. Like all West African dogs, its close descent from the jackals and wild dogs was apparent in its rangy body, erect ears, short hair, and suspicious eyes.

Inside the Queen's Hotel a dingy corridor led to a row of tiny rooms, one of which was my very own. An iron bed sagged under soiled cloth; the walls were grimy and colorless under a naked light bulb. An ancient floor-standing fan loomed in the corner like a '50s robot, beside a scratched and wobbly table. At the dark end of the hall, a shared bathroom of slimy bare concrete smelled of urine and mould.

The thing of it was, Kumba was not especially poor. It had been a prosperous market town since German colonial times, serving a rich agricultural area to its northwest, and also had fresh-water fishing at a nearby crater lake. The town boasted a rail link to Douala to transport its goods, and the roads connecting it with the coastal and northern towns had been built with American aid money in the '60s.

A certain level of material wealth for the citizens was apparent too, among what came to seem like a *spiritual* poverty. From the hotel gate, above the mean shacks in that squalid alley, I counted nine television antennas, and a large color TV played in the bar of the Queen's Hotel. People appeared well-fed, and though their dress was slovenly, it was not ragged. I had seen much poorer places than Kumba, in China and in other parts of Africa, and would see many more-impoverished villages around Cameroon. But none would be as *miserable* as Kumba. Its wretchedness was not a product of poverty; something else was at work.

As we took turns rinsing ourselves in the uninviting bathroom, I heard rain on the metal roof, and the pleasant smell of wet dust briefly replaced the reek of garbage and mould. Clean and changed, I sat in the bar waiting for the others, and had my first opportunity to watch Cameroon television. I took a seat on the red vinyl couches with three young locals who were watching a West African pop group of about twelve singers and musicians. A lead singer wailed over chanting vocal refrains, all in French, to a rhythm of pulsing bass drum and syncopated snare stabs. The music was fetching and soulful, but the monotonous song continued without pause or modulation for about ten minutes — great dancing music, if a little tedious for listening.

But it ended suddenly after all. The power went off, and when the others came up to see what had happened, the manager told us the electricity had been "seized." Whatever he meant by that, it was seized for the rest of the evening. (When we returned from town, he told us the power had been on again for a short while, but now it was seized once more. "Dang!" said Leonard. "We have missed the window of opportunity!")

We walked to the market in search of food, threading the alleyways past the wrecked cars, scurrying chickens, smouldering refuse, mournful-looking people, and the corrugated metal shacks, which seemed on the verge of collapse. The market was closed, empty, trash-filled and desolate, and in a West African town, if the market is closed, the town is closed. The market is the heart of the place, in so many ways; people even measure time by it. A week was a "market week," sometimes four or eight days, and the villagers would say that something happened "three markets ago," like the American Indians measured time by moons. The market was the meeting place, shopping mall, community center, playground, the arena of salemanship and social graces, and the forum of discontent.

But in Kumba, there was no produce on the tables, no bright-colored heaps of fruit and vegetables and grain, no talk and laughter, no crowds of people, and at first we could find nowhere to eat. Finally David stopped at a particularly grubby stall, and the sour-faced woman agreed to fix us something.

"Mmm!" I said, as she ladled out bowls of rice with beans and *ndole* (the green sauce). "Rice with junk on it again."

Else looked up, "Are you getting fed up with the food too?"

"No, not at all. I like rice with junk on it. Um — I guess you don't?"

She made a negative sound and shook her head. I took a drink of lemon soda and thought to myself 'well, she's complained about the heat and the hills every day, the forty-eight mile ride today, and now the food. There's not much left.' If she didn't like the cycling or the food, and certainly the hotels weren't much to look forward to, with the enduring exception of the Atlantic Beach in Limbe — it was going to be a joyless journey for her.

As we strolled the alleys of Kumba in search of bottled water, a few calls of "male caucasian!" assailed us, along with hisses and indecipherable muttered comments. The waters of Mount Cameroon were commonly available and seemed safer than the local water, so I decided to stay with that as long as it remained cheap and plentiful. But when I asked the price of Tangui water in an untidy little shop in Kumba, the rodent-faced proprietor tried to double the price. I shook my head and put down what I knew to be the real price, and he took it with a shrug. Then, as I walked out of the shop, stepping carefully over the uncovered cesspool of a ditch, a sneering layabout called to me, "Hey, give me your water!" Again I shook my head and walked on.

What was *with* this unfriendly and slovenly town of Kumba? Why were these people so unhappy and impolite, so lacking in pride for themselves and their surroundings? An ironic little card in my hotel room admonished the guest, "Have respect for yourself and your surroundings." Good advice for the town, rather than the guests.

I don't know what "kumba" meant in the local language, but I ran across it in the Swahili dictionary. In the lingua franca of East Africa, *kumba* means "to clear out, take away. Sweep out a place and collect rubbish." This too would have been good advice for Kumba, the most wretched and miserable little hell-hole I have ever visited.

Post-modern, avant-garde wall painting.
Outside a bar in Togo.

hotel happy

The English have a saying about their neighbor to the north: "The only good thing about Scotland is the road leading out of it." Petty chauvinism aside, you could not say that about Kumba. As pleasant as it was to be leaving that hell-hole, the road was no better than purgatory.

At dawn the streets were hazy in the dust and half-light. A fetid miasma hovered over the ditches, and the smouldering garbage gave off its own reek. Shabby figures shuffled in the gloom; women on the way to market carried basins of dirty yams on their heads. Men leaned against the abandoned vehicles and called out the unwelcome greeting, "White man! White man!" Women and children huddled silently around the water tap, waiting their turn.

Passing trucks and minibuses stirred the road into choking clouds as I pedaled down the main street, and I pulled my bandana up over my face like a bandit. A crumbling bridge led out of town, past garbage and wrecked cars tumbled down the side of a sad little stream. I looked up the hill to see the one nice building in Kumba: the Catholic church, of course. The House of God was in order, but not the House of Man. Beside me a young guy called out, "Wrong way!" and I wondered what he knew that I didn't.

Perhaps he knew about the road. My wheels sank into the soft earth of a bumpy and rutted track of red dirt, and I had to steer carefully to aim for the higher parts. Traffic was scarce: a couple of trucks, a moped, a bicycle with an ancient chainsaw strapped to the back, but the "male caucasian" calls continued from field workers. Passing minibuses answered them for me: "Let Them Say" and "Loving Brother."

By 7:00 the children were on their way to school, the girls in blue dresses and the boys in blue shirts, and I smiled as three of them began jogging beside me. The two girls' rubber sandals flip-flopped along; the boy's bare feet slapped the earth, and I heard the rhythm of their breathing. They said nothing, hardly even looked my way, just trotted along beside me for more than a mile. Somehow cheered by their presence and their unsmiling stamina, I stopped for a moment to give them each one of the colorful pens I'd brought for just this purpose.

Away from Kumba the friendliness of the country people returned, and I began to hear calls of "good morning" and an occasional *bonjour*. Men raised their cutlasses in greeting, and one voice called out, in *basso profundo*, "Hello guy!" Many more children walked along the road on their way to school, and, less taciturn than my "running escort," called out to me. A pair of old ladies tottered along together, and one of them offered my favorite greeting: "Welcome!"

But as the people became friendlier, the road became less so. The soft earth gave way to rocks and gravel glued together with dust, and I had to pick my way carefully, eyes always down on the road, steering the bike across and back to avoid the larger stones. The other riders soon caught up with me. Their mountain bikes, with fatter tires and wider handlebars, were more suited to this kind of terrain than my touring bike.

On one rocky hill I chose an unfortunate course. A large stone deflected my front wheel to the side, and I jerked desperately for balance as my bicycle headed for the ditch. On roads like that I left my toe-clips loose so I could get my feet out in a hurry, but there was no time. Suddenly I was on my back, sprawled on the stones with the bike on *top* of me. I felt a stab in my spine, and my camera and tape recorder went spilling out of the open handlebar bag into the dust. I muttered a curse, but seemed to be okay, though I reached back and felt a tear in my shirt and the wetness of blood. Pushing the bike off my legs, I got to my feet and brushed off the dust. David and Leonard were just ahead of me, at the top of the hill, and called down to see if I was all right. Like Pee Wee Herman, I told them, "I *meant* to do that."

"Nice break-dancing!" Leonard called back.

By noon we had only covered twenty-five miles of that terrible road. Riding in front of the pack again, I was stopped at a guard post just before the junction with a paved road, and the gendarme asked me, in French, where I was going. Disgruntled and unwilling to recount the whole story, I answered "N'djamena," which *was* our ultimate destination, though it was three weeks and more than a thousand miles away.

His eyebrows raised, and he said: *"C'est possible?"*

"Oui, c'est possible," I assured him wearily, and he went on to ask me why I was traveling by *velo* — bicycle — rather than by *voiture* — vehicle. I told him the usual story about how you see more traveling by bicycle, meet more people, and it's a better way to travel. Shaking his head at my foolishness, he waved me on, then stopped David to ask him the same questions.

That guard post represented the former border between English and French Cameroon, and even after more than twenty-five years of amalgamation, few roads cross that frontier. Apart from this dirt track from Kumba to Loum, the highway we had ridden between Douala and Tiko was the only other one, and much political noise had been made at the opening of that "Highway of Reunification." This, then, had been the "Dirt Road of Reunification."

Since we were in a French-speaking area once more, *"Homme blanc!"* replaced "male caucasian," though I also heard a pleasant *"Bon courage, mon frère."* Yet another security check interrupted my passage, soldiers this time, but they spoke English, and when they asked what we were doing, they seemed glad to learn we were tourists, traveling in their country just to see it.

From there we turned north again, happy to be back on a paved road, with painted lines and even a narrow shoulder as sanctuary from the speeding traffic, though it was hilly country, with a lot of climbing in the midday heat.

Hot and thirsty, I stopped at a drink shop in the busy hillside village of Manjo, and sat in front of it drinking grapefruit soda — *Pamplemousse* — and watching the schoolchildren return to their afternoon classes. A crowd of them gathered around my bicycle and me, staring and giggling, until a stern schoolmaster came along. He stood there and yelled at them, delivering a loud tirade of abuse and chasing the loitering boys around, swatting at the backs of their heads until they all ran away.

He reminded me of my Grade One teacher, Miss Jenner. An Anglophile spinster (she spent her summers in England and always returned with a new Austin or Morris) Miss Jenner shared a house with our kind and soft-spoken principal, Miss Gilleland. One winter day I saw Miss Jenner drive by in her prim little Austin while a bunch of us were throwing snowballs at each other — *blocks* away from the schoolyard — and when I got to school she grabbed me by the collar and dragged me to the office. She asked why I'd been throwing snowballs, and I said something like "Well, some guys threw snowballs at us, and Tommy said 'let's get 'em,' so we threw snowballs at them."

Her ruddiness deepened by quivering rage, she cried: "You stupid, *stupid* boy!," and laid into my hand viciously with the heavy woven "strap" that was the favored instrument in those days of scholastic capital punishment. Even at the time I was wounded by her insult more than the injury, not understanding why I was a "stupid, stupid boy," and I would always wonder why a friendly snowball fight well away from school grounds so enraged her. Just as I wondered why this African martinet reacted so violently to his charges' crime of looking at a white man and his bicycle. I suspect they each had other frustrations than us children, and found us convenient "whipping boys."

Leonard and Annie rode up together, Leonard cool as ever in big sunglasses and a blue bandana over his head, and Annie with her glasses crooked and hair sticking out of her helmet. They joined me for a Pamplemousse and a seat on the ground. Time went by, along with several more Pamplemousses, and when an hour and a half had passed, we began to worry a little. Finally David pedaled up, looking weary and broken, and announced that Elsa was having a tough time with the heat and the hills. He'd had to wait for her on every hill, and, he reported, she'd even been putting on the brakes on the *downhills.* He was going to put her in a taxi for the last ten miles to Nkongsamba.

Elsa walked slowly up the last hill, pushing her bike, and collapsed beside us. She too was weary and broken, and her silence was bitter, spreading in a slow wave over us all. When David had arranged the taxi for her, and loaded her bike into it, the rest of us started off again, up and over the wooded hills.

I felt badly for Elsa, but I could imagine what David had endured as well, his patience stretched to the limit by having to stop for her again and again, as well as receiving the abuses of her frustration. She'd been ready to give up, catch a bus to Douala and go home, and only David's urging had brought her this far. But I knew he'd receive no thanks, either for his patience or his encouragement.

No one ever did. And what good is self-denial if no one *appreciates* it?

A minibus roared by, its sign offering a Nietzschean piece of advice for Elsa, David, and all of us: *"Volonté."* Will.

Seeing David riding ahead of me, downcast but stoic, I rode up beside him and said, "Good news. I've been talking with the Pope, and he agrees that you should get a sainthood!"

He grinned and replied "But Neil, I'm Jewish!"

"I'm sure that's not a problem; it's been overcome before. I understand most of the Holy Trinity, and even the Holy Mother of God bore the same stigma."

He laughed and nodded, then we crouched down to concentrate on a fast descent between the trees. High volcanic mountains rose on either side, wooded slopes, bare shoulders of pale green, and higher mountains of cloud piled on top of them. A sign announced the village of Ngwa, and at the end of a row of twelve huts, back from the road, crouched a witch-doctor's house, set apart by carvings and idols in the yard. A sign advertised cures for everything from madness to sterility.

And finally, Nkongsamba (the "N" silent in local pronunciation) where David left me at the crossroads to wait for Leonard and Annie, while he climbed the hill into town to check on a hotel. A crowd of youths gathered around and politely asked about my travels. I took it as a tribute to the quality of my bluffed French that one of them asked me if I was from Paris(!), while another asked if I carried a notebook and an *appareil-photo* — camera — to record my travels in his country. That was an unusual and incisive question, and I smiled and nodded, telling him *"Oui."*

On the side of a steep road overlooking the suburbs of Nkongsamba perched a collection of irregular buildings with pink walls, topped by an uneven roof of corrugated metal, part flat, part peaked, and one end rising to a pyramid. The only sign announcing it as a hotel was a bizarre cartoon figure painted on the wall, a pipe-smoking biped with horns and tail carrying a sign reading "STOP — HOTEL." Across the wall beside it the word HAPPY was repeated several times.

David cycled up to the market to fetch Elsa while the rest of us carried our bikes inside, to another variation on the M.C. Escher interior we'd seen at the Hôtel Kontchupé in Douala. I squeezed my heavy bike around winding corridors, lugged it up two or three steps only to wrestle it back down two or three steps, then down another narrow hallway.

I had a room to myself at the Hotel Happy, though it was on an inside corridor, so that rather than enjoying a view down into the valley, my tiny window looked out on the dark, airless hall. The room too was tiny, with robin's-egg-blue walls barely six inches on either side of the bed, but the bathroom was vast, big enough to park my bicycle in. In fact, as a bathroom it made a *great* garage, because there was no water. "It has been seized," pronounced Leonard solemnly. However, buckets of rain water were delivered to our rooms, and a wash and shave improved my appearance and even my mood.

David led us up to the main part of town, walking along the dark road with our little flashlights. We passed the walled-in marketplace, *La Grande Marché*, a bakery, and bright shops full of canned goods and imported liquors. A few Mercedes and an unlikely Renault Turbo Fuego tooled down the paved streets. Yes, it was about as unlike Kumba as could be: a clean, prosperous, and friendly town, where the people smiled and greeted us, or at worst minded their own business without passing rude comments to pale-skinned visitors. We liked it there.

And we liked the *Restaurant Touristique* too. After a week of market-stall chop-houses, and the longest, hardest, and hottest day yet on the bikes, we were truly ready for a real restaurant meal. A sandwich-board on a side-street directed us into a small turquoise building, where we sat around a small table and checked out the menu.

"Look what they have," Elsa said. "Salad!"

"I think I read ... um ... that salad is, like, the worst thing you can eat in Africa," Annie said.

"That and ice cream," I said. The waiter brought us a jug of water. "And water."

"Yeah, a lot of times greens and things aren't washed too well," David advised, "but it's probably okay here. It's a good restaurant, and I'm going to take the chance."

"Yeah man!" Leonard said.

The salad was good (though I would pay for it later). Then came plates of chicken and french fries, with, of course, bowls of rice with junk on it — to remind us where we were. We laughed over the tough and scrawny chicken, commenting that we'd seen the hard life it would have led, constantly running to escape the wheels of speeding minibuses.

"These," Leonard said, "are *really* free-range chickens."

Elsa had recovered from her heat exhaustion, and had regained her usual manner. She "hadn't expected it to be so hot" (What *did* she expect in Equatorial Africa?) and she "did just fine when it wasn't too hot" (she didn't) and to David: "Why did you have to pick such hilly roads?" David — the newly-beatified Saint David — just shook his head and laughed.

Back at the Hotel Happy, my room was sweltering and stuffy. Even the little window into the hall had been shuttered for the night. I ministered to the cuts on my back, the scrapes on my hip, the myriad of red bug-bites on my arms and legs, took my anti-malaria tablet, chased a large beetle across the room and under the door, and tried to fix my camera. The roads and my break-dance tumble had pounded it to death.

When I'd managed to resurrect it, I settled into bed. Sigh. It sagged like a hammock, and I was able to touch three walls without moving. But, I *was* moving — tossing and turning as two fists wrestled inside my stomach. All those meals in filthy little stalls hadn't affected me, but the first one with some pretense of elegance (clean glasses, knives and forks on a plastic tablecloth) seemed to have disagreed with me. 'Probably the salad,' I reflected with a healthy dose of rue. My cuts and scratches chafed against the rough blankets, and the insect bites itched. I was really having fun now.

And with all that, it was a noisy place — another "quiet night in Cameroon." The same song seemed to drone and throb for hours from the bar across the hall, while I shifted and twitched in the airless heat. In the room beside me an enterprising woman entertained a succession of "gentleman friends," while the walls reverberated with her wheezy giggle and the deep, swaggering laughter of her companions.

An occasional few minutes of silence, then another knock at the door, the tinkle of glasses, and the laughter began again. She was doing a brisk business at the Hotel Happy.

Carvings on the Fon's secret hideout, near the Fon's secret beer.
Fon's Palace, Bafut.

the larger bowl

In this reporter's opinion, insufficient research has been devoted to the effects of Third World stomach distress on one's dreams. Personal experience in China and Africa has proven that the most vivid and bizarre dreams are created under these conditions, far beyond the wildest hallucinations of any "mind–expanding" drug. My advice to those substance-abusers who seek cheap thrills and momentary elevation by way of addictive and messy chemical concoctions, "Stop wasting your time and money — try dysentery instead." I'll start a foundation, print up some buttons. "Just say *o-o-o-o-o-o-h*."

I awoke in a dizzy fog, sprawled sideways on the bed with my legs entwined in the sheets, and shook my head until my cheeks rattled. What a *weird* dream. An armored helicopter had carried me from Toronto to the east coast of Canada, where we flew into the back of a truck, which drove us through a tunnel under the Atlantic Ocean, to Halifax(?). Apparently I was there to do an interview, but I found myself in a clothing store, doing a *phone* interview with a guy named Fletcher. Anyway ... a song was playing in the store, a plaintive ballad called "The Larger Bowl." Something about loneliness and the misfortunes of life, I recall. No such song as far as I know, but I like the title. While I listened to the song I read a review of it in a trade paper, written by my friend Rod Morgenstein — who is a great drummer, but *not* a record reviewer for *Billboard*.

The Hotel Happy was silent at last. The monotonous pounding music and the wheezy giggle of the courtesan next door had ceased, and with a sigh I got up to go to the bathroom. Again. A little after 5:00, while it was still dark, an eerie wailing resounded from somewhere far away. A *muezzin*, the Muslim "cantor," sang out from the top of the minaret, and called the faithful to bow toward Mecca.

"Prayer is better than sleep," goes one of the opening lines, and although I'd contest that assertion (especially at 5:00 a.m.), I do find a haunting quality in the song of the *muezzin*. The strange music somehow transcends religion in a way that hymns and gospel music never do (when you don't understand the words, they can't *preach* at you) and the exotic Arabic scales and language obscure the underlying *meaning*.

The neighborhood roosters soon joined in the *muezzin*'s song, creating a discordant morning concert as I loaded my bicycle and hauled it over the steps and down the dark hallways. While I sat on a low wall outside and waited for the others, the sky faded to pale gray, then pink. Far below, tendrils of mist lingered over the jumbled rooftops of the town, where winking lights gradually disappeared. The looming presence of Manengouba *Massif* rose in a dark shadow to the west.

"Paved, flat, hilly and mountainous" announced the itinerary for the ride to Bafang, and though I don't remember much of it being "flat," the "hilly and mountainous" bits stand out clearly in my memory. The hills came one after another, some of the climbs pulling me steadily upward for an hour or more at a time. Elsa was to refer to it as the "Bafang Death March," but it was the kind of cycling I enjoy — the challenge of the climb, the long struggle upward rewarded by the adrenalin-rush of a fast descent. On one of the longest hills the name of a passing minibus gave me more good advice: *"Don De Patience."* Gift Of Patience.

Many snakes lay squashed on the road that morning, the largest a three-foot length of dry, flat snakeskin. I had yet to see a live snake, though Elsa had encountered one the previous day. She told us she hadn't been sure which of them was more frightened, as the snake reared up like a cobra on the road in front of her, then slithered off into the grass. In general, West Africa has fewer snakes than one might imagine. The people don't like them and have been killing them off for hundreds of years. Since you don't often see a snake, it's easy to grow complacent. However, one time in Ghana I saw a freshly-killed python, about eight feet long, lying beside the road, and from then on I was more careful when I waded into the bushes for a pee.

Things Women Carry On Their Heads, Volume XIV: Big woven baskets full of greens, metal basins, plastic tubs and wooden bowls full of fruit or cassava roots, burlap sacks bulging with something, maybe yams. I even saw a few men for once, toiling along under burlap sacks, but strictly the *old* men. Generally, it was the women who carried The Larger Bowl.

We paused for breakfast in the village of Melong — actually Melong 1, for there were two of them, signed Melong 1 and Melong 2. Melong 1 was built along a ridge, just after a wide brown river, and a group of men stood by the road selling dry–looking *brochettes*. "Yum," Leonard said, "Pig guts on a stick!"

A tinny speaker filled the streets with a bizarre kind of organ music, as we found a chophouse and parked our bikes by a urine-reeking wall. A middle-aged couple ran the place, the man taking our orders and passing them on to his wife, who fried us each an onion omelette, accompanied by fresh bread and Nescafé. The loud music continued to float and waft on the air. I use those verbs advisedly; it was the strangest music one could ever hear in an African village. Through the crackle of distortion and static, an old-time Wurlitzer organ warbled through a series of watery melodies. Foot-pedal bass and the built-in primitive rhythm box played Latin beats to roller-rink standards like "Guantanamera" and "Yellow Bird." (I think I heard "The Larger Bowl" in there too.) The music and its submarine effect were like the soundtrack from *Eraserhead*, weird and incongruous, and Leonard and I snickered as each new melody wobbled into life.

"*Where* did they get this *music*?" Leonard wondered aloud.

"Traditional African folk tunes," David said, with a deliberate poker face.

This finally "seized" and switched to *real* African music, just as we saddled up again and pedaled into the mid-morning heat. Many miles and many hills remained on the "Bafang Death March." Our route followed a main road, and I often glanced up to my helmet-mounted mirror to keep an eye on the fast-moving traffic: lots of minibuses, big Mercedes trucks, several Mercedes sedans and even a couple of limousines. (Africans have a special name for the tribe of Mercedes-Benz owners, *wabenzi*, and in Togo, the wealthy market-women in the capital city of Lomé are called "Nana Benz.")

Those steep hills had been as hard on trucks as they were on cyclists, and many broken-down behemoths were parked where they had stopped, blocking one side of the road. Stones had been placed behind the wheels, and the approaching hazard was signaled in the usual West African way, clumps of grass torn from the roadside and placed up and down the road in lieu of flares.

Dangerous corners were identified by the number of mangled cars rusting at the roadside, every removable part stripped away.

Whenever I approached a blind corner and saw three or four abandoned hulks sticking out of the leaves at unnatural angles, I automatically moved closer to the side of the road, out of the way. The previous night at dinner David had explained that many of these wrecks occurred at night, when drivers raced at their reckless daytime rate, or sped through the blinding rain until they met a fallen tree.

During the midday hours there wasn't a scrap of shade anywhere. The benevolent early–morning glitter became a blinding radiance on the tin roofs. The sticky tar crackled under my wheels and sweat streamed down my face, arms, legs, and stomach. My T–shirt clung wetly along my back. An occasional hot breeze tossed the palm fronds and the roadside grasses, but there was no coolness, no evaporating sweat.

The villages were quiet in the heat. An old man looked up from under a tree and greeted me with a smile, *"Bonjour papa!"* A group of idle youths sprawled under an overhanging tin roof, and hissed at me as I labored past them. I had experienced the hissing in the Caribbean before, and knew it wasn't as rude as it seemed. The long sibilant call is directed at friends as well as strangers, an attention-getting variation on "Hey!" or "Yo!" These guys were only hissing to make me turn around — to make sure I *noticed* them. (I became so used to the hissing that once when I had just returned from West Africa I was cycling through Toronto and heard a truck's air brakes, and turned around to see who was *calling* me.)

My head-down determination on the climbs put me ahead of the others, and a few miles before Bafang I started to look for a place to stop and wait. A small open-fronted shack was decorated with soft-drink signs, and I pulled off there for a rest and a warm Fanta.

While I sat on the stoop wiping sweat away with my bandana, a family of children played and toddled around the shop, eyeing me curiously from their pleasantly dirty faces. The five smaller children were watched over by an affectionate older brother of about thirteen, who reprimanded them gently when they became too bold or careless. He was kept especially alert by a bossy and brassy five-year-old boy, who strutted around commanding and tormenting his siblings. Those who didn't do what he wished got a smack or a kick for their resistance. He gave me a cocky smile and a defiant look, puffed out his little chest and raised his fists as if to attack me. I laughed and called him *"Le petit patron,"* the little boss.

One of his sisters I thought of as *La serieuse*, a sober-faced little darling of six or seven who squatted silently in her ragged dress, glancing shyly at me and watching the antics of the other children. *Le petit patron* was the most "antic," of course, as he pulled out his penis and ran around waving it at everyone. He was finally captured and subdued by the older brother, who made him sit down on a stool. That lasted nearly a minute, until the guardian was distracted by another toddler who sat chewing up mouthfuls of dirt.

I went to my bicycle and pulled out a package of mint candies, and passed them around to the children. *Le petit patron* snatched one away from me quickly, while *La serieuse* waited for hers without a word or smile or change of expression, then sat with her sad eyes fixed on the white candy as if she expected it to disappear.

You never saw children make candy last so long. No sucking or chewing; each of the children held the little mint between a grubby thumb and forefinger, only occasionally taking a lick. By this economical method, they made the candies last for fifteen or twenty minutes. Except, of course, *Le petit patron*, who soon devoured his own mint, then went looking for one to steal. He chased and tormented another small boy until the victim broke the remainder of his mint in half and split it with the tiny tyrant. It was easy to see who had "the larger bowl" here.

Leonard and Annie rode up and joined me for a warm drink on the stoop. Then David and Elsa arrived at last, both looking exhausted — though each for different reasons. Elsa slumped wearily down to lean against the wall, and stayed there while the rest of us walked over to a nearby waterfall.

A footpath led away from the road and into the trees, then to a precipice overlooking a deep gorge. I stepped carefully to the brink of the rounded cliff, then held firmly onto a tree and looked through the leaves. Two streams flowed into one at the top of an eighty–foot drop, and a thundering rush of white water cascaded to the bottom. Cool air wafted up from the cloud of mist steaming over the round pool at the bottom.

A hand-lettered sign was placed near the waterfall, demanding 200 francs for looking at *la cascade*, and 400 for the privilege of photographing it. A beer can had been broken in half and set beneath the sign to receive our "contributions." *"Malheur à qui ne paye pas,"* admonished the anonymous collector. Misfortune to whomever does not pay. We decided to take our chances.

Together we pedaled up the last hill into Bafang, welcomed by a few young layabouts shouting and hissing at us, then pulled up at a small hotel on a back street, *Le Grand Hotel Le Paradis*. If not quite so grand or paradisial as its name, it did have water and electricity — and both at the same time.

It was Leonard's turn for a single room, while David and I took turns washing our laundry in the sink and bidet (men *can* use them too). We hung our dripping clothes on a rope which David had strung across the room and back again a dozen times. When the room was completely blocked in by dangling T–shirts, shorts, and socks, I decided to take a walk through Bafang.

Music was everywhere as usual, blaring out of the shops from tinny megaphone speakers. A record shop had a big pair of cabinets on stands in the street, but those impressive-looking speakers had been beaten into submission by long abuse, and were limp and distorted.

The buildings which lined the main road were two or three storeys of cinder-blocks, with a parade of dusty shops on the ground floors. Car parts, hardware, bakery, cigarettes, and a sad–looking little tailor shop. Many of the upper floors sported breeze–block balconies with wrought-iron railings, like an echo of New Orleans.

But try cashing a traveler's cheque. I entered the bank and stood in the "line" (*bunch*, really) in front of the counter. When I finally made my way to the teller and laid the cheque before him, he only shook his head. When I asked why he wouldn't cash it, he lost me in a flow of heavily-accented French, and I surrendered. I would seek my fortune elsewhere.

Crossing the street, I stepped carefully over the boards which covered the open drains, and entered *La Banque National Camerounaise*. 'This is more like it,' I thought, seeing a much larger business area, and two prominent VISA stickers on the glass around the teller's cages. I stood confidently at the teller's window and handed him a $50 traveler's cheque and my passport, which he took away to an office in the rear. To my surprise, he returned shaking his head, handed back the cheque and my passport, and turned away. When I called him back and pointed at the VISA sticker and the matching logo on my traveler's cheque, he just turned around again, not even trying to explain. I continued to protest in stumbling

French — doing a fine imitation of an obnoxious tourist — until he called over his superior, who explained to me that they didn't have enough money to cash my cheque. I pointed to the teller in the next cage who was counting through a brick-sized wedge of cash, but he only shook his head again.

Shaking my own head by then, I gave up and headed back to the hotel. The curse of the waterfall, *Malheur à qui ne paye pas.* Misfortune to whomever does not pay. Or is not paid. They wouldn't cash my traveler's cheque, and now I had no money. Of course I didn't need much, as David paid for the hotels and dinners, but as a rule I hate having no money in places with names like Bafang.

And more misfortune was about to descend upon us. When I got back to *Le Grand Hotel Le Paradis,* Elsa rolled out the Apple of Discord ...

• • •

Inevitably, when a group of strangers with very different backgrounds and personalities shares a trip under difficult circumstances, friction will arise. In Bafang the conflicts in our disparate bunch began to surface. Maybe the dance was getting tougher, and the masks were beginning to slip.

Earlier in the day, when we'd first arrived, we had waited outside the hotel while David negotiated with the manager. As I straddled my bike and wiped a bandana across my face, I heard Elsa grumbling to Annie about the distances we'd been riding every day (though that day's ride had only been thirty-three miles), and I heard her say something about David pushing us too hard. 'Aha,' I thought, 'mutiny already.'

Annie listened agreeably with her open-mouth smile, then turned to me. "You've been on a lot of bicycle tours. Are they usually this hard?"

I had to say that they were usually harder, at least the cycling part (I should have added "so far"). But we'd only been averaging about thirty miles a day; the longest ride had only been fifty, and all the roads had been paved. On my first-ever bike tour, in China, they gave us several punishing eighty-mile days in a row, and later when I joined tours with friends in Europe or Canada, we usually rode seventy or eighty miles a day and some days up to a hundred. And that's in the Alps, the Pyrenees, or the Rockies. It's axiomatic that if you want to see anything, or get anywhere, you've got to cover some miles.

Although David had planned for a day-off in Bamenda, which was only two days away, I heard Elsa suggest to Annie that instead of taking a day-off we should reduce the mileage every day. Just then David had emerged from the hotel entrance, and Elsa went silent.

Later in the afternoon, when everyone was back from town and lounging on the open corridor between the rooms, Elsa announced that she wanted to have a meeting. Books were closed and, in the case of Leonard, eyes were opened, while Elsa bent forward, her sharp features stern and business-like.

Hesitant at first, not wanting to admit anything like defeat, she suggested we split the next day's ride in half, and, instead of having the day free in Bamenda, we could spend more days covering the same distance. David spoke up. "Well, we *could* do that, but I don't know. Once we start messing with the itinerary..." He tailed off, wondering how best to be diplomatic, and yet not let his own plans slip away. "I think you'll find that a day off the bikes is the best thing you can do — have a good rest for a whole day. Even not having to get up and pack your bags for once makes a nice break. I don't think we should give that up. Bamenda is an interesting town, and worth spending some time in. But," he spread his hands to the group of us, "it's up to you guys. If that's what *everybody* wants to do, then I guess we can, but..." He shrugged and looked down.

Annie was the malleable sort who just wanted "everyone to be happy," and she would gladly have gone along with Elsa. Leonard was easy-going enough to agree to whatever was decided, so I knew they wouldn't argue too much. My feelings were more complicated, and my sympathies more with David than with Elsa. "Personally, I don't want to start riding twenty-five-mile days and miss out on things we might have seen, or places we might have gone. And David's right, a day off is a wonderful thing on a bike tour. I don't think we should give that up either." I turned to Elsa, "Why don't you just take it easy on yourself, swallow your pride, and if one of the rides is too much for you, just take the bus like you did the other day?"

But she was having none of that. "Well, that's not what I really want to do. And I don't speak French, so someone is always going to have to arrange it for me. I do okay until the heat gets too much," (David's eyes met mine), "and I'd rather be able to ride if I can. The day I had to take the bus I just wanted to pack it in and go home."

I tried to reason with her. "Well, if you just accept that you can stop anytime you want — take the pressure off yourself, and realize that if you're *hating* it, you can always take the bus. Just keep in the back of your mind that if it gets too horrible for you, every mile could be your last."

I hadn't meant "every mile could be your last" to sound quite so *mortal*, but there was a chorus of laughter from the others, which at least broke the tension. "I don't know if I like the sound of that," Elsa said dryly.

David spoke again, "Remember, there's nothing to *prove* here, Elsa. This is the toughest bike tour on the market, much harder than any of the others I lead." He framed our little group with his hands, and said "Look, I could only get four people from all of North America even to *try* it! So it's not a question of being tough enough to pedal every mile. You were tough enough to try. That's the thing."

Facing this resistance, Elsa gave it up, and trailed off with "Well, taking the bus is not really what I came here to do, and not what I *want* to do. But I guess I can if I *have* to."

We went back to our rooms until dinner time, then met in the hotel restaurant. As the chicken, steak, spaghetti, rice, fried potatoes, greens, and good French bread were being delivered to us, a conversation bubbled up and boiled over into a dinner-table debate that so engrossed me I hardly tasted the food.

The discussion began innocently enough, with all of us agreeing on our concern for "environmental issues," not an unusual subject for bicyclists to agree on. But if we agreed on the *effects*, we sure didn't agree on the *causes*. I found myself battling the amazingly widespread notion that some mysterious confederation of power-brokers is pulling all the strings, and we are all puppets and victims. This conspiracy theory always seems to include the idea, as indeed it must, that everything people do is a result of *conditioning*; that the whole human race responds to a Pavlovian "mind control" which is programmed by the evil tyrants of government and business. So many times I have argued this, and though I've never *lost* the debate, I've never exactly *won* either. People seem content to believe that a few unnamed manipulators are clever enough to control all the other people in the world, who are stupid enough to let themselves be controlled.

Elsa started it. People only burn fossil fuels, she said, because of some unspecified "arrangement" between government and the oil companies. "People only drive cars because they are *forced* to."

No way a lifelong car-lover could let that lie — my first *word* was "car." "Wait a minute," I said, "don't you think people *choose* to drive cars?"

"Only because they have no other choice. The government doesn't bother building good mass-transit systems."

"Isn't that because nobody wants to *use* them?" She shook her head, but I went on. "Do *you* drive a car?"

She dodged that with "The government doesn't make trains available to me," and the battle was joined. Leonard, to his credit, remained silent through the whole debate, but David and Annie aligned themselves with Elsa.

I dove into the fray. "Surely it's people themselves that have made that choice. People have *always* preferred the convenience and privacy of automobiles, ever since they were first built at prices they could afford — the old Model T."

I couldn't imagine anyone could argue with that, but I was met with a chorus of dissent. Still I went on fearlessly. "And it's not like gas engines were the only ones *offered* to the public. There were steam and electric cars built right from the beginning, since the turn of the century" — and here all those years of interest in cars paid off — "the Stanley Steamer, the Baker Electric. In fact, one called the Detroit Electric was built right up until World War II. The reality is that no one *wanted* them. The gas engine was more powerful, more convenient, and more efficient."

Then David jumped in, "Well what about solar power and wind power? They've been around for forty years, but they've never been properly applied. No research goes into them. The government and the oil companies have kept them buried."

And Elsa, "Meanwhile they spend all this money on things like the Tennessee Valley Authority, and —"

I cut her off: "So now there's something wrong with hydro-electric power too?"

"Well no, but..."

I was getting mad now, and turned back to David's statement about solar and wind power having been "buried." "That is so *obviously* untrue. Yes, the technology has been around a long time, but it's never been perfected. You must have seen those forests of windmills out in California? Could they even light up a small town?

"I had a solar heater for my swimming pool once, thinking it was such a great and modern idea, but it didn't *work* worth beans. And you live in *Seattle*. How much good is solar power when it *rains* every second day? Both solar power and wind power are being tried all the time, and are even in limited use, but they're simply not *powerful* enough. And this idea of 'big business' as the villains who are holding back great ideas — the carburetor that gets a million miles-a-gallon, the light bulb that lasts forever, the perpetual motion machine — *well*.

"How about this? They have a big race in Australia every year for solar-powered cars, to see which one can go the farthest and the fastest. And who do you think won this year?"

I answered the shrugs with a defiant "*General Motors*, for heaven's sake, the biggest car-maker in the world. And there was a solar-powered race in Switzerland this year too, and that was won by Mercedes–Benz. If these corporations are supposed to be trying to *suppress* these alternate energy sources, why is it they're at the leading edge of the technology?"

No one stopped me, so I kept going. "If there is money to be made on those ideas, those same people will be *in there*. In the first place, I don't believe businessmen and politicians are *smart* enough to get together and coordinate a giant scam like that, nor could you get two of them to *agree* on anything long enough to make it work. And in the second place, I don't believe people are that stupid."

"People *are* stupid," Elsa said. My adrenalin boiled, but the others, except Leonard, just murmured their agreement.

"You really think that?"

"Yes, people are stupid," declared Elsa. "Why —" she gestured with her fork. "Well, look at cigarettes. All those American movies from the 'thirties and 'forties, everybody puffing away like crazy — just tobacco company propaganda. And then all the young people thought it looked *sharp* to smoke."

"Then how do you explain China," I wondered, "the heaviest smokers in the world? Or right here in Africa, look how many people we've seen smoking. Do you think *they've* seen many black-and-white American movies? It just doesn't wash. Can't you accept that some people actually *like* to smoke?"

She was horrified: "Oh no, it's such a dirty habit. And people that smoke smell bad."

I was beyond reason now, heart and mind racing ahead of me. "Well, people who eat *garlic* smell bad too. Smoking is bad for you, of course, but lots of things are bad for you. I try not to smoke, and you've never seen me smoke, but I happen to *enjoy* it, and if it wasn't bad for me, I would smoke all the time."

David jumped in again. "I think smoking *looks* stupid."

And so it went. Elsa introduced themes from her little "Beyond War" cards: *the responsibility to work for creative solutions; a sincere search for truth and a spirit of good will; work together with others to build a world beyond war; pray or meditate on this thought until it becomes reality.* She said, "The Russians are ahead of us now in disarmament and the search for peace."

In vain I protested ... collapsing economy ... political maneuvering ... budget cuts twisted to save face. I cited the exiled Soviet writers, and the too-easily forgotten conditions of life in Russia at that time (1988). The few who "got out" told the story for all who cared to *listen*. Not a single voice ever escaped from the Soviet Union to tell us all how *wonderful* it is there.

How is it that so many people in the West are jaded and cynical about their own governments (with good reason, unfortunately), and yet are perfectly willing to swallow the "good intentions" of *another* government? Even Soviet Russia, whose history was so ugly, brutal, and murderous, and was only then making feeble efforts to crawl out from the yoke of collectivism — from what would *finally* come to be accepted as a "discredited ideology," in the West *and* in the East.

After seventy years of glowing support from Western so-called "intellectuals," using their media powers to praise that "noble experiment" even in the face of Stalinist genocide, the tide had turned, at least on the editorial pages and to objective internationalists. But not yet for that bitter attitude carried by the America–bashers, so many loud citizens of Western Europe, Canada, the Third World, and — worst of all — Americans *themselves.*

David offered his view that the *Chinese* were leading the world in reforesting, cleaning up their environment, and cutting their military budget.

"But — but — but," I was shell-shocked now. *"China?"*

He nodded complacently: "Sure."

"But China's always been *proud* of pollution. They point to their smokestacks with pride, as a sign of their *progress* and late-blooming industrialization. When I was there, only three years ago, the rivers were a black solid–waste dump you could almost *walk* across. Reforesting? Northeast China has been deforested for *three thousand years*, and with a billion people, every inch of it is under cultivation. There's just no room to reforest, except maybe the Gobi Desert. And cutting their military budget, *Goddam!* That wouldn't be hard, nearly everybody's in uniform! All they'd have to do is create some real jobs for their youth, so half of them wouldn't have to be employed by the *army*."

He folded his arms. "Doesn't matter. They're doing it."

I was overwhelmed and outnumbered. The more facts I offered, the more I protested that neither the Soviets nor the Chinese were doing any better at fixing up the world than we were, the more I met with stony resistance. They believed otherwise, and nothing I could say was going to modify their opinion that the rest of the world was better than their own country, and smarter too. I brought back the greatest horror of all, the "people are stupid" outlook, the issue I couldn't accept or let lie.

"How can you set yourself above the rest of humanity like that? To say that *you're* smart enough to see that everyone else is stupid? Don't you think we all just need to be *educated* about how to look after the world? Don't you think people are educable?" (I had my doubts about that word, "educable," but Elsa picked it up and ran with it.)

"Oh sure, they're *educable*."

"So they're not *stupid*; they're just ignorant?"

"I guess so, if you want to put it that way."

"Well, it makes all the difference. It's the difference between hope and hopeless, don't you think?"

"I suppose," she said reluctantly.

Leonard added some much-needed humor at last. "Yeah, well, what about the CIA selling drugs in our schoolyards?"

And Annie came in as conciliator. "The important thing is that we all *care* about these things, right?"

So the Great Debate was allowed to subside, as we pushed back our plates and rose from the table. But I was still all worked–up inside by this intellectual exercise, and it kept me awake for hours.

The worst result of the day's disagreements would be that a series of wedges had been driven into the fragile unity of our little group. Less than a week had passed, and we had only begun to forge some kind of working relationship, but after this day of open discord we would each retire into a wary solitude. Polite, civil, and not openly tense or hostile, but still — the possibility of something more was gone.

On every other occasion when I'd thrown myself into a group of strangers like that, cycling in China, camping in Tanzania, or climbing Mount Kilimanjaro, I had forged new bonds with former strangers, had made enduring friendships that sometimes, as in the case of friends made in China, had led to sharing other travels together. Difficult times and the state of being apart from one's "context" make fertile ground for intimacy and trust, and a warm relationship with another person can develop quickly and completely. But that would never happen on this trip; I knew it already. I was sad to see that "window of opportunity" closed.

Leonard would always be friendly and funny, always warm and always cool, and because of his easy-going equanimity he would become a kind of anchor for us all. I would always feel comfortable with him, and enjoy his company and his humor, but we were both too reserved. Two shells take longer to crack than one. For me, it is easier to respond to my opposite, the gregarious type.

Between David and me — well, there had always been a thread of tension. We seemed to coexist on a fine line of mutual respect, and a shared passion for cycling and interest in the world, but the ways in which we were *alike* (our stubbornness, our healthy sense of self-esteem, our independence) worked against us, and we would maintain a wary distance. I would always be happy to travel with him, but we would always travel apart.

Annie, ah, Annie. We were so very different, and yet she was the classic "good heart." Even when she was most exasperating, you had to love her.

But between Elsa and me, the Cold War had begun.

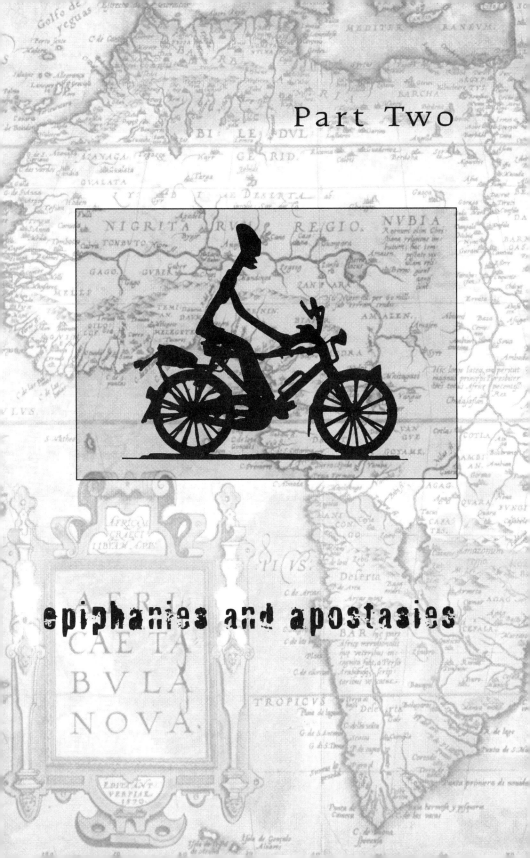

Part Two

epiphanies and apostasies

Mary Poppins in Africa.

epiphany at vespers

We gathered in front of *Le Grand Hotel Le Paradis* in the haze of first light. It had been another of those "Quiet Nights In Cameroon." Music raged from the downstairs bar until the small hours, when the action continued in the nearby streets. People shouted and laughed, engines revved, tires squealed, radios blared. But all was silent now, and fog sprawled over Bafang as we pedaled down the main street. A few figures moved in the shadows, a few hisses, a few hollow shouts.

Annie was pale and silent, and I heard Elsa tell David that her room—mate had been up many times through the night. Annie's turn for Third World stomach distress. She said nothing about it herself, no complainer our Annie, but as we got rolling I rode up beside her and offered my sympathy. She shook her head weakly and muttered: "Oh, um, it isn't so bad." But I knew it was.

The fog lifted with the sun, and soon I was sweating and gasping my way into the hills, moving ahead of the others with the previous evening's debates still rattling around in my head. The day's route would take us north, over a succession of long, steep hills and up into a region called the High Plateau, the country of the Bamileke people. Their dwellings were distinguished by pyramid—shaped roofs, always in sets of two or four. In former days these decorative roofs had been thatched, but now they gleamed in shiny metal, scattered like silver tents among the furrowed green hills.

David caught up with me, taking a rare break from his dutiful escort of Elsa, and together we pedaled at a good pace up, around, and down the hills, then stopped at a small eating-house in the village of Bandja. While David arranged for some food, I sat on the ground in the sun and watched for the others.

A young white girl walked purposefully along the tree–shaded village street. Tall and slender, with long dark hair, she wore a blue–flowered dress, and carried a book under her arm. I wondered what a girl so young was doing in such an unlikely place, and certainly not dressed for traveling. From behind me I heard David call out, "Hey Peace Corps!" The girl, startled, turned and walked over to us.

As David had surmised, as a Peace Corps veteran himself, she was the local volunteer, and taught in the village school. She had just begun her two-year stint, and was finding it a little lonely and difficult, but she was "getting along all right." From TV commercials and magazine ads, I had always thought of the Peace Corps as a bunch of kids working together in some exotic place, a kind of "summer camp" atmosphere of adventure and camaraderie. But here was the reality. A college graduate barely out of her 'teens, stuck alone in a remote place for two long years, the only American, the only white person, for many miles. She couldn't have known what she was in for when she signed up at her Midwestern college. She seemed so young, so fragile, her dark eyes veiled and defensive, her chin a little high and forward as if to defy her surroundings and her own vulnerability. After a few minutes of diffident conversation, the Peace Corps girl gave us a shy smile and said, "Well, I must get to school. Have a good trip," and turned and walked off down the road. As we watched her go, I said to David, "She seems so young."

"Just out of college, nineteen or twenty."

"Such a remote place, it must be a hard life for her. Tell me, do many of them give it up before their two years are up?"

"No, I don't think so. Most of the ones I knew stuck it out."

"Hmm," I nodded. They had my respect.

Another omelette and Nescafé, and back to the hills. David had chosen to stop in Bandja because he knew the *really* big hills began right after it, a series of long climbs to the High Plateau. As I followed the winding road up through the village, passing the children on their way to school, a line of them fell in behind me, until about twenty had joined the procession, laughing and chattering in my wake. As I stood on the pedals, cranking slowly up the steep hill, I glanced over my shoulder and smiled through clenched teeth at their beautiful faces and innocent joy, glad to have them with me.

Suddenly there was a stern voice from the roadside, and a fat policeman in a brown uniform and red beret stepped in front of me and held up his hand. My smile faded and I unwillingly came to a halt, losing the momentum of the climb. For no reason I could see, the obese officer started shouting at the children and chasing them away, waving his arms and making runs at them, like shooing chickens. Then he turned to me, and gruffly demanded my *Carte d'identitée*.

I produced my passport, and he turned the pages and stared at them dumbly for a minute. While he frowned in concentration I looked him over. The enameled badge on his barrel chest was red, yellow and green like the flag, his bulging stomach strained the buttons of his brown shirt, and he carried a gun in a worn leather holster. I wondered why this fat, surly policeman, like the head–smacking teacher in Manjo and my own Miss Jenner, had become so irate at the children for simply having fun. What was his real problem?

"Où est le nom?" he demanded, and I showed him where my name was, even though, being a Canadian passport, all the information was indicated in both English and French. So my corpulent interrogator couldn't read. *"Où est le numero?"* I showed him the number. He pulled out a scrap of paper and a pencil stub, and slowly, laboriously, copied down my name and number, and handed my passport back. As I slipped my foot into the toestrap and prepared to push off again, I watched him plod morosely down the road, ready to darken someone else's day.

As I continued the low-gear battle against gravity, I was grateful for the mercy of the overcast sky, but it was still plenty warm. Beside the road, scattered people tended their plots of coffee and beans, some calling out greetings as I sweated by and waved. A fat woman rippled all over as she walked heavily down the hill toward me, wearing one of the loose dresses with the heraldic design. This one featuring the pope's face rather than the distinguished visage of Président Paul Biya. I wished her a *"bonjour."* A young boy murmured *"du courage!"* as I climbed past him, and I smiled and said *"merci."* An incoherent stream of yelling came from above me, and I looked up to see an old man sitting on his porch, holding a jar of creamy-white palm wine at a careless angle while he berated the world at large. Out of his mind at eleven in the morning. 'Good idea,' I thought as I blew the sweat off my nose, 'I should join him.'

Occasional villages grew up beside the highway, each with a small market at its heart, and I began to notice that not all of these villages were friendly. In some of them the people seemed surly, and either ignored me or muttered something in my direction, without smiling. Instead of cries of "Welcome!" *"Bonjour!"* or *"Salut!"* I heard guttural calls of "White Man!!" or *"Homme Blanc!!"* Young guys lounging by the road yelled phrases that I couldn't make out, though one I heard a few times seemed to end with *"mon cul"* — my ass — and probably wasn't friendly or welcoming.

But, the next village would be friendly again. "Welcome!" *"Bonjour!"* *"Salut!"* Most of the places we had visited had been friendly; yet there was Kumba. David had told me of another town he stopped at during his last trip, called Bafia, where the people had been so unpleasant that he would never go back.

All of the villages were equally poor, and the people descended from the same tribes, so the difference must run deeper. Maybe sometime in the past there had been a chief, or a succession of chiefs, who were grasping, insensitive, suspicious, or simply rude. They would deal with their people in that fashion, and whether or not the people emulated the chief's attitudes, they would be forced to emulate his behavior. The chief's world-view, however twisted, would become the example, and soon the way the villagers treated each other. And if the men dealt with their neighbors by dishonesty or suspicion, so too would the women on market day, and the sons and daughters after them. It would become the manner in which people *related* to one another, defensive and cynical and me-against-the-world, and before long the whole village would function by that *modus vivendi*. (There's even an international parallel there.) The opposite would also apply, in the ripples radiating from a chief who was confident and personable, who treated his people fairly and with affection. His village would have time for friendliness, and room for self-respect.

Could hell be a place where there is no self-respect? A place where people have no pride in their own existence or behavior, and thus would have none for anyone or anything else? Was that what had made Kumba so unnerving? The town so slovenly and repellent — not because of poverty, but because the people didn't seem to care if they dumped garbage in the streets, if they were rude and unpleasant, if the ditches reeked, if the roads and buildings were falling apart. That sign in the hotel room about showing respect for yourself and others, that was a great way to ask people to behave themselves. Aristotle would have liked that.

• • •

After one climb had pulled me upward for more than an hour, I pedaled gratefully along a ridge, catching my breath and a drink of water. Then I looked ahead and made a face at the hated sign, the red circle with white outline and a horizontal black bar reading "HALTE GENDARMERIES." Another roadblock, and once again the friendliness of the local people was displaced by the menace of armed authority. A few guys with guns can spoil everything.

And at that moment, out of nowhere, the origin of the word gendarmes came to me. *Gens d'armes* translates freely as "guys with guns." I like those sudden flashes of understanding, like the time in France when I was pedaling by a county line and noticed that the word for county, *comté*, was like the word for count, *comte*. Then I saw the connection. A *comte* rules over a *comté*, just as a count rules over a county. An interesting thing to know, simple, neat, and, like so many facts, useless. Like guys with guns.

The barricade was a long stick laid across a metal barrel to block half the road. Three soldiers sat around a languid spiral of smoke beneath a shelter of woven palm-fronds. Spying me, one of the soldiers hauled himself up and waved me down. Holding out his hand for my papers, he demanded to know where I was coming from and where I was going. While I straddled the bike and sourly watched him leaf through my passport, I noticed that most of the buses and cars continued around the barricade without pause. Only occasionally did one of the other soldiers heave himself to his feet to wave a vehicle over. One who hadn't paid his "dash," I guessed.

In front of a small shop across the road, three dead rats hung from a pole by their necks, bloated gray bodies and mouths gaping with pointed teeth. I wondered if they were an exterminator's trophies, or the makings of rat stew ("bush meat," the locals would call it). The soldier finished grunting out his questions, then frowned deeper and nodded once as he handed back my passport.

The road curved down from the plateau, winding around in a long descent and bringing me out into a valley beneath a suddenly open sky. All at once the two-lane blacktop became a modern four-lane expressway, and I stared around in amazement like a character in *The Twilight Zone*. Neatly painted white and yellow lines divided the perfect ribbons of asphalt; signposts with international symbols indicated speed, curves, merging and yielding traffic; and a brand-new overpass and cloverleaf interchange served another highway above it. Ahead I saw a Mobil service station, brand-new, starkly modern, and yet deserted. On the other side of the empty expressway sat its twin, a cubicle of glazed brick with four shiny white gas pumps bearing the red Mobil Pegasus.

Then, the "expressway to nowhere" came to an abrupt end. A sign gave the symbol for "narrowing road," and my wheels rolled back onto the simple two-lane blacktop I'd been climbing up and coasting down all morning.

It was all very splendid — *but what was it for*? There was no town in sight, no sudden crush of traffic, no *reason* for this incongruous little section of superhighway. A piece of misguided foreign aid? A monstrous error by the highway engineers? Like, all this was supposed to have been built somewhere else? A prestigious "decoration" to impress visitors on their way to Bafoussam? Probably all of the above.

The map of West Africa is dotted with bizarre monuments of that nature, and Ghana is a perfect example. In 1957 Ghana became the first black African country to win independence, and Britain left the new nation with half a billion dollars in foreign exchange reserves. The new government launched itself into nationhood by decorating the capital city of Accra with a conference centre for sixteen million dollars, a drydock for seventeen million, a state house for eight million, a huge monument in Black Star Square for two million, and a showcase superhighway, like this one in Cameroon, which was twenty-three kilometers long, under-used, and cost nine million bucks. In less than ten years, Ghana found itself a billion dollars in *debt*, and entered a long, dismal period of decline from which it is only now beginning to emerge.

In contrast, the Ivory Coast, Ghana's neighbor, was the great success story of West Africa. Instead of kicking out all the Europeans, as most African countries did at independence, the Ivory Coast, like Kenya in East Africa, invited them to stay and help get the new country rolling. Thus those two countries, though not without problems of their own, had truly become "developing nations" rather than surviving on the handouts of foreign aid. Some Africans, however, explain it a different way.

One night in Ghana I fell into conversation with a young Ghanaian, and he was telling me of his concern about Poland and Eastern Europe. Well, not concern *about* them; he was worried that American aid money would all be going there, and *not* to Africa. I asked if he didn't think we should help them too, and he said: "No. You have to support Africa."

"*Support* Africa?" I asked, intrigued by the choice of word.

"Yes, you *owe* it to us!" When I asked him why, he explained, "Because of the terrible things that happened." Then followed a discussion of why it was *America's* responsibility to make up to Africans for the scourge of slavery, when it had been *Africans* who started the slave trade, first selling their people north across the Sahara to the Arabs, then south to the coast and the Europeans — who, after all, had been the ones to carry the slave trade overseas. There hadn't even *been* an America then. The Portuguese had first brought African slaves to the New World; why wasn't my Ghanaian friend concerned about *their* aid? Et cetera. Then when I mentioned that billions of dollars in aid money had been coming to Africa for thirty years, he sneered and said, "Oh yes, to Kenya and Ivory Coast," as if their success was only attributable to receiving more handouts. He finally admitted that Ghana had received a lot of money, "but we've had a radical government, and none of it's done any good." To which I replied, "If none of the money has done any good, how will you know the difference if it starts going to Poland or East Germany?"

But get these politics out of here. None of *that* stuff is what makes Africa so special to me; it's the people. As I left that strange bit of superhighway behind me, my whole morning was altered, divided into before and after, by a five-year-old girl in a yellow-flowered *pagne* and kerchief. As I pedaled by her, grumpy and fed up with everything, she turned to me, all dark eyes and shy smile, and said the softest little *"bonjour m'sieur."* That's all she gave me, this tiny angel, but all at once I was transformed. I forgot about the heat, the hills, guys with guns, and African politics, and pedaled on with a glow.

A few miles before Bafoussam I pulled off the road and parked my bike against a big shady tree. Pulling off my helmet and gloves, I wiped my sweat-sticky face and arms with a bandana, and sat back against a stone wall. Water bottle beside me, I took out the *Ethics*. Maybe I couldn't use Aristotle's clear reasoning to understand a stretch of superhighway in the middle of the African bush, but I was getting some insight on the Doctrine of the Mean — called the "Golden Mean" by everybody *but* Aristotle.

Philosophy can be scary stuff, but sometimes, like *comte* and *comté*, or *gendarmes*, it can be simple and clear if you just look at it right. Unfortunately, like African politics or the Bible, people can twist it around to suit their point of view. The Doctrine of the Mean states that moral virtue lies in the middle between two extremes, courage between cowardice and rashness, generosity between meanness and prodigality. Clear enough. But so often the idea of this Golden Mean has been corrupted, and used as a plea for moderation, for mediocrity, for temperance. Benjamin Franklin said "all things in moderation." Did he mean eat, drink, do anything you want, but be *moderate* about it? Like say, shooting heroin?

Aristotle makes this distinction clear. *But the rule of choosing the mean cannot be applied to some actions or feelings, which are essentially evil.* Under this heading he includes murder, adultery, and theft. I'm sure he would have put heroin in there, and probably guys with guns too. Later moralizers have corrupted this concept to their own purposes, and I was pleased to find in the introduction to the *Ethics* that other philosophers besides Voltaire and Nietzsche have a sense of humor. The writer of the introduction addresses the self-appointed "fun police" thus:

> If the Doctrine urges us not to drink too much
> wine, it equally urges us not to drink too little — that
> is something which the moralizers usually find it pru-
> dent to ignore.

And moralizers were the order of the day for me. Once we regrouped and cycled together through the busy town of Bafoussam, past another three police and army roadblocks, we were into the country again, and on our way to spend the night at a monastery.

M oN aST e R e
MONASTERE
SAINT BENOIT
BABÉTÉ
1,5 KM

---

said the little handmade sign where a rutted lane led into the trees. We pedaled along the track for a mile or so, then emerged into a wide clearing. Ahead of us was a long, low building with varnished wood doors and louvred-glass windows, and to our left was a new church, three storeys tall and mustard-colored, surrounded by bare earth, heaps of stone and dirt, and bits of construction equipment. The new reddish-brown metal roof seemed out of place against the ancient forest behind it.

We dismounted, and David pulled on his long trousers and went inside. He came out accompanied by a tiny nun, perhaps seventy years old, in gray and white habit. She gave us all a grandmotherly smile, her wrinkled face kind and sort of *blessing* us, as she greeted us in French. David and I did our best to answer her questions about our journey. We stood, stiffly respectful, by an arch of woven branches and wild flowers over the doorway. The Sister told us that the Mother Superior would be returning that evening from a visit to Switzerland, and the arch had been erected by the Sisters to welcome her back. Not, she said with a twinkle, to welcome bicycle riders.

She led us back along the lane to an enclosure of other buildings, three plywood-paneled rooms containing rows of iron beds. On each bed was a pillow and a home-made blanket, the loosely-woven "afghan" type that generations of grandmothers have sat knitting by the fire, or, these days, by the TV. I remembered my own grandmother turning out dozens of them, for her beloved United Church to send to "missions in Africa," and I smiled at the irony — me, the impious one who made a point of donating only to *secular* charities, on the receiving end of missionary aid.

We had the whole dormitory to ourselves, and we each chose our beds in scattered corners, with empty beds beside us on which to spread our gear. At the far end a communal bathroom was a welcome sight, a row of shower stalls and two toilet cubicles, one western-style, the other in the eastern mode (a porcelain pan at floor level, with rough tiles on either side for good footing while you squatted over it). Talk and laughter echoed between the shower stalls as we washed away the dirt of the road.

The Sister had told us that Vespers would be held at 5:00, and we were welcome to attend. I was eager to experience this unknown ritual, with such a beautiful name. Vespers, like a soft, musical whisper. After a quick shower (a cold shower always seems to be quick), I changed into long trousers and my one "respectable" shirt, and walked quickly up the lane. Annie came running up behind, and together we crossed the churned-up dirt around the new church. Just then a line of gray-and-white nuns emerged from the main building, like an illustration in a children's book. Annie and I searched along the portico, but could find no open door, so I suggested we look around back where the Sisters had gone.

The door was unlocked, and I entered the hallway warily, Annie just behind. We tiptoed and whispered, wondering which way to go, when all at once the singing began, a gentle chord of echoing voices. I found another door, and whispered to Annie that it was unlocked, asking if she thought I ought to try it. She nodded, and I turned the knob, the two of us crowding up to the opening in curiosity.

The eyes of the old Sister went straight into mine as I found myself facing the line of nuns, all of them singing in adoration with their hands outstretched — toward *us*. I stood frozen for a moment, feeling like a fool, as I realized we were *behind* the altar. For all I knew of Catholicism, we might have been committing a grave blasphemy. Red-faced, I closed the door, and we walked outside again to find a side door had been opened.

I made myself as small as I could and slipped into the umber-colored interior, Annie and I each taking one of the bamboo benches which served as pews. The afternoon light was filtered through narrow arched windows, and tinted by a large stained-glass window behind the altar. The Sisters faced the image of Jesus, the central figure in the square of colored light, which was designed in a proto-Cubist (i.e. African) style. The seated Jesus, with cross-racial features, was bracketed by a pair of colorful saints, a chorus of angels, and the words "Alpha" and "Omega," the Beginning and the End.

As the singing continued, our other three cyclists tiptoed in, and the old Sister who had welcomed us stooped back to where we sat, handing us each a copy of the Vespers service. I opened it to *Vendredi*, Wednesday, and saw that they were singing Psalm 102, a lonely prayer for mercy in the wilderness.

The voices of the six nuns reverberated around the walls of the cavernous interior, accompanied by the gently strummed guitar of a young African Sister in the same gray habit and white headdress. Four novices in bright *pagnes* and kerchiefs sang, like the others, with their hands out to their sides. The priest sat back a few rows, bowing his white-tonsured head as he rounded out the sopranos with the low organ notes of his voice. The high and low voices singing in delicate French and the ringing sustain of the guitar were enhanced by the returning echoes in the vast church. I felt the music resonate within me — my eyes, my throat, the pit of my stomach. It was mostly the music, but it was also partly a spiritual response to the simple faith in this worship.

As they sang the second and third Psalms, I divined a kind of rhythm to the ritual. They began seated, intoning a soft hymn of praise, then at intervals they rose in unison, standing in a half-bow and singing with more feeling, their hands cupped before them in a poignant gesture of supplication. Then they stood straight, hands wide and voices raised in a gentle crescendo of adoration which left me profoundly moved. The voices rose and fell in shimmering waves, a fragile melody that seemed so elusive, and yet would haunt me forever.

'Epiphany,' I thought with a little smile, 'religion has come to me at last. I didn't think it would happen in *Africa* — and I didn't think it would be Catholicism.' Growing up in a nominally Protestant home, with my grandmother's austere Puritanism serving as a model of religion, I had tended to see Catholics, in the most innocent and even admiring way, simply as "Them." I didn't really understand what it was about. We all lived in the same neighborhood, and even played on the street together, but everything else seemed to be so *separate*. Even their schools were called Separate Schools. For some reason I couldn't fathom, they seemed to be "special," these Catholics, so I took this to be true, that they were somehow set apart.

Every day on my way to school I passed the Star Of The Sea, the school where the Catholic kids went, and saw them all playing behind the chainlink fence. This gave me a strange sense of isolation and puzzled wonder, as if there was something denied me. They had to have a separate school from "us," even a separate high school, and their church was so much grander and more ornate than the simple brick Protestant churches in my little town, and this too would naturally appeal to a child.

I was impressed, and a little bit in awe, but then I grew up, learned a little history and current events, and realized the "specialness" was entirely the old illusion of possessing the exclusive Truth — an illusion shared by all other religions. Wars, Inquisitions, Northern Ireland, pedophile priests — these, I learned, were the other side of the Star Of The Sea's small-town grandeur, and the other side of this touching and innocent Vespers service in the hills of Africa.

Epiphany now? Epiphany *here*? Not really. Just when I thought I had it, it was gone.

I've always thought I'd like to make a collection of Epiphany and Apostasy stories I've heard, how different people have adopted or rejected religion in their lives. For example, the father of a friend of mine came to Canada from Eastern Europe after World War II, accompanied by hope, a multi-syllabic name, and his young bride. Both of them had been brought up as Eastern Orthodox Catholics, and carried their beliefs with them to a new country. His wife was stricken by disease soon after their arrival, and died, leaving my friend's father wretched with pain at this meaningless loss, and he rejected his religion forever. "A God who could do this to me is not my God."

My brother Danny feels that the greatest sadness in life is to lose a beloved mate; but he has no children. It seems to me that the deepest, most cruel sorrow must be a mother losing her child. No bonds can be tighter, or more painfully broken. As a boy I once saw a photograph of a Vietnamese mother holding her dead baby and wailing. This seemed to represent the greatest of human suffering, and I have never forgotten that image. And yet all the platitudes that are trotted out, "that's the way God planned it;" "God has called her to Him;" "she has found a better life." How does a mother lose her innocent child, and still keep her faith in such a cruel deity? And yet they do.

I don't remember ever really *believing* in religion. As a child I was merely ambivalent. Every Sunday morning we were sent off to Sunday School, pulling on the itchy gray pants, clipping on the fake tie, polishing the clunky Oxfords, putting on the hand-me-down jacket that smelled of my grandfather's cigars. And I remember sitting there in the United Church basement looking at the portrait of Jesus (long hair, soft beard, limpid eyes, all in sepia tones) as I mouthed the words to "Jesus Wants Me For A Sunbeam" and wondered, 'Does He really?'

One day while my friend Rick and I walked along Main Street he told me about a book he'd found called *The Passover Plot*. He said this book claimed that all Christianity was a big lie designed to control people. Being an adolescent, I was impressed — my very first conspiracy theory. It's in a book, after all, and when you're young and impressionable those kind of things carry weight, just as one becomes enamored of "ancient astronauts" and "unexplained mysteries." However, it was then that I first *dared* to disbelieve. I had learned that somebody else did, so maybe it was all right.

I was fifteen in 1967, and was allowed to paint the ceiling of my bedroom with the graffiti of the day, "Flower Power," peace symbols, LOVE. In the corner, without thinking anything of it, I sprayed another current catch-phrase of the time, "God Is Dead" (all unaware of its Nietzschean origin). My father was outraged, not surprisingly, and demanded that I take it off. My mother said, "your grandmother would flop over dead if she saw that." So demonstrating my continuing ambivalence, with a few strokes of the aerosol can I changed it to "God *Isn't* Dead," and everyone was happy. I didn't really care one way or the other.

But there was still another Epiphany for me. At around the same age I remember going to a hockey game at the arena, and as I walked among the seats I was thinking, like a typical fifteen-year-old, about sex. All at once my mind was overwhelmed by the intricate pattern of human sexuality: arousal, male and female anatomy and their responses to each other, the great mystery of reproduction, and with a blinding flash it all seemed too complex to be accidental. There *had* to be a great Mind behind it all. This is known as the "argument by design," I believe, but it left me confused and wondering for a long time afterward. Until now, in fact.

Sure, I still wonder. As infuriating and senseless as organized religion seems, and with all the abuses of the evangelists and fanatics, I am still intrigued by the romance, the ritual, and the *security* of a Higher Power. Like most everyone, I'd like to believe in something larger than life, especially for those times when life seems small and mean. But, after I've admired the poetry of the King James Bible, appreciated the peaceful wisdom of Buddhism, recoiled from a vengeful Allah or God, wondered about the secret societies of Freemasons and Illuminati, in the end I return to reality, and believe in Life. And that seems good to me.

I can worship Nature, and that fulfills my need for miracles and beauty. Art gives a spiritual depth to existence — I can find worlds bigger and deeper than my own in music, paintings, and books. And from my friends and family I receive the highest benediction, emotional contact and personal affirmation. I can bow before the works of Man, from buildings to babies, and that fulfills my need for wonder. I can believe in the sanctity of Life, and that becomes the Revealed Word, to live my life as I *believe* it should be, not as I'm told to by self-appointed guides.

There are holy virtues too in this Life-worship: artistry, integrity, love, ideas, and discovery. Yes, even laughter. And no other system permits the one instinctive first cause: your own existence. You'll never be asked to *die* for Life. At least not for a while.

Carvings
Fon's Palace, Bafut.

the missionary position

Back at the dormitory I found David talking with two German missionaries, part of a group of Lutherans from all over Cameroon who were meeting at the monastery. I'd thought it strange that they were guests of the Catholics and yet took no part in their services, but I was, of course, naive to the politics of religion.

One of the missionaries was tall, bald with a fringe of gray, a shy smile, and a kindly twinkle behind his glasses. The other was short and wide, with a heavy beard and a crooked blade of a nose, and dressed in a pajama-like costume of blue cotton pants and shirt, in a sort of tie-dyed print (gone "native"). Both spoke fair English, though heavily accented, and were interested in our travels. "Vere haff you been zo far?" "Ah, I zee. Und zo — vere are you goink nixt?"

The short bearded one, whose square build made me think "dwarf," worked in Buea, while the tall gray-fringed one had a mission in a remote part of the Northwest, where no roads at all were shown on the map. He told me that their German Lutheran Church had taken over the work of the old Basel Mission, and a few things I'd read in *A History Of The Cameroon* clicked into place.

• • •

Under German rule at the turn of the century, the Basel Mission had become the most important missionary group among all the churches who had already divided up the country like conquering armies. British Baptists, American Presbyterians, German Catholics, Paris Evangelicals; they had all staked out their "turf," like warring gangs. In 1886, the "rights" to part of the country — the "soul futures" — were actually *sold* by the Baptists. The Basel Mission picked up those "options," and also took up trading with the Africans (to finance the more seemly business of harvesting souls).

The Basel Mission had been a fairly benevolent force in Cameroon, often defending the native people in disputes, continuing to educate them even against Germany's wishes, and fighting for fair treatment of the workers by the plantation owners. By the time World War I turned everything upside-down, the Basel Mission had established 631 mission schools, teaching 40,000 people, and thus could be seen as one of the positive aspects of colonial rule.

. . .

The dwarfish German seemed interested in cycling, and took one of David's Bicycle Africa newsletters, saying that he'd like to go on a tour like ours. Then he asked how old Elsa was, and when David told him, he wrinkled his forehead with doubt, and his response was surprising. "You must haff to vait for her often," he shook his head regretfully. "Zere must be a lot of vaiting."

Everyone else we met remarked how great it was that Elsa was *doing* this thing, or that we were all doing it *together*, while to the Cameroonians it was positively miraculous that a sixty-year-old woman could even *ride* a bicycle. But this good Christian was only concerned that we might be held up by having to wait for a weaker rider (a basic Christian metaphor, no?) and this possibility obviously darkened his whole view of the affair.

Missionaries are hard people to figure. Some of them are undeniably doing great things, like the American doctor in Togo with his makeshift hospital, and one has to admire them. But not all missionaries are so active in actually *helping* people. Some of them consider "saving souls" to be more important than saving *lives*. People become missionaries because of their religion, and their "mission" is to spread the word of God. That's really what it's about. If all they wanted to do was help people who need it, there are plenty of secular organizations who would welcome them as volunteers. What people in West Africa and throughout the Third World need is *clean water* — that can save more lives than anything. But missionaries don't come to a village and dig a well; they build a church (or bribe the locals to do it).

And if these missionaries like to call themselves "teachers," too often that means they teach *religion*, period. That is their *mission*, though they often dress it up to look more humanistic. The West African capitals are dotted with offices called "International Institute of Languages," or variations on schools of "Linguistics," or "Literacy," and they're all run by the churches. Not to teach *literacy*, but to teach the *Bible*.

The Pope himself came to Africa with a message against birth control and Western civilization: "Birth control programs carry a powerful anti-life mentality. They suppress the African people's healthy love of children. You must beware of the streak of crass Western materialism in development."

Yes, crass Western materialism *will* encourage these struggling people not to bring more children into a hungry family. Those who have actually *looked* at those faces can only agree. One Catholic missionary in Cameroon advised the women of her village to *use* birth control, explaining to them, "the Pope might not like it, but I don't think *God* will mind."

All dogma aside, it is nakedly humane and truly compassionate not to want people to suffer, whether or not someone says it is "God's will." That must be the simplest of truths, the kind that can only be contested by people who place dogma *above* life, and those are the people, whether communist, fascist, Muslim, or Catholic, who must represent the enemy to those of us who worship Life as the supreme good, and the supreme god. Or to those who just want to *enjoy* it.

• • •

In the cool evening we walked up to the the monastery and found the refectory, a large dining room containing a dozen round tables and chairs. One of the tables had been set for five, so we sat down at it, just as the Lutherans began to arrive. About ten children came bouncing and yelling into the room, followed by six women, then lastly by the two men, all of them taking their places around three tables. The adults' faces all reminded me of Baader-Meinhof *Terroristen* posters in Frankfurt airport.

A woman who seemed to be the taller missionary's wife, a sad-faced, wearily plodding *frau* with a harried and distracted expression (and the most facial hair I've ever seen on a woman) carried a baby in a sling in front of her, while she herded two small children ahead. Curious, I thought, only the two men, yet there were six women, and ten children and...

"They're polygamists!" Leonard whispered, and we looked at each other with raised eyebrows. Our prurient conjectures were interrupted by the arrival of the nuns, who spread an assortment of steaming bowls on a neighboring table. A bass voice began singing behind me, quickly joined by the rest of the Germans, and we sat quietly as they delivered their Grace. In contrast to Vespers, this performance was loud, most of them singing at full voice, and it was proud. The women sang ever higher, and even veered off into harmonies, "projecting" their songs to the Lord with their heads erect and their chests puffed out. It wasn't prayer so much as a Wagnerian *performance*. Their eyes alone were frightening, burning like a hawk's at the kill, with pure fanaticism and an attitude I can only describe as "vainglorious."

Why, if the nuns were so beautiful in their worship, was there something so profoundly *ugly* about this?

There is sometimes a disturbing cast to a face which has nothing to do with features or expression. Perhaps the inner light of smugness, of being in possession of the truth, and the mean pride of worshipping that truth *better* than someone else. I had seen that face before, without knowing what I regarded.

On the Caribbean island of Montserrat, where I was recording at Air Studios (before Hurricane Hugo razed the island and closed the studio), I once stood with my wife Jackie outside the tiny airport, waiting to put her onto a flight to Antigua and home. A large group of tourists crowded out by the runway. They wore ordinary clothes, and had ordinary bodies and faces, but there was something about them that made me uneasy. I whispered to Jackie with a laugh that it was the "ugly people's convention," but they weren't *definably* ugly. It was just something I sensed.

Their matching baggage tags identified them as a Canadian Evangelical Crusade, visiting Montserrat — one of the most unspoiled and well-adjusted islands in the whole Caribbean — and why? For the same reason we were, I'm sure. Montserrat is a wonderful place to visit, and no doubt all the better if your church is paying for it.

The man I had marked as the "scariest-looking of all," with a Velcro smile and opaque eyes, turned out to be the leader. He waved goodbye and took off in his private plane, while the other shepherds and sheep crowded onto the commercial flight with the unfortunate Jackie. Perhaps she was well defended against acts-of-God, but a smart deity would see through those faces too.

And now in Cameroon I was seeing those same faces again, only this time I understood why. Pride, the first deadly sin. The Lutherans' loud performance of Grace was not worship, it was not adoration or prayer, it was "Look at me! See how I sing for my God! He has given me this voice and I'm damned proud of it!"

But, if the Lutheran Grace was a little excessive, the Catholic meal was pretty good. The first soup we'd been offered in Cameroon, rice in a thin broth, was followed by large bowls of rice and cabbage, a sauce with a rumor of meat in it, and, oddly enough, a tray of fried eggs, sunny-side-up. Bottles of beer and orange soda were lined up on a side table, with a list of prices on the side of a slotted can. The "honor system," no less. Leonard leaned over to me with an evil smile. "Psst — Hey! Let's rip off the nuns!"

As the Lutherans finished their meal, the women rose from the tables in a great flurry, collecting dishes and stacking them at the sink in the corner of the room. As soon as our plates were empty we carried them over and offered to help, but they waved us away. "*You* can do eet een ze moaning," one of them said.

The most "normal" looking of the German women — the only one you might not be afraid to be caught sitting beside on an airplane — was careful to explain to Leonard that she was "just the nanny." Her fleshy face was tired-looking and pale, red hair in untidy wisps, and one could only guess at the joy of *her* existence.

The older missionary remained seated, talking quietly with a child on his lap, while the dwarfish one in the blue pajamas made a great show of playing with the children, who had lined up the empty chairs to make a "bus." He laughed and yelled louder than anyone as he patronized each of the children in turn, but his performance seemed false, contrived to impress, and lacked the innocence that playing with children should evoke.

• • •

The stars were bright as we strolled back to the dormitory and lay on our scattered beds. For once it really *was* a quiet night in Cameroon, the only one we'd experienced so far, and it was especially appreciated after the riotous all-night action in Bafang. I asked Leonard about the book he was reading, *The Roswell Incident,* and he told me it was an exposé kind of story, claiming that a spaceship had crash-landed in New Mexico in the late '40s, and was recovered by the Air Force, who kept it secret all that time. "Either it's a big lie, or one of the most significant things ever to happen," said the fair-minded Leonard.

It wasn't long before I looked over and saw him asleep with *The Roswell Incident* open over his face. I got up and turned off the overhead light and climbed into my sleeping bag, and read a while longer with the flashlight on my shoulder. In *Dear Theo*, Vincent had renounced religion for art (an excellent alternative), and his letters became much more interesting. Now the tender-hearted Vincent had taken up with a "woman of the streets," and was determined to rehabilitate her. And he too had experienced his apostasy:

> Often when I walked in the streets quite lonely and forlorn, half ill and in misery, without money in my pocket, I looked after them and envied the men that could go with them; and I felt as if those poor girls were my sisters, in circumstances and experience. And you see that it is an old feeling of mine, and is deeply rooted. Even as a boy I often looked up with infinite sympathy, and even with respect, into a half-faded woman's face, on which was written, as it were: Life in its reality has left its mark here.
>
> That God of the clergymen, He is for me as dead as a doornail. But am I an atheist for all that? The clergymen consider me as such — be it so; but I love, and how could I feel love if I did not live, and if others did not live, and then, if we live, there is something mysterious in that. Now call that God, or human nature or whatever you like, but there is something which I cannot define systematically, though it is very much alive and very real, and see, that is God, or as good as God. To believe in God for me is to feel that there is a God, not a dead one, or a stuffed one, but a living one, who with irresistible force urges us towards *'aimer encore,'* that is my opinion.

'Mine too,' I thought as I switched off the flashlight and turned on my side. The music of Vespers still wandered through my thoughts, and two epiphanies in one day had been too much for a linear-thinking agnostic like me. The small girl that morning, okay

— it had been the sense of her *life* that had shaken off my world-weary mood so suddenly, had lighted up my darkness with a simple greeting.

As for Vespers, that was more complicated. Had it been a choir of monks, say, or boys, it probably wouldn't have touched me so deeply; it was the *voices* of the Sisters, and the feeling behind their gentle song. And I wondered if it was partly about sex. *Gender*, really. Not sexual desire, but sexual polarity and appreciation.

When we were among the children of Cameroon, Annie once remarked that I seemed to love the little girls most, while, she laughed, it was the boys who attracted her. And it was true, I might give the boys a friendly smile, but it was the sweet little girls who melted my heart, and made me theirs. Nothing Freudian about it, just appreciation for your opposite. Daddy's little girl and Mommy's little boy. I have a female friend who shares my enjoyment of Italian opera, but for her it is the basses and the baritones who are the attraction, while for me it is the sopranos of *Madama Butterfly* or *Tosca* that carry me away.

Most of us learn at some point that sex is more than the dirty words chalked on the schoolyard wall, but we can still be surprised how deeply it runs in our cells. And for humans, certainly it has long transcended its biological imperative — or at least we have dressed up that imperative in so much significance, protocol, and ritual that it begins to overwhelm even that of the Catholic Church. (Though not quite, for a lot of people: "Beware the streak of crass Western materialism in development...")

As an act, we no longer accept the basic reproductive coupling; we want it to be an *idealized* experience, a romantic, as well as physical, catharsis of intimacy, pleasure, and trust. The threads of that desire (or *need*, as a courageous high-school Health teacher once dared to tell our class) become the fibres of existence on so many levels, and manifested in so many ways.

Some relations are easy to see. Rock 'n' roll music is about sex, sure, implicitly and often explicitly, but so are nearly all popular songs. Perhaps, in subtler ways, opera and ballet are about sex too, and about *spectacle* — another common denominator that a Rossini fan might not admit to sharing with a Rush fan. But the romance, the live *presence*, the magic of lighting and the dramatic illusions of staging, all appeal to the same taste for the sensational and fantastic.

Entertainment preferences also tell some tales in broad generalities of gender (perilous earth, I know), though in this case it seems as if we don't respond to our *opposite*, but rather to the ideal gender-type of our own. It's fair to say (and easy to show) that many females are attracted to an ideal of sexual *magnetism*, exemplified by romance novels, movies, pop music, and its ephemeral faux-rebels. For males, the ideal of sexual *strength* often attracts — contact sports, paramilitary heroes, and aggressive music. A heavy-metal audience will be ninety per cent male, and the audience of the latest teen idol will be ninety per cent female. This is not a stereotype; this is *choice*.

So, if we can accept that the yin and yang of it all is sensitivity and aggression, perhaps that explains why so many great artists have been homosexual, whether active or latent. In that other perilous earth, the gray area between the sexes, is found the sensitivity to feel something the artist wishes to say, and the aggression (or arrogance) to go ahead and try to do it.

One thing, though, doesn't change for most of us. Boys like to look at girls, and girls like to look at boys. As a male friend of mine once said, "Men may be the stronger sex, but women are certainly the *sexier* sex."

• • •

A morning prayer service called *Matins* was to be held before dawn, and by 5:00 I was awake, dressing quietly and slipping out of the dormitory into the darkness. The opportunity for another epiphany was not to be missed, though my companions felt they could do without it, and slept on. The moon had set, but in that remote place the stars were bright enough to see by, and all was silent as I stood near the church looking up at the sky.

My eyes were drawn to the clear diamond of Orion, directly above me, and the necklace of the Pleiades beside it. The Pleiades are always "my stars," the constellation I look for at night, wherever I am, and feel comforted. My stars. My grandmother used to say that all the time, often as an oath of exasperation with me — "my *stars*, boy!" Or even "you can thank your lucky stars . . ." I'd never reflected on what it meant before. Astrology? Superstition? Certainly not Puritanism.

Eyes fixed on the heavens, I felt immersed in the starscape above, all other senses suspended. Awareness became only a projection, not *what* I was, but *where* I was, and for a brief moment the stars truly became my universe. I existed only as another point of light among the galaxies, looking out from a microscopic planet, and an abstraction called Africa. I was *out there*; the Universe was my home, and the Pleiades were my family. My stars. Then a bug bit me.

Trees and buildings began to materialize in the yet-imperceptible light. Still no sign of life in the church, and only a dim glow of moving light inside the monastery building, so I decided that *Matins* must be a time of private prayer. Then I smiled to think what it had been for me — a chance to escape self-consciousness, and to send myself outward instead of inward. A time of private prayer as it *ought* to be, not the begging of favors and forgiveness, but a pure kind of humility and selflessness.

My mask was slipping. I shook off this religious fervor, this uncharacteristic humility and selflessness, and went back to my monastic quarters to doze for a while until breakfast.

Later I walked up to the refectory with the older of the missionaries, the tall gray-haired one whose eyes had seemed kind. From down the hill we heard a class of children singing out their lessons, and I remarked how exuberant they sounded. To my surprise, he shook his head sadly. "*Ja*, it is always like zat." He pointed to his forehead with both index fingers, "Zey are *zinging*, but zey are not *sinking*."

I was silent, trying to make out exactly what he meant (and I don't mean his accent). Was it a condemnation of the Catholic teaching methods, or a comment on the inability of Africans to think? Everywhere in the world children are taught things by rote — first they learn the symbols, the words and numbers, and later in life they can worry about their abstract connections. How can children know that the numbers they add with such effort will someday be the symbols of life and death, of survival or starvation? Or that those numbers will be used to decide their fates, add the number and nature of their responsibilities, the reward they are given for their work, the debts they owe for their needs? Why do children *have* to know that? Let them sing.

• • •

Breakfast was simple, bread and hot water for tea or instant coffee. But there was *butter* for the bread, another first, and even jam, though it was a sickly-sweet paste. There was another mysterious jar, the contents of which no one tasted, though everyone took a sniff of the molasses-like liquid that smelled of prunes.

We agreed that Elsa should leave early to get a headstart in the cool morning, and sent her down the road while the rest of us cleaned up. The Bicycle Africa team moved into action; Leonard and David gathered up the plates and cups and brought them to the sink, while I began washing and Annie picked up a towel to dry. Soon we were loading up our bikes on the lawn by the dormitory, and saying goodbye to our Catholic hosts, and to their Lutheran guests. Breakfast and dishwashing made a late start for us, nearly 9:00, and the morning was already hot.

In David's itinerary the route was described as "paved, roller coaster, and climbing" for a distance of thirty-five miles, and I looked down at the map on my handlebar bag, eyes tracing the black line of highway N-6 to Bamenda. The black line had a lot of squiggles in it, a sure sign that it was not flat. Ahead of me the highway receded over a series of hills like a gray serpent, and soon I was grinding upward. Minibuses raced by in both directions, and the lizards ran for cover. A large butterfly, black velvet wings with bright turquoise stripes, perched on the road in perfect beauty. Dead, but perfect. "A Disappointment Is A Blessing," read the signboard on one of the passing minibuses, and I thought about that for awhile.

Nearly everyone I passed, man, woman, or child, smiled and waved, and I returned their greetings happily. When I went by the old women as they hiked along the road with baskets on their heads, I noticed they often smelled of woodsmoke, no doubt from years of hunching over open fires in tiny houses.

After two long hills I was well into the rhythm of the day, but my pace and my internal monologue were interrupted by a roadblock just before the village of Mbouda. The green-uniformed soldier who interrogated me barked his questions rudely, then demanded my passport, which he spent long minutes scrutinizing. Finally he handed it back, and nodded toward the highway, indicating "get lost."

Another security check awaited me on the other side of Mbouda, and I spied a pale figure in light-colored clothing and white helmet — Elsa, stopped at the side of the road in front of two soldiers. If I'd caught up to her already, when she'd had more than an hour's headstart, I presumed she'd been stopped there for awhile, and smelled trouble. After the unpleasant grilling I'd just received, I felt my body tense again, suspicious nerves activated and prepared for a hassle.

Riding straight over to them, I straddled my bike and struck a defiant pose, asking Elsa what the problem was. But no, there was no problem. These soldiers were friendly, and merely curious. One of them had been chatting with Elsa in schoolboy English, asking about her travels in Cameroon, her home in California, and her family, while the other looked on, smiling and listening. The talkative soldier took my passport as he continued asking about our journey, now addressing me more comfortably in French. Once I'd explained where we'd been, and where we were going, he handed the passport back without even looking at it; his partner nodded and smiled widely to us, and they waved us on.

When Elsa disappeared behind me on the first climb, it occurred to me that if it had taken her over an hour to travel three or four miles, she was in for a long day. And so was David, who felt obliged to stay back with her when no one else would. David seemed infinitely patient, and I admired him for that, but privately he'd admitted he didn't enjoy spending his days riding in circles at the top of every hill while Elsa made her way up, then having to stop while she had a drink and complained for a while. He had advised her against resting at the *top* of a hill, stewing in the heat of the climb, when the best relief of all was simply coasting down the other side, with no exertion and the cooling wind of speed. He'd also tried to get her to drink from her water bottle while she rode, instead of stopping every time. But like the proverbial old dog, she wanted no new tricks.

Now, Elsa was sixty years of age, and fully entitled to be slower than the rest of us, but sometimes a slow rider has nothing to do with strength or age; it can be a mental thing. There's probably a metaphor for life there. At whatever speed, sensible riders choose their pace and stick to it, taking breaks at considered intervals, and if a hill is too steep they'll *walk* up it. But they keep going.

On other trips with groups of cyclists, I have noticed that the slow riders are often the last to be ready in the morning, still packing their bikes, or looking for water, or pumping tires when everyone else is ready to go. Also, they are often the ones who dally at every stop, and stop more often than they need to. Obviously it's not laziness, or they wouldn't be on a bike trip in the first place, but a certain lack of focus, a sloppiness of mind, seems to carry over from their personalities to their cycling, and it slows them down.

That would be fine, of course, but a negative attitude is often part of that temperament — a loud resentment of the hills, the food, the hotels, the guide, and how *long* it's taking to get there. In the "group dynamics" of a bike tour, that's the real problem. Not waiting for the slower riders, but listening to them complain.

Some riders like hills and some don't. Another metaphor for life. In many ways a challenge is its own reward, but in this respect I've always felt the equation was simple: you go up, you get a view. And I like views.

When I parked my bike against a tree outside Bamenda several hours later, I knew I'd have a long wait, but at least I was at the top of a hill — I had a view. From the edge of an escarpment, a sheer cliff called a "fault scarp," I had a panoramic overview of the town far below, a sprawling array of low buildings, the brown earth of the market area, and a green soccer field. Green hills rippled away into the distance.

The road beside me made a hairpin turn as it started down the escarpment, then twisted across the steep wall in switchbacks. Nearly every driver turned to stare at me as he started into that first corner, and I began to worry that I was about to witness a busload of innocent passengers hurtling over the precipice, while the driver rubber-necked at me. Tires squealed as the distracted drivers went into the turn too fast, or at the wrong angle, and I finally moved back up the road, away from the corner, so the drivers could get over their shock and curiosity in time to look back at the road *before* they had to negotiate the hairpin. This was a true act of altruism, for I had to move away from the shade and bake in the sun, and I'm sure by now the people of Bamenda have erected a statue to me.

Leonard was the first to arrive, bathed in sweat as usual. He took off his sunglasses to wipe his face with a bandana, then peeled off his shirt to wring a stream of water from it. Propping his bicycle on its stand, he fixed his umbrella upright on the back and sat on the ground with his legs curled up to squeeze his whole body into the small patch of shade. He swore he was getting a terrible sunburn, but I laughed and told him he didn't look very *red*.

Now Annie — Annie *was* red, from the heat and exertion as well as the sun, as she rode up with her glasses askew and her dark hair poking out of her bandana in every direction. "Whew!" she said, "heh-heh, quite a ride!"

Yes it was, and it was quite a *wait* too. We sat there by the side of the road for an hour and a half in the broiling sun, Annie taking shelter beneath a tree across the road and Leonard under his umbrella, before David and Elsa finally arrived. They both looked grim, though for different reasons. Elsa was silent, stern, and frustrated, while David was silent and resigned, even *his* beatific patience stretched to the limit. With a weak smile, he pedaled on by us without pause, determined not to give Elsa another excuse to stop. She continued behind David as he coasted around the first sharp curve, and the rest of us mounted up and followed.

At the bottom of each fast descent, crouching into the wind, hands down on the bars, the road turned back on itself in a sharp hairpin, forcing me to squeeze the brakes hard and carefully lean into the curve. The cars and big trucks strained against *their* brakes as they roared up behind me, urging me into the side of the road as they passed. There was no enjoying the view.

At the bottom we followed David through a maze of streets and onto a wide boulevard. Tall trees hung over the rooftops and softened the squareness of the buildings, and behind everything was that spectacular escarpment, a distant waterfall tumbling down it. Two- and three-storey buildings lined the boulevard, banks, restaurants, gas stations, and shops selling hardware, books, furniture, crafts, portable stereos. Shirts and dresses on hangers, displayed above the tiny shops, moved gently in the breeze. Street pedlars offered racks of cassettes, tables of used books, and food — the little pyramids of peeled oranges, bananas, and *brochettes* (pig-guts-on-a-stick). The market was buzzing; masses of people thronged the stalls; women squeezed through with baskets of produce on their heads, and the boys carried neatly-arrayed baskets of cigarettes. The competing blasts of music mingled with the talk and laughter, and an occasional voice sang out from the crowd. The people seemed friendly, the streets relatively clean. There was a good "feel" about Bamenda, and I was glad we'd be spending an extra day.

• • •

Sometime during the night I woke to the sound of voices outside, the busy, murmuring undertone of many people on the streets. My first thought was of the citizens of Bamenda on their way to work, or to market, but I looked toward the window and saw it was still dark. And I heard no other sounds, no cars, no buses, no music. Strange. I felt for the Casio on the floor beside the bed, brought it up in front of my face and found the stupid little button to illuminate the digits, it was only 1:00. Maybe it was a revolution, an uprising, a mob coming to *kill whitey*.

'Better wake up Leonard,' I thought, 'He can hold them off while we get away.'

Curious, I crept out of bed and over to the balcony, looking down from our fourth-floor room over the main street. The row of streetlamps in the center of the boulevard cast circles of light, and crowds of people gathered under each one in faint silhouettes. They moved slowly about, as if aimlessly, like a bunch of escaped lunatics, and all the while the constant muttering babble. Talking and laughing and calling out to each other, each individual voice lost in the mass.

Shadows whirled above the street — big enough to be bats, but whirling in dizzy orbits around the lights. Occasionally one circled out from the light and fell to the ground, and a dark figure raced for it. One young boy ran around filling a Coke bottle, while others picked them up with one hand and filled the other with their harvest. I stood on the balcony trying to make sense of it. 'Okay, they're harvesting locusts. But what for?'

'Bait for fishing?' I thought, 'or maybe they make something out of them? Furniture?

'Ha — I know, they probably eat them.' Back to sleep. Just before dawn I awoke for good, to find the streets silent and empty.

Things Women Carry On Their Heads, Volume VI: Looking down from the balcony of the International Hotel at sunrise, I watched a woman carrying a five-gallon pail of water on her head. It must have weighed fifty pounds, and she didn't spill a drop.

We made an early start for the village of Bafut, leaving our panniers in the rooms. My unladen bike felt light and supple as we wheeled throught the back streets of Bamenda. Children batted at the trees and shrubs with sticks, hunting for any leftover bugs. In front of one house a hand-lettered sign was posted, "No Trespassing To Catch Grasshoppers." I asked David about this insect harvest, and he told me that people did indeed eat them, and that when fried the grasshoppers produced a rich oil.

"You ever try them?" I asked him.

"Yeah, once. Not bad. Wouldn't you?"

I thought about it for a moment. "Yeah, I guess I would — if they were offered to me." (Years later, in Mexico, my bravado was put to the test. I ate them. They were good.)

We were on our way to visit the palace of an important chief, a personage locally called a "Fon." (Leonard came out with one of his shameless puns. "Tell me; what exactly does a *Fon do*?" to a chorus of groans.) Bafut was only ten miles away, and the road was paved, but it spanned a few hills. I stopped once at the top of a long climb to wait for Elsa, and when she finally came struggling up I smiled and waved her on. "Go ahead."

But my smile quickly faded when she snapped, "What do you mean 'go ahead?' Don't you people even stop to blow your nose?" and she sneered and pulled a handkerchief from her bag. Stung, I answered sharply, "No — we stop to wait for *you*!" and pedaled away.

I thought of other older people I'd traveled with. On safari in Tanzania with a group of mixed ages and nationalities, there'd been Ray and Day, a sunny New Zealander couple, both near seventy years of age. Through miles of heat and dust, they had bounced around in the back of that old truck all day with the rest of us, then helped lug the tents to the campsite, set them up and tear them down every day. They had *never* complained. In fact they were smiling and happy, and always more solicitous of others than themselves.

Or my friend Gay. Pushing fifty, and by her own admission no athlete, yet she had cycled all over Europe, and in China and Australia, had pedaled over the Alps, the Pyrenees, and the Rockies with our group, and had never been heard to complain about anything. If the climb was too much for her, she simply got off and walked, enjoying the music on her Walkman and waiting for the top, so she could earn the great pleasure of going downhill — her favorite part.

But Elsa didn't seem to *have* a "favorite part," nor any "great pleasure," and I soon learned that others were aware of this too. In the village of Bafut, we had to make a turn to reach the Fon's Palace, so the four of us stopped at the crossroads to wait for Elsa. Minutes went by, ten, fifteen, then twenty, until David finally said, "You know, she could be stopped just beyond that hill, waiting for someone to come after her. I wouldn't put it past her to do that — just out of spite!"

Annie giggled; I made a wry face and nodded; and Leonard laughed in agreement.

Elsa finally appeared, slouched over the bicycle and wearing a martyred look, and David turned and whispered, "Quick, get moving. Don't give her another excuse to stop," so we pushed off and continued down the dirt track.

Just where a market came into view on our right, a homemade barricade was stretched across the road, bits of rope and strips of rubber tied together. A short, fat man strutted out and raised his hand officiously. "Where is your pass?"

A few other layabouts stood at the roadside looking on, as David said politely, "We are going to visit the Fon's Palace, we don't need a pass."

"Yes you do," said the frowning man. "You must have a pass."

David asked him, "Are you a gendarme?"

"Yes, I am a gendarme."

"Where is your uniform?"

"I don't need a uniform." He pointed at the pathetic barricade, "This is my uniform."

"And is this how you welcome visitors to your country?" David said.

The "gendarme" looked a little unsure, but said nothing. (Like the mayor of Limbe, he was "taken aback.") I noticed his handful of tickets marked "Hawker's Pass," presumably for sellers at the market, and said to David, "Looks like a hustle."

We resisted the temptation to be rude, to challenge his homemade barricade and his homemade authority, and just stood there, straddling our bikes, and stared at him silently. Finally he realized we weren't about to offer him a "dash," so he turned and muttered something to his companions. One of them dropped the barricade, and we pedaled on, feeling as if we'd got away with something.

We stopped at the market to ask about breakfast, and were directed to a small clay hut. Inside, a big stone-featured woman motioned us to a pair of rattan benches, and went to work at her tiny kerosene stove. We enjoyed a new culinary delight, with the sneezy name of *achu* (a grayish dough of pounded yams) along with rice, hard-boiled eggs and papaya. Then it was off to see the wizard.

As we parked our bikes against the high brick wall outside the Fon's Palace, locking them together and pulling out our cameras and long trousers, a woman came out and asked if we wanted to visit the Palace. She told us she was one of the Fon's wives (one of *ninety-seven* wives, we learned). She was tall and graceful, in her early thirties, dressed in a well-made dark blue dress with a red and gold floral print, and a matching kerchief. Her shoes looked Italian, and her speech was cultivated and articulate as she told us that it would cost us a thousand francs each to tour the Palace. There was a bit of humming and hawing about that, but I pulled out my wallet and said, "Come on, it's only a few dollars. When's the next time you'll have the chance to visit a Fon's Palace?"

The Fon's wife led us inside, telling us as we walked that the Fon was thirty-five, and that only four of his ninety-seven wives were legally married to him; many of the others were widows or destitute women for whom he was responsible, along with 415 children. *"Whoa!"* Leonard said, impressed. The wives lived in rows of little brick houses which lined the outside of the vast compound. On the far side of the courtyard was an impressive stone and glass building where visiting chiefs and dignitaries could stay.

In the middle of the compound was an open lawn shaded by tall trees and a single jacaranda tree, spreading clouds of mauve flowers over the courtyard. A gatehouse along one side was painted with lions (a symbol of royalty from England to Cameroon) and above an archway a sign stated the obvious: "Fon's Palace." This arch opened into a courtyard of white-painted stone, where the Fon would sit on his elaborately carved throne and listen to petitions and disputes among his people, or consult with the sub-chiefs.

Beyond the small courtyard was the tallest building of all, its stone steps leading up to a bamboo pavilion with a tightly-thatched pyramid roof. There the Fon conducted his secret ceremonies and rituals, and as we admired the intricate decorative work of carved idols and animal heads, I caught a glimpse of a white-robed figure gliding past the doorway. The Fon himself, though he didn't come out to greet us.

I stretched up on tiptoe to admire a chair with beautifully carved humanoid figures forming the legs and arms, and beside the chair I smiled to see an empty bottle of Heineken on its side. Perhaps the Fon had just been enjoying his morning beer when we interrupted him with our tour. Hopefully the five thousand francs we were contributing to his coffers would be some consolation. When I pointed it out to Leonard he laughed and said, "Here we are in the Fon's Palace, beside the Fon's Pavilion, there's the Fon's Chair, and here's the Fon's Beer!"

We gathered back outside by the bicycles, where for the first time I noticed a small thatched hut on a stone platform in the middle of the square. In front of it stood a big slit drum, carved from one giant log, but as I moved closer to look at it, a voice from across the road warned me away. David tried to approach it as well, but was also waved off. The Fon's wife told us this was the den of the Fon's secret society, a tradition which was also tied up with the *juju* enforcers, and that no one else was permitted near it. The price of admission for a woman was death.

• • •

The rest of the day was spent in a pleasantly lazy fashion. We cycled back to Bamenda for lunch, pushing through a beaded curtain at the Star Restaurant for a meal of rice with tomato and meat sauce, and the green sauce called *ndole*. I spent an hour waiting to cash a traveler's cheque in the bank (not bad for an African bank, and great compared to Bafang, where I hadn't been able to cash one at all), then wandered the streets for awhile, looking in the shops and enjoying the music which played everywhere. A sign above a clothing store advertised "Isometric Shopping," a concept about which one could only wonder.

Bamenda was the largest town in the English-speaking part of Cameroon, and was well-supplied with bookstores, always a favorite haunt for me. Some of the shops were large and spacious, others just small kiosks piled to the ceiling with schoolbooks and assorted western novels. I was surprised to see the *Compact Oxford Dictionary* in one tiny shop — the *C.O.D.* is "compact" only by comparison to the twelve-volume set it replaces, by reducing the typeface to microscopic size. But even so, it's a sizeable two-volume set, with its own little magnifying glass in a drawer in the binding, and would have been worth hundreds of dollars. I wondered who they thought was going to buy it.

In a small grocery store I discovered a faded-looking tube of Smarties, which sparked a chocolate fever, and also a bottle of water and some cookies. (I smiled to see the trademark on the cookies: "Barbara Dee's," made in Marietta, Oklahoma.) I carried my treasures back up to our room, and lay back to browse through a newly-purchased *Geography of Cameroon*.

Leonard returned from his shopping excursion, and sat down for a moment to watch the exciting activity of David and me reading. He seemed a little down, perhaps struck by the same homesickness that had afflicted me a few times that day. After a few minutes he got up again and said he was going down to get some "Vitamin B." He returned a few minutes later with some cans of beer, and announced that he was going to "sit on the balcony and get fucked-up." This he proceeded to do.

The drum makers, Ghana.

encounters

Only one incident would mar my good impression of Bamenda. Next morning, as David and I cycled together on our way out of town, I heard running feet behind me, and turned to see a hand snatching the bottle of water from the top of my rack. I stopped, straddled the bike, and looked into the belligerent, sneering face of a well-built man in his thirties, neatly dressed in white shirt and black trousers, and holding my precious water. I called out for David to stop, and asked the water-snatcher, "What do you think you're doing?"

"Black man is faster than white man," he said tauntingly, then played the extend-it-grab-it-back game a few times. I dropped my bicycle on the road and swiped the bottle from his hands.

"Black man is faster and stronger," he sneered, "I can break you in two."

David spoke up with his excellent phrase, "Is this how you welcome visitors to your country?" But, while that thought often changed people's attitudes, it had no effect this time.

"This is Black Africa," the man said, with a note of defiance.

Two other young men had stopped, and they looked embarrassed and apologetic. One of them spoke to me shyly: "He is not," he groped for the word, "He is not..."

"He is *crazy!*" supplied the other.

The first man danced a little as he jeered at us, "Black man is stronger; black man is faster!"

David tried another diplomatic tack, turning away to ignore him. He pointed to a sign which read Baptist Heliport, and told me that the Baptist Church kept their own helicopter there, and had more airplanes than the Liberian Air Force.

"This is *Black* Africa," repeated the man.

To me, David said "I don't remember this road being paved," then he turned to the man, hoping to mollify him with a civil question. "How long has this road been paved?"

But he took offence at that as well. "How long have the roads been paved in your country?"

David shrugged, "Different places, different conditions."

"Yes, that's right," the other man replied defensively. "This is Black Africa."

Just then Leonard came riding up, and Mr. Black Africa must have thought he'd found an ally, saying to him, "This man just asked me a funny question."

"Oh yeah?" Leonard said, looking at us and wondering what was going on.

"Yes, he asked me how long this road has been paved."

David spoke quietly to Leonard. "Forget it. Just go on ahead, this guy's a little belligerent."

Annie and Elsa came into view as we mounted up again, and I turned once more to Mr. Black Africa. "He only asked you that because he has been down this road before, when it *wasn't* paved — Mister Friendly."

"Okay, Mister *Enemy!*" he taunted again, as we pedaled away.

We struck off to the northeast on a dirt road. Stones jostled my wheels and dust swallowed them up. Passing trucks and minibuses churned that dust and trailed a thick, choking cloud. Once more I pulled the bandana over my face, though even then my throat began to ache from inhaling the opaque air. I thought I must have picked up something in Bamenda, one of those Upper Respiratory Infections which are common in the Third World. My throat felt swollen, talking was painful, and my voice had a hard edge.

In the village of Bamboui we stopped for breakfast at "Jimmy Brown's *Achu* [Gesundheit!] Eating House," which was furnished with a swaybacked old couch and matching easy chairs. The walls were decorated with posters of Michael Jackson, Bob Marley, and multiple collections of World Cup soccer teams, African heads-of-state, and women from different ethnic groups in traditional costumes. Jimmy Brown served up a good omelette with onions, and a cup of tea soothed my raspy throat. David pointed out different faces on the African heads-of-state poster. "This guy's been deposed, this one's been shot, this one's in exile..."

We compared the photos of Michael Jackson at various stages of his career, from an Afro-topped child prodigy with the Jackson Five to the booted-and-buckled cosmetic-surgery and skin-bleaching testimonial of *Bad*. Looking at a series of images like that, you can trace all the "enhancements" to his nose, lips, eyes — even his skin color. "Poor Michael," I said aloud.

"Why do you say that?" asked Annie.

"Well, there's no question he's very talented, but I have to wonder if he wouldn't have been a happier person if the family had just stayed in Gary, Indiana, and he'd gone to work for Ford or something. Think about it: what's he going to look like when he's fifty, and *parts* of his face still look like Diana Ross?"

"Scary thought," Leonard said.

"Nah — he'll just have some more operations," David laughed, "and work in Vegas!" (Prophetic remarks, no doubt.)

The day's itinerary gave the cycling conditions as "dirt, rolling, and big hills," and so it was. The "dirt" and "rolling" were bad enough, but the "big hills" were a real torment. After Bamboui we began a series of climbs up a steep escarpment, winding around rocky cliffs and bare, corrugated hills. The fine dust which coated the road was like talcum powder, and would have been a joy to walk in barefoot, but cycling in it was hell. The steep incline was right on the limit of my gearing, right on the limit of traction, right on the limit of strength. If I leaned forward to put more weight on the front wheel for steering, I lost grip on the rear wheel, while if I sat back to keep my weight on the rear wheel for traction, the front wheel hopped uselessly in the dust.

At least there was no "break-dancing" that day — I stayed on *top* of my bike — but several times my wheels began to slip from under me and I tasted fear. My bandana went up when the minibuses strained by, then down again when the air cleared, long minutes later. Panting and sweating in the baking heat, I put all my strength into making the pedals go around.

Sometimes I was charmed and comforted by a soft "*ashea*" from women or children, but I learned a new word from some of the men: "*nasarra*." From "Nazarene," or Christian, *nasarra* is the Arabic equivalent of "white man" or "*homme blanc*," and was another word I would grow to hate in coming days.

As I slowly climbed higher, occasional signs on dusty laneways indicated Catholic schools and missions. Once again these cooler highlands had been deemed the best places for soul-saving. And that day my own soul was saved, or at least *soothed*, by Psalm 102, the melody that had so affected me at Vespers. I had thought it would be too elusive and would slip away, but during that endless climb the fragile melody floated up from my subconscious, a little at a time, and came together as a calming mantra, spinning itself out again and again.

The scenery was another consolation, as always on a climb. You go up, you get a view. Below and behind me lay the highlands of Bamenda (I guess we were in the "super-highlands" now) silver roof-tops shining, and low purple hills disappearing into the haze. A few cinder-cones towered in the distance, volcanic rock frozen into gray columns. Waterfalls tumbled from the cliffs, nourishing the grassy hills and a few spiky palms, and the sight of moving water was a temptation to drop my bicycle and run across the hills to stick my head under it.

A small village sprouted from the highest plateau, where the climb finally leveled out, and the road was bordered by neat thatched houses in swept yards. Two boys on horseback trotted by, turning to stare all the while, then urged their horses into a wild gallop through the grass. Along the road came a woman and two men, tall with sharp features and thin lips, and dressed in flowing headdresses and long robes. This was my first encounter with the Fulani people, a once-nomadic tribe thought to be of North African descent, who had moved into the north of present-day Cameroon in the eleventh century, at the height of the great Fulani Empire.

Like the Maasai of East Africa, the Fulani had been proud and fierce warriors, overwhelming the indigenous tribes and mounting slaving expeditions among them. At first the Fulani violently opposed the spread of Islam, then later became equally frenzied converts and mounted a long, bloody *jihad* against the pagan chiefs. Only the arrival of the Germans halted their hegemony (one of the few real benefits of colonialism in Africa was interrupting the internecine tribal wars for awhile) and in post-independence Africa the Fulani had dwindled to a scattered, pastoral tribe who, like the Maasai again, counted their wealth in cattle.

Traditional, Eurocentric Western history tends to gloss over not only the great dynasties of China, but also the ancient empires of West Africa. Medieval times were not necessarily "dark ages" in other parts of the globe; beginning around the tenth century a series of highly developed societies evolved on the southern rim of the Sahara, at the crossroads of the rich trade in gold, salt, ivory, and slaves. (In those days salt was so valuable it was traded ounce-for-ounce for gold.) Kingdoms like Songhaï, Mali, and Ghana became wealthy and sophisticated, and built great cities, like Timbuktu, which became centers of commerce, religion, and learning.

Strangely, none of these great empires had a written language, but remained dependent upon Arab scholars and bookkeepers. In all of sub-Saharan Africa, only two tribes ever developed alphabets: the Vai people of Liberia, and a sultan in Cameroon — though he got the idea from hearing about Arab and German writing. It is sometimes disparagingly said of Africans that "they never even had the wheel," though it can be argued that they didn't need the wheel. Writing, however, they needed, and would continue to import. The Arab scholars and bookkeepers became the "International Institute of Languages," just as the wheel became the Nissan minibus...

... which raced by me in a cloud of dust as I rode out of the Fulani village. Having reached the top of this high plateau, now I had to go down the other side. And if the way up had been hell, the way *down* — what should have been the reward — was worse. No question of a wild and joyous freefall, no exultant downhill rush after the heat of the climb; as the road plummeted down the mountainside through jolting rocks and slippery dust, I squeezed hard on the brakes, trying frantically to control my speed. I had to stop often to rest my hands from the constant gripping, and to let the wheel rims cool. Heated by friction, they were too hot to touch, and added the danger of a blowout.

One stretch of road was so steep it had been necessary to pave it, to allow even the trucks and minibuses to make it up and down. I appreciated the break from the treacherous sand and stones, but the steep, one-lane strip of asphalt only urged my heavy bicycle to go faster.

While I anxiously squeezed the brakes against the force of gravity, Leonard sped by, tossed me a "yo," then disappeared around a

sharp bend below. Both tempted and challenged by Leonard's reck-
lessness, I followed him the rest of the way down, and what had
taken three hours to climb took about two minutes to descend. Relieved to feel the road return to an unpaved track and level out,
Leonard and I pedaled together across the Great Plain of Ndop. Volcanic hills stretched along the northern horizon as we continued to
the east, bandanas up against the tides of red dust trailed by passing traffic. By the time we reached the village of Ndop, a coat of red
powdered our clothes, skin, and bikes, and I felt the grit between my
teeth, and in my nose and ears.

Up in those hills, not far from Ndop, was Lake Wum, the scene
of a bizarre tragedy. On an August night in 1986 a cloud of toxic gas
bubbled up from the lake and rolled down into the valley. Thought to
be of volcanic origin, the gas killed everything in its path — more
than 1,700 people died in their sleep. Yet I hadn't even heard about
it at the time. Just as Western history takes little account of great
chapters in African or Asian history, so too are their current events
all but ignored by the Western media — except for the occasional
"spectacle" of famine or genocide. If an earthquake hits San Fran-
cisco and kills forty people, we hear about nothing else for days, but
if a cloud of poison gas wipes out 1,700 people overnight in Africa, or
an earthquake kills tens of thousands in China, it's only worth a few
column-inches in the newspaper. To every tribe, the farther away
something occurs, the less important it seems.

Leonard and I stopped at a humble building of clay blocks and
corrugated metal. No sign indicated its name, but the fluttering line
of brewery pennants across the front and the deserted bar inside
seemed to identify Ndop's only lodgings, the Festival Hotel. No one
answered our hellos, so we settled in the shade of the low porch to
wait for the others, leaning against the stone supports and sipping
at our water bottles, rinsing away the grit. Leonard pointed back
the way we'd come, to where a flock of vultures circled in the sky,
and laughed softly. "I bet they're over David and Elsa!"

Annie arrived next, another apparition in red dust, and her
habit of riding with her mouth open had dotted her front teeth with
red mud. As she pulled a bandana from her unruly hair and wiped
at her face and arms, Leonard smiled at me, then turned to her and
said, "your teeth."

She looked perplexed. "Huh? Um ... what do you mean?"

I told her, "Your teeth, they're kind of *muddy*."

"Oh — heh heh. I guess that's what I get for riding with my mouth open!"

"Catch any flies?" asked Leonard.

"Ha-ha ... Hmm."

An hour later, David and Elsa rode out of the late morning sun. Against Leonard's prediction, both were still alive, though Elsa barely so. She'd walked much of the way uphill. David asked how we'd enjoyed the ride.

I answered in mock D.J. hypertalk, "Hey! I thought it was pretty *horrible*! What a road! I'm not sure which was worse — going *up* or coming *down*!" Elsa nodded silent agreement; I knew it had been harder on her.

David seemed offended. "Well, I would have hoped you'd be appreciating the scenery up there, rather than just getting upset over the road."

I smiled and nodded. When people lead you somewhere they've been before and you haven't, they sometimes take any criticism of the place, even in fun, personally.

David was able to find someone at the Festival Hotel to give us some rooms, and we pushed our bikes through the bar to a row of doors in a dingy passage out back. At the end of the hall, two dismal closets served as "bathroom," if three buckets on the floor merits the term. A stained and broken toilet could be flushed occasionally by filling the tank with water, but the smell suggested previous users hadn't bothered.

The few guest rooms at the Festival seemed to have been tacked onto the back of the bar, and were more likely used, like those at the Hotel Happy, for a short-term purpose. A more *festive*, more *happy* purpose than sheltering passing travelers. I leaned my bike against a tilted wardrobe, kicked my shoes onto the concrete floor, and lay back on the sagging bed. I looked up at the ceiling, at the flyspecked light bulb. The curtains bellied inward on the breeze, the pattern of upside-down ducks and reeds looking as out of place in Ndop as I was.

I felt low. My throat was still raw and swollen, my stomach wrung with distress, and a nervy edginess sapped at my energy and good spirits. Thoughts of home and family were a physical ache. It was the kind of mood when you ask yourself all the "why" questions: Why am I here? Why do I — no, why *did* I — want to do this? Why don't I go home?

While I tried to distract myself from this edgy depression with *Dear Theo* (reading about Vincent's edgy depression) there was a knock at the door. David was reading beside me, and got up to answer it. I heard him say, "Oh — you want to talk to *him*," and suddenly there was a tall young African standing at the foot of my bed.

I sat up, looking a question, and he said, "You are a musician?" His face was earnest, and I noticed he held a battered cassette tape in his hand. I knew what was coming, but collected myself, nodded, and shook his extended hand.

"They told me out there," he pointed toward the bar, "that one of the other bicycle riders was a musician. Maybe you could help me out."

I thought of the old joke: 'Sure, how did you get in?' but only asked him "How?"

"Well, I am a songwriter, and I thought you could help me become successful. Maybe you could listen to my songs, and give me some advice."

I had faced this situation a thousand times, but still hadn't become adept at it. "Well, let's start with what you want to *be*."

"I want to be a musician."

"What instrument do you play?"

"Well, I don't exactly play anything. I just ... my friend plays a little guitar, and while he plays I make things up and ... sort of sing them. Then we record it."

"But you want to be a *musician*?"

"Yes," he nodded solemnly, "that is what I want."

I had to smile, but tried to make it look encouraging. "Don't you think that first you should learn to play?" Here was another young African who dreamed of *having* rather than doing.

"Well, yes. But I don't know how."

"The best thing would be to find a teacher, someone who can teach you about music, and show you how to play the guitar, or the piano, or whatever instrument you want to learn. Then once you learned how to *play*, you could start making your own songs."

He nodded silently. It was starting to sound a little difficult. "That would take a long time."

"Yes, it would, but there is no fast way to learn anything as difficult as being a musician. There is a lot to learn, and it takes many years."

I could see his enthusiasm was sinking. Then he suddenly brightened. "Maybe you could give me your address, and I could write to you for advice!"

I summoned my feeble powers of diplomacy. "I'm afraid I couldn't be any help to you. I live in Canada, a long way away, and already many young musicians from Canada and the United States send me their tapes. I get them all the time, hundreds of them. I can't listen to them all, so I make it a point not to listen to any. I am not a record company or a producer, or even a teacher, and can't do anything to really *help* these people. I can't help them become successful; I can't help them make the kind of music *they* want to make. I can only give them my encouragement, as I give it to you. I'm sorry I can't do more."

"Well, I think you have given me some good advice already."

"I hope so. I wish I could make it easier, but it's a difficult thing."

"Yes, yes, I see that it is. I thank you."

"Not at all. I know how hard it is to become a musician anywhere, and it's probably even more difficult here, but I wish you luck if you decide to try."

And with that he went out again, leaving me feeling inadequate, as such an encounter always does. Other people might have handled it differently, maybe better. I could have listened to his tape, then simply said, "It sounds very promising; keep up the good work." Whether or not it was true, perhaps both of us would have felt better. (Well, *he* might have, anyway.) I could have said, "Sure man, just leave it with me. I'll check it out," and thrown it away. Or I could have said, "Go away kid, you bother me." But I'd tried to be honest, and as is often the case, being honest didn't feel as good as it ought to.

• • •

The town of Jakiri lay over the next hill, just around the next bend on the red-dust road. Rather than ride the rest of the way into town, and wait for the others amid a crowd of staring eyes, I parked my bike by a tree and lay down in the shade. From my distant vantage point I admired Jakiri's hillside setting, pale houses dominated by a huge Catholic church in gray stone — a church presided over, David's notes indicated, by a "sour father."

To look at my immediate surroundings, I might have been resting by a country road on a summer day in southern Ontario, or the American Midwest. Across from me a line of evergreens, cedar-like with soft tufts of foliage, bordered a field where the wind blew waves through the yellow grass. As I lay back, the sun winked through the leaves overhead. A swallow flitted by, a ladybug crawled across my hand, and cattle lowed from a distant valley. I *might* have been on a country road in North America — except for where I'd been, where I was going, and how I felt.

The day had begun in misery. I awoke in the middle of the night with a vicious wrestling match in my guts. Doubled over and wracked by cramps, I lay in the dark writhing and stifling my groans. After two hours of grinding spasms and cold sweats, I was obliged to stumble down the dark hall to the "bathroom," to squat amid the stench and squalor. My intestines were treated to a good cleaning-out, a complete purge. My journal described it thus: "Unleashed a load of fury."

Drained and weak, I staggered back to the room and slept fitfully until dawn. Then I was up to "unleash" once more, pack my bike, and push off into the cool morning, feeling bad. Our route continued east along the Ring Road, an urban-sounding, and perhaps rather grandiose name for the dusty track which pounded my bicycle, swallowed my wheels, and did my troubled stomach no good at all. Elephant grass bordered the road in fifteen-foot walls, leading across the Ndop Plain toward the green hills which marked its eastern border.

My mood was lifted somewhat by a little more varied bird life than usual. White Cattle Egrets picked at the fields, and a big chestnut-colored Coucal made its characteristically awkward flight from the road in front of me. Even more awkward was a black sparrow-sized Whydah trailing a pair of foot-long tail feathers which made it look more like a tropical fish than a bird.

The rest of the route to Jakiri had been a mirror-image of the day before, twenty-seven miles of dirt and big hills. The same modest distance on paved roads might have been covered easily in two hours, three at most, but each of those days had demanded nearly six hours of real struggle. By the time I parked under the tree overlooking Jakiri, I was worn and battered and feeling like hell. Waiting for Elsa was no problem; I was glad to lay down for awhile. Leonard soon caught up and lay back in the shade beside me, but eventually we became restless and pedaled the rest of the way into Jakiri.

Jakiri's few streets radiated from a roundabout, a circle of stones in the red dirt surrounded by low shops, a bar, and clay-block houses. Like us and our bicycles, the metal roofs were rusty-red from the dust thrown up by the trucks and minibuses which plied the Ring Road. The dust gave the impression of a desert crossroads, an oasis in reverse — an island of parched dirt amid the forested hills.

Leonard and I parked in front of a store, sitting on a bench with bottles of warm Pamplemousse. Fifteen or twenty local lads crowded around, but their curiosity was directed more at the bicycles than at us. A Sunday parade of colorfully-dressed women with their prayerbooks strolled by, or alit from the dust-coated minibuses.

Always the women doing *everything* — going to church, carrying things on their heads, working in the fields, cooking in the eating-houses, selling in the markets. What on earth did the men do all the time? (I know, as little as possible.) In contrast to that, in Jakiri a few men in Islamic robes strolled by, yet none of their wives. Perhaps the Islamic women and the Christian men were kept locked up at home on Sundays. Or got together for a party.

A boy in a Michael Jackson T-shirt encouraged another bizarre imagining, as I pictured that hero of world youth driving into Jakiri in a white Testarossa convertible (actually, he couldn't have *driven* it over those roads — maybe they brought it in a truck), to delight these remote admirers, who would never have the privilege of paying fifty dollars to sit in the outer reaches of a football stadium. Or be able to pay a surgeon to carve away their African features.

• • •

Jakiri's *Auberge* (inn) was another low, metal-roofed place, and like the Happy and the Festival before it, more saloon than inn. As we entered the deserted bar in front we were assailed by blaring music, a distorted cacophony playing for no one. David told us that when they saw him ride up they'd first cranked up the music, and *then* talked to him about rooms. Perhaps it was the customary welcome for travelers, or to give the place an air of gaiety and celebration. In either case, it failed.

My turn for a room to myself, one of four tiny "guest" rooms in back of the bar — once again more likely supplied to bar patrons for short-term use. A big number "4" was scrawled in chalk on the rough plywood door, and I turned the long old-fashioned key, pushed open the door, and bumped my head. At the other end of the blue-walled cell was another doorway, where I bumped my head again, so eager was I to inspect my very own *bathroom*.

A stained toilet was a welcome sight, though of course there was no toilet paper — a commodity still in frequent demand, and the roll I carried with me was shrinking. A sink hung out from the wall, but it had no faucet handles. An ancient shower-head stuck out of the ceiling, and, standing back, I turned the tap on the wall. Nothing. I unpacked a pair of pliers from my toolkit and turned the faucet on the sink. Nothing. Pulled the chain on the toilet. Nothing.

Sigh. I stood for a moment with my hand on the chain, head down in abject discouragement, while the ceaseless music rattled the walls. From outdoors, the roar of a diesel generator competed with the roar of the music inside. Anger welled up, and I turned quickly, banged my head on the door, swore, crossed the room, banged my head again, swore louder, and stalked into the bar. A young guy sat nodding his head to the music beside the flickering meters of an amplifier. I shouted at him, a little louder than necessary, "CAN YOU TURN THE WATER ON?"

He turned in shock and cowered visibly, eyes bugging as he hunched away outside. I returned to Room 4 — *ducking* this time — and stretched out on the spongy bed. A few minutes later, I heard the toilet tank filling with water.

• • •

At six o'clock next morning we pedaled through a silent Jakiri. David led the way out of town, his white helmet seeming to glow in the half-light of dawn. Since we would be spending another night at the *Auberge*, we had left our panniers in the rooms, and the bikes felt light and nimble. Our destination was Kumbo, a market-town twenty-three kilometers farther along the Ring Road (and not to be confused with Kumba, the hell-hole).

Elsa had chosen to stay behind and rest, so the four of us made unusually good time, though the road was a recurring nightmare of dust, stones, and steep hills. My stomach was better, but since I had eaten so little the previous day, it was also very *empty*, and often distracted me from the torments of the road and the pleasures of the view.

From the hilltops I looked down into green valleys dotted with silver roofs, and the red road snaking across the valley floor toward the far side. Once again, it was hard to say which was worse — the panting, jarring struggles upward, or the breathless, jolting high-wire act of the descents. On balance, I guess I hated them both.

Cranking up the last long hill, graced by a suddenly paved surface, we rolled into Kumbo a little before eight o'clock, just as the sun was gathering strength. The houses and shops were spread around a hilltop, narrow winding streets running down from a roundabout. Like Jakiri, the town was dominated by a massive Catholic church, and dwarfed by its stone tower and belfry.

We stopped for an omelette and Nescafé in a tiny chop-house, where a local schoolteacher gave us directions to the Fon's palace. At the end of a steep lane we came to a wide square walled in by buildings, and stopped, uncertain which way to turn. I leaned against my bicycle and looked around at the strange, decaying arrangement of buildings, once grand but now falling into ruin. The walls of the square were weathered stone and crumbling plaster, the scarred surfaces pierced by intricate doorways. I laid my bike on the ground to walk up for a closer look. The frames and lintels were elaborately carved in dimensional relief, like totem poles, each one a different pattern of humanoid faces, geometric symbols, and guardian spirits.

As ever, a crowd of small boys seemed to materialize out of nowhere, and gathered around to stare at us and our bicycles. By now it seemed as if the same group of boys was following us wherever we went, like Grateful Dead fans. One of the Fon's wives must have heard of our arrival, and came out to greet us (this Fon had a mere eighty wives — the Fon of Bafut had ninety-seven — but at least this one didn't charge admission).

We left our bikes in a courtyard and followed her to a small room, where a row of chairs faced a modest throne. She told us to sit down; the Fon would see us soon. A pair of tall carvings stood in the corner, male figures with friendly faces and calm Buddha-smiles. A set of framed certificates hung on the wall, commendations from the Boy Scouts, a signed portrait of Lord Baden-Powell, and, even more curiously, a personal blessing from the Pope to the "Fon of Nso" — who was a Muslim. Every potentate we encountered seemed to have been similarly "blessed," and I found it strange to think of the pope sitting down to sign all these autographs for the heathens and infidels of Africa.

A young man entered the room, neat and professional-looking in a beige leisure-suit and a brown cap. He introduced himself as a Prince, the Fon's son, secretary, driver, and translator, and sat behind the desk as the Fon himself made his entrance. David reminded us of the protocols before a chief: No shaking his hand (people avoid direct contact with the Fon, who is considered too potent, and also he is protected from the taint of a commoner) and, for some reason it was taboo to cross your legs.

But still, if we knew what *not* to do, we didn't know what to *do*. Stand with heads down, sit with eyes averted, or bow and scrape and grovel? There was a last-second meeting of anxious eyes between Annie, Leonard, and me, but it was too late — the Fon was in the room. I sat awaiting a cue from David, but he gave no sign, so I watched the Prince, hoping for an eloquent signal of appropriate behavior. He was no use either, looking the other way. So there we sat like kids in the Principal's office, while the stout, white-robed Fon moved regally to his throne. (And I was *sure* he looked at us pointedly. I wished I knew what to *do*.)

Later I learned how it *ought* to be done. You are preceded by a retainer, you clap your hands to attract the Fon's attention, and wait demurely until it is granted. You don't sit unless he invites you to, and when you address him you avert your eyes, bow your head, and cover your mouth with a hand. So, we did *everything* wrong — but he was still nice to us.

The Fon wore a headscarf of small black-and-white checks (the "tea towel" variety of burnouse like Yasir Arafat wears) and his perfect white robe reached down to his ankles. His face was dark and wrinkled, cheeks swollen by a beaming smile which displayed his even teeth and crinkled his eyes until they nearly disappeared. This was no ceremonial mask — this was for real, a warm, friendly, and welcoming expression of joy-in-life which charmed me immediately. 'Louis Armstrong,' I thought to myself, remembering an old photo of Satchmo wearing the biggest smile known to man. The comparison seemed apt — the same roundness in the Fon's features, and the breadth and permanence of his fabulous smile. Even his lips had the swollen look of a trumpeter's *embouchure*. So perfect and symmetrical were his teeth that I began to think they might be false. But no matter; that *smile* wasn't. It was the kind of face which appeared at rest, at ease, when wearing a wide smile.

While David described our journey, the Prince translated, and the Fon seemed enthusiastic and interested in where we had been and where we were going. He asked many questions about the bicycles, what luggage we carried, what spare parts, how we repaired breakdowns. He told us he had ridden bicycles as a boy, and later had been fond of motorcycles, but — he spread his hands as the Prince spoke for him — now that he was Fon, the people did not want to see him on a motorcycle. His Satchmo-smile widened as we laughed at his little joke.

I asked about the miniature Canadian flag on his desk, and the Prince told me that Canadians had installed the town's water system, and so were their good friends. Annie asked if the Fon spoke English, and was told that he understood it a little, but only spoke his tribal language, *Lanso*, and 'Pidgin English' (a scrambled colonial variant, something like the Jamaican patois). He was only the second Fon ever to embrace Islam, after his father, and had earned the Muslim honorific *Al Hadj* by making the pilgrimage to Mecca. Annie asked shyly if we might be permitted to photograph the Fon, and he graciously consented.

The Prince led us outside to a small courtyard which served as the Fon's audience chamber. On a low dais at one end stood three chairs, each of them hewn from a single section of log. Legs, arms, and backs were carved into animal icons, human figures and faces. The stonework on the floor was laid out in the design of the spider icon, the symbol of wisdom, and when the Fon settled himself in the middle chair and flashed his ivory smile for our cameras, he put his dusty lace-ups on a footrest carved into a double-headed leopard, the symbol of the Fon's power. Traditionally, he had the right to the pelt of any leopard slain within his kingdom (scarce these days) and it was believed that a Fon could sometimes change into a leopard, just as it was accepted that the leopard could change to human form.

Decorating each of the steps leading up to the Fon's dais were stickers, reading:

PAUL BIYA
Mon Président
My President

but it was only later, when I had the photographs developed, that I noticed the statue in the corner. A carved wooden figure, covered in multi-colored beadwork, held aloft a bust of a neatly-groomed man in a gray suit, white shirt, and tie. Closer scrutiny revealed the man in the gray suit to be Paul Biya, and the features on the figure *supporting* him were suspiciously similar to a slender Louis Armstrong — or a younger version of our Fon.

As is so often true, these small details, unnoticed at the time, told a big story. They showed that behind the Satchmo smile worked an astute political mind; that to be a Fon in the late '80s was not unlike the balancing-act of becoming and remaining pope. Scheming and machinating between sacred and secular, dominance and submission, Allah and Biya, chiefs like our friend the Fon of Nso had to tread that fine line. They had to be seen as absolute rulers among their own people, in a traditionally feudal background; yet they had to submit to a western-style central government in a modern African strong-arm republic. Give obeisance to the President, but hold the respect of your people. As the Fon of Bafut's wife had told us when we asked her what happened if a Fon was unjust, "Oh ... things can happen ..." Yes, things can happen. The people can poison you, and the government can shoot you. With those stickers and that carved tribute to the president, the Fon demonstrated his loyalty and devotion to the central forces, and at the same time kept himself out of

trouble. The government could think, 'Now there's a harmless fig-
urehead setting a good example for the peasants,' while his people
could think, 'See how our wise Fon gives lip service to the Feds, but
does what *he* wants.'

The Fon sent us on a tour of the palace, guided by the Prince.
The main buildings surrounding the courtyard were built of stone,
many with glass windows framed in blue and white, and European
paneled doors. A lawn-chair of blue and white vinyl seemed an unlikely detail, as did the calendar from a German bank, but these ac-
corded with the other anomalies — the Fon's lace-up shoes, the Canadian flag, an old-fashioned telephone-in-a-box on the desk. In
spite of these false notes, the decor remained unmistakably African,
tall wooden figures and chairs everywhere, carved and painted
doorframes against the stone walls, and the combination of wood
and stone was nicely organic.

In contrast, the Fon's wives lived in monotonous rows of handmade brick huts with metal roofs. A network of swept earth path-
ways ran among them, but they and the shuttered houses were silent and deserted. The Prince told us that the wives were away in
the country, working on the Fon's coffee farm. On one of the
unpainted shutters a poem was printed in chalk.

> WHEN LIFE IS FULL
> OF UPS AND DOWNS
> WE SAY IT IS ARROW
> OF GOD
> ANY ATTEMPT TO
> ACHIVE SUCCESE
> THINGS FALL APART
> BUT AT THE END
> OF NO SUCCESE
> WE ARE NO LONGER
> AT EASE

I was intrigued not only by the pessimistic insight and idiosyn-
cratic spelling, but because only the previous day I had started reading a novel called *Things Fall Apart*, by the Nigerian author Chinua

Achebe. From its introduction, I knew that the title had come from a poem by W.B. Yeats, and that it formed a trilogy with two other novels, *No Longer At Ease*, and *Arrow of God*; so those titles had been the inspiration of this poet's muse. And too, the poem's message reflected the themes in Achebe's novels, which deal with the changes this century has wrought in Nigerian life, and by extension, in West African life. I couldn't quite make out the signature after the poem, but it sure looked as if it said "Mom."

The largest building of all was the Fon's ceremonial chamber, which stood apart from the others. It was square, built of upright poles with mud plastered between them, and a heavy thatched roof in the shape of a pyramid. To my surprise, we were permitted to go inside, where the tribal rituals and death ceremonies were performed. As we ducked through the low doorway I felt a tingle of excitement.

Like many sacred places, it was not in itself a spectacular sight. As my eyes adjusted to the dimness I made out a ring of stones surrounding a long-dead fire, a few dusty benches and carved stools, that was all. But I thought I *felt* something. Maybe it was just my own anticipation, or knowing that it was a forbidden place; those could have been the sources of my excitement. But I think a place does become imbued with the magic of what has transpired in it. I have felt the power of the great boulders of Stonehenge, the deserted rows of consoles at Mission Control in Cape Kennedy, or the empty stage in a concert hall. And in the Fon's ceremonial hut, I could imagine that fire glowing red on the stones as it burned low in the night, flickering on a circle of masks, voices chanting in unknown tongues, drums throbbing.

We emerged into the sunlight again and walked back along the path between the wives' huts. I looked back and saw the Fon watching us, leaning easily against a dusty black Peugeot with his arms folded across his chest, and smiling that smile. He joined us as we returned to the courtyard, and stood for a few minutes inspecting our bikes and watching us prepare to depart. David presented the Fon with a Bicycle Africa newsletter and a cycling calendar, and was rewarded with a smile of thanks.

Just then the Prince reappeared, and presented us with *our* gift from the Fon — a live chicken. The terrified bird flapped and squawked as the Prince shoved it into an open-weave basket the size of a shopping bag. The poor chicken continued to cluck in outrage as David fastened the basket onto the rack of his bicycle, and the four of us were laughing in pleasure and puzzlement — what were *we* going to do with a live chicken? But we had to be gracious.

We thanked the Fon for his hospitality and his gift, shook hands with the Prince (but *not* the Fon), and straddled our bicycles. The Fon stood in the courtyard watching us go, still beaming that infectious smile.

· · ·

Feeling elevated by our audience with the Fon, and cruelly amused by the occasional clucks from the chicken on David's rack, we headed for the Kumbo market to buy some meat. We'd met the local Peace Corps volunteer the previous night, and she had offered to make us hamburgers if we brought back the meat. After weeks of rice with junk on it, some homemade burgers sounded like a fine idea.

Near the market we heard a loud call of "Hey White!"

"Hey Black!" David called back.

"What you doing in Black Africa?" came the shouted response.

"Penance," I said quietly.

"Just visiting!" called out Leonard.

We wheeled into the truck-park outside the market, dark faces turning to stare at us. Small pickup trucks and minibuses were parked haphazardly, loading and unloading produce and passengers. We leaned our bikes against a big tree in the middle, and David went off to shop for some meat. He disappeared down a crowded passageway and left the rest of us to guard the bikes. "And the chicken," he reminded me with a smile and an admonishing finger. "With my life," I promised.

And for once I really felt as if our stuff *needed* guarding. A crowd had immediately closed around us, fifty scowling, shuffling youths muttering among themselves as they slouched ever closer — too close. No smiles, no greetings, just a dense circle of unfriendly faces giving us and our bicycles appraising looks. Fingers reached out to touch the shifters, brake levers, handlebar bags. I stood as near as I could to the bikes and put a nervous hand over my beltpack, feeling unwelcome, conspicuous, and an easy mark. My eyes flicked from David's bicycle to mine and back again, then to the crowd that seemed so menacing, trying to watch everywhere at once.

Annie giggled nervously, saying, "Not a very friendly bunch, are they?"

"Just like at home," I said, "guys with nothing better to do, acting tough and hanging around the mall."

Leonard laughed, "Hanging around the mall — Yeah." But then he abandoned me, pushing his bike through the crowd to inspect some of the cheap cassette players on sale at a nearby stall.

Annie turned to me, "Do you mind if I leave my bike here?"

I looked around at the mob of scowling faces and considered whether I wanted to be left completely alone to watch over three bikes at once, to defend them against an imagined thief. I decided I felt uneasy enough as it was — maybe even a little paranoid. How simple it would have been for one of those sour-faced punks to grab something, even a whole bicycle, and disappear into the hostile crowd. I could have done nothing.

"I'd rather you didn't," I said to her.

"Oh," she said, nodding and seeming surprised. "Oh, okay then."

So I stood there, tense and vigilant, wishing David would come back so we could leave. He returned at last, holding up the parcel of meat with a wave of success. As we pedaled through the roundabout and left Kumbo behind, I heard another shout of "Hey White!" and turned to face the sneering caller. "Don't call me names," I snapped, with new insight into the ugliness of racism, and he watched me in stunned silence as I pedaled by.

On the road back to Jakiri I bounced and pounded along beside David, feeling better in mind and body, though sorry for the chicken squashed into the basket on David's rack. However, the object of my pity accepted its punishment quietly for the most part, only occasionally offering a cluck of protest. My own protests were less restrained — breathing out curses every time I took an especially violent pounding.

• • •

In the late afternoon we went to visit Kim, the Peace Corps volunteer, at her little bungalow. Kim was twenty, strawberry-blonde and freckled, and was near the end of her second year as a math teacher at the local school. She told us she was one of 160 Peace Corps people scattered around Cameroon, and had enjoyed her time in Jakiri, despite its remoteness and the odd bout of malaria — one of which had put her in a Yaoundé hospital. Guests were rare; she'd even put on makeup for us.

An elephant-head mask and a gamelan (thumb-piano) decorated her living-room wall, and a line of books, mostly well-used paperbacks, stretched across the top of a cabinet. No doubt inherited from other Peace Corps volunteers, they offered an inviting and varied collection of good reading: Faulkner, Steinbeck, Tolkien, Dickens, *Zen And The Art of Motorcycle Maintenance*, *Atlas Shrugged*, *Dune*, *Out of Africa*, *Great American Short Stories*, as well as a row of college textbooks. With little else for entertainment — no television, no radio, no newspapers, no cinema — books were an important resource among the Peace Corps people. While glancing through one of the newsletters from Peace Corps Cameroon, I noticed the prominence given to book reviews, and the volunteers even advertised for specific books. "Wanted: *The Sun Also Rises* and *Tender Is The Night*. Can trade for something you want. Brian, posted in Yaoundé."

Two other guests joined us for dinner. One was a Peace Corps supervisor visiting from Bamenda, named Chris. He told us he was from Dallas, though somehow he had escaped with barely a trace of Texas in his speech. (Probably a CIA cover.) The other guest was a tall Cameroonian man of about forty, named Paul, who was dressed in a knee-length cotton shirt and embroidered cap. Paul's relation to Kim was unclear, but he seemed to be a kind of "houseboy emeritus," as she had one of her students to do the fetching and carrying. Paul had been born in Jakiri, then had lived in Nigeria for many years, though now he admitted to us that he hadn't liked it there ("too crowded") and was glad to be back in Cameroon.

Our visit to the Fon of Nso sparked much of our conversation, the four of us still excited about our reception, and delighted by the hospitality the Fon had shown us. We told how we had been allowed to enter the Fon's ceremonial chamber, and the conversation turned to *juju*. Kim mentioned that the masked spirits sometimes appeared in the middle of Jakiri, causing the local people to disappear from the streets in a panic. "I must admit," she said, "they even frighten me. My mother visited me here last year, and you should have seen her face when we walked out of a shop to see one of them running at us!"

Paul nodded thoughtfully, and said, "Yes, there are some I am very afraid of, but others are not to be feared."

"Some of them are even funny," Kim said, "like jesters."

Annie made a puzzled look. "But what do they *do*?"

David, the most knowledgeable about Africa, took up the explanation. "In one way they are agents of social order, kind of like police. The dancers are members of the Fon's secret society, and each mask represents a certain character, usually an ancestor. Some of them are fierce and others are kind of comical, but all of them are supposed to possess magic powers. When they put on their masks and costumes, people believe they actually *become* the ancestral spirit."

"Yes," Paul said, "with the mask they are no longer human."

"I think they must drink a lot of palm wine before they come out, maybe even take some kind of drugs," Kim said. "They are supposed to have amazing strength."

David went on, "In the old days they had unlimited power in the village. They could beat up or even kill a bad man. The Fon didn't have to look like a mean guy, and it also kept the punishment anonymous, like our old hooded executioners. These days the masks are not so powerful, but they are still feared."

Kim emerged from the kitchen bearing baskets full of golden fried potatoes, then a platter of hamburger patties and sliced rolls. The conversation halted, and all of us gathered around the table to admire this western vision: burgers, fries, mustard, tomatoes, onions. I felt a twinge of cultural guilt, the way I had once felt going into a Burger King in Paris, like a typical North American tourist — but I put it aside. I'd earned this. We all had. Silence reigned in pious devotion to the god of Burger, until Leonard and I had split the last one and left the platter bare.

"Wow," I said to Kim, "that was great. You should start a burger joint here in Jakiri."

"Yeah," Leonard said. "You could call it The Burger Fon."

By the time the meal was done darkness was coming on, and we soon rose to go. We said goodbye to Paul and Chris, and offered our thanks to Kim for a rare treat. With the highest token of tribute we could muster, David presented her with our chicken.

After a brief interval of delicious quiet back in Room 4, the generator came to life with a clanking roar, and the music from the bar blasted through the walls and throbbed in my head. Before leaving home, I had laughed to see "earplugs" on David's suggested packing list, but now I saw their use and their wisdom. Quiet nights in Cameroon. Occasional cramps still twisted my insides, my throat still ached, and homesickness and non-specific depression continued to sap my spirits. I tried to close my mind to the relentless generator and the distorted noise from the bar, and opened *Dear Theo*. And once again, poor Vincent echoed my mood in a letter to his brother:

> I long to hear from you, for notwithstanding the beautiful scenery I feel gloomy. I am overcome by a feeling of discouragement and despair. Though I wish it were not so, I am extremely sensitive as to what is said of my work, as to what impression I make personally. If I meet with distrust, if I stand alone, I feel a certain void which cripples my initiative. What I want is an intelligent sincerity, which is not vexed by failures. Two persons must believe in each other, and feel that the work can be done and must be done; in that way they are tremendously strong. They must keep up each other's courage.
>
> I take it deeply to heart that I do not get on better with people in general; it quite worries me, because on such contacts depends so much of my success in carrying out my work.
>
> When I look around me, everything seems too miserable, too insufficient, too dilapidated. We are having gloomy days of rain now, and when I come to the corner of the garret where I have settled down, it is curiously melancholy there; through one single glass pane the light falls on an empty colour-box, on a bundle of brushes the hair of which is quite worn down. It is so strangely melancholy that it has, luckily, almost a comical aspect — enough not to make one cry over it.

The Sultan's happy-laughing throne, all in red, blue, and yellow beadwork.
Sultan's Palace, Foumban.

the good heart

When people say that a person has a "good heart," they often *really* mean "he's an idiot, but harmless." That kind of snotty put-down, damning with faint praise, needs no introduction. Like "she has a nice personality," "nice legs, shame about the face," or that classic character, the whore with a heart of gold.

But when a person is described as "good-hearted," the implication is different, inferring that *on top of* other sterling qualities, the person also remains compassionate and gracious. Intelligent and accomplished, say, but also possessing that much rarer quality — a good heart.

Annie, for example, had a good heart. I mean, Annie was good-hearted. Oh, she could sometimes drive a person to distraction, but you couldn't really get *angry* at her. You felt instinctively that she was the kind of friend who would do anything for you, if you asked. Not the sort who was *thoughtful* — who would do something nice for you spontaneously — but she would willingly do you a favor, if you asked her to.

But because of that quality, she assumed that everybody else was equally ready to serve her, if only they were asked. She'd be standing beside a stone wall organizing her panniers before we set out in the morning, and automatically start passing *you* her glasses to hold, or her water bottle, or her helmet, rather than simply sitting them on the wall beside her, or on the ground. Little things, but continually repeated. Without thinking anything of it, she was always recruiting others in unnecessary ways. "Can you hold this?" "Can I borrow that?" "Will you do this for me?" Although you couldn't get angry at her, as the days and weeks passed it grew a little wearying.

Like the time back in Mutengene when she was waiting for us to leave, with *her* bike stacked in front of everyone else's. That scene was repeated more than once. Or the morning we left Buea. Annie had neglected to buy enough water for the day, and asked me if she could "buy" some of mine. Of course, I gave her half of my spare bottle — but then *both* of us had to worry about stopping to find more water. Or on the road to Mbouda: Leonard and I stopped for a break, and Annie came riding up and sat beside us under the tree. "Heh-heh ... it's hot ... does anybody have anything to drink?" And then, "Um ... does anybody have anything to eat?" Soon she was resting comfortably, reading *David's* book, drinking *Leonard's* water, and eating *my* food.

David remarked on the same thing another time, in Bamenda. Annie had been out all afternoon wandering around the shops and the market, then came to our door in the evening, as we were going out, and asked David if *he* could pick up a bottle of water for her. David came back into the room shaking his head and muttering. I began to call her "Blanche Dubois" in my mind — always depending upon the kindness of strangers.

I know other people who are like that, and they are so opposite to me that I often find I like them very much — despite my exasperation. It was that way with Annie. Sure, she could be thoughtless of others in little ways, but it was an innocent and blameless kind of *true* thoughtlessness. She simply didn't think about it. Her thoughts, like her speech, seemed to be halting and insecure, filled with gaps and ellipses ... um ... heh-heh ... yeah.

And if Annie could be thoughtlessly inconsiderate, so too could her "good heart" lead her to the opposite extreme. When the opportunity to be nice was plainly thrust upon her, she was gullible and could be exploited. In Jakiri, one of the local youths was eager to try out her bike, and soon cajoled her into lending it to him "for fifteen minutes." Fifteen minutes passed, then an hour, then two hours, until she started to worry.

The rest of us scoured the town on our bikes looking for it, but when we returned to the *Auberge* with no news, for the first time I saw Annie lose her composure. Her eyes misted over behind the thick glasses, and she pounded the wall, blurting out "I'm so *stupid!*" No one said a word. Eventually, on our way to Kim's house for dinner, we found the guy — in front of a bar, straddling Annie's bike and jawing with his friends.

So Annie's thoughtlessness was never arrogant or cruel; she was inconsiderate more-or-less accidentally. But Elsa was different. Her heart seemed full of bitterness, and the mask of "humanitarianism" she affected couldn't hide her basic contempt for humans. Or, perhaps she really *did* love humanity, but just didn't like *people* very much.

Maybe she hadn't always been that way. We had heard about her two sons and her grandchildren, but she didn't talk about her husband — ex-husband, we gathered. Once she told us a story about hiking in the Sierras with another woman, then added drily "now she's my husband's wife." Maybe a long-harbored bitterness had hardened her heart. Maybe she used to be different.

• • •

We left Jakiri when it was barely light, beginning a forty-three mile ride down a steep plateau from the highlands, then across a sweltering plain and into the city of Foumban. The first part of the ride was downhill, yes, but it was *that* kind of downhill — a bouncing, churning, heart-in-the-throat kind of daredevil descent which left my hands aching from straining at the brakes, my muscles cramped from the tension of the nervous balancing act, and my whole body stiff from the constant jarring. At the end of each of those four days on the Ring Road, I'd noticed that my muscles were sore, not from *exertion*, but from absorbing the constant shocks and body-blows transmitted up from the pedals, the saddle, and the handlebars.

When the road finally leveled off, the five of us spread out along the dirt track once more, rolling across a treeless savanna. Just ahead of me, halfway up a particularly rutted hill, Annie stopped to take a photograph. She didn't trouble to move aside, but stopped on the *only* navigable strip of the road, and as I struggled to go around her I went careening through the dust and gravel, nearly tumbling into the ditch. "Thank you, neighbor!" I called out.

Startled, she lowered the camera. "Oh ... heh-heh ... um, sorry!" As with so many good-hearted people, sarcasm was lost on Annie. I bounced on, my eyes raised to the heaven of Good Hearts.

By eight o'clock the heat was already becoming oppressive, and we stopped in a village for a makeshift breakfast, pushing our bikes into the deserted market. Spirits seemed low among our little group as we nibbled at the oranges, bananas, bread, and peanut butter.

No one said much, or offered the usual little jokes or comments, not even any remarks about the horrors of the road. David seemed especially silent. There was no apparent reason for this mood, at least not yet, but it seemed to hang like a pall. Everyone was in a bad mood.

This condition should not be shared; a bad mood is a sullen, solitary state, which has no real cause, and no real cure either. It just has to go away. A bad mood is not like misery, or even depression — it does not love company. It is not to be shared, and no improvement is gained by letting others have some of it. Only bitterness or unintended hurt. And if two bad moods collide, there will be trouble.

Also unlike other negative dispositions, this is a *responsive* state; a bad mood only exists in relation to other people. Although I am not often stricken with this condition, I have noticed that I often don't even *know* I'm in a bad mood until I come into contact with others. Then suddenly I notice that I have an urge to be surly, and don't wish to "open up" to people. And the barriers go up. If I'm on a concert tour, say, and spend the early part of a day alone in my hotel room, I might feel fine — reading, writing, watching TV contentedly. But as soon as I have to go out into the world I discover, by my *response* to others, that it is a zero-tolerance day. I fold into myself; friends seem annoying and self-satisfied, strangers seem invasive and contemptible, and I just want to be left alone. Sometimes it helps to go for a bike ride by myself.

So when we set off again, I pedaled ahead and rode out in front of the group, letting everyone keep their moods to themselves, and gradually increasing the distance between us. The plateau diminished to a hazy rampart behind me, and all around the brown grass was peppered with low trees, like the East African savanna. The only sounds came from my bicycle, the dust-caked chain grinding through the derailleurs and around the gears, tires crunching against the stones. The panniers banged against the rack, and an unidentifiable rattle came from somewhere down on the frame. Time was measured only by the occasional passing of a minibus, speeding by me in a roar of tossed stones and trailing a long plume of weightless dust. When I saw a reddish cloud approaching from in front or behind, once an hour or so, I pulled the bandana up over my face until long after the minibus had disappeared, .and the dust had settled. I sipped at my dwindling water, but my mouth was immediately parched again, dust grinding in my teeth. My skin felt gritty and salt-sticky, the sweat evaporating instantly into the dry air.

When I finally reached the outskirts of Foumban, I stopped in the shade of an abandoned truck to wait for Leonard, then together we rode into town. Spotting a drink shop behind a petrol station, we pulled in to investigate. Wonder of wonders, the drinks were kept in an electric cooler, and were *cold.*

Leonard wandered around the side of the building, where a young guy operated a "car wash" — a hose and some rags — serving the local taxi owners and their Peugeots, Renaults, and Nissans. Almost at once Leonard was back, stripping the bags off his bike and pushing it away. He'd made a deal to have his bike washed for 300 francs — only about a dollar, but probably more than the washer usually got for doing a whole car. Recognizing the wisdom of his idea, I followed Leonard's example, stripped everything off my bicycle, and rolled it around to line up behind his.

The car washer was about twenty, and full of the arrogance and confidence of youth. He wore a dirty shirt open to the waist and trousers rolled up to his knees. These clothes were suited to his work, but the car washer was one of those people who look proud even in rags. He wore them like an Armani suit.

Leonard once made that comment about Elsa, how even after suffering through a long day of dust and sweat she always managed to arrive looking neat and composed. David had laughed and turned to Annie, eyeing her grubby dishevelment, and said: "while Annie looks ..."

"Heh-heh — like somebody who doesn't *give* a damn," she finished, with a trace of defensiveness masking as pride. How often one sees that reverse vanity — people who are proud about not being proud, or vain about not being vain.

The car washer's handsome face wore a permanent smirk, and he swaggered about his domain of cars and mud, every gesture flamboyantly graceful. He had a small audience of local boys who hung around to watch him work and serve as the laugh-track for his steady flow of comments. Without understanding his speech, we knew his offhand remarks were delivered at the expense of his friends, us, and the rest of the world, a world under his command. The only one who would never be the butt of his jokes would be *himself.*

When I raised my camera to take a picture of him at work on my bike, he twisted like a dancer to face me, then crouched with his knees bent and arms thrown wide, like *The Jazz Singer*. As soon as he realized I could speak a little French, he began to work his unsubtle wiles on me, telling me how he "needed a beer," and could I "bring" him one.

Perhaps a Coca-Cola? I suggested.

No, he said, I don't like Coca-Cola. I like beer.

I laughed and nodded, and went to buy him a cold beer.

We spotted Annie coming along the road, and I ran out to wave her in. We told her about the cold drinks, and as she leaned her bike against the wall, she asked if someone could get her one. With a wry smile and a little shake of my head, I went. Dear Annie.

When I returned, I saw her trying to rub the layers of dust from her face with a dry bandana, while Leonard looked on and laughed at the futility. He suggested she start with her teeth. "Oh ... heh-heh ... the mud-tooth." Annie moistened the bandana and made another pass at her face, but this time only succeeded in smearing her cheeks with swirls of red mud, while Leonard and I continued our cruel laughter. "You guys," she said in dismay, "do I look all right or what?"

"You look fine," I lied.

Despite Annie's claim that she didn't "*give* a damn," she was often very concerned about what others thought. One time, as she climbed off her bike and wound the *pagne* around her waist, I kidded her about it, saying "One of these days you're going to learn how to put those things on." She'd laughed at first, but a few minutes later came up to me with a look of poignant vulnerability. "Does it *really* look okay?" I had to assure her once again that she looked fine. Or when we went shopping in the craft markets of Foumban, and I helped her make a good bargain for a small carving; when she'd bought it and we were walking away, she asked me for the third time "Do you really think it's okay?" Yes Annie, it's fine.

But if Annie sometimes cared too much what others thought, Elsa ran to the opposite extreme. That afternoon, after we'd checked into the hotel, I sat down and cleaned my bicycle, oiled the chain, pumped up the tires, and prepared it for the next day's ride. Elsa walked right by me as I sat on the floor working, but it never occurred to her that she ought to take care of those things too. Then the following morning all of the others were out early to do the same maintenance on their bikes, while Elsa was the last to appear, forcing the rest of us to stand around and wait while she oiled her chain and pumped her tires. When it was done, she stood up and seemed to notice us for the first time. "Oh, are we ready to go?" Yes Elsa, we are.

But, at least that day I gained some insight into the difference between David and me. While I bounced along the road to Foumban, it occurred to me that although we shared a love of cycling, we didn't share the same *reasons*.

There are two ways one can appreciate cycling. As a means-to-an-end, it is the perfect way to travel in an unfamiliar place. Fast enough to cover some territory, but slow enough to experience that territory. But as an end-in-itself, spinning the pedals and devouring the road is a rhythmic, exhilarating, and challenging action which sets the mind into a steady, soothing groove. The world is a friendly place from the saddle of a bicycle, and anything you can't actually *see* from that vantage point tends to recede into unimportance.

Even in a tense American city, people will smile at a cyclist, even speak to you if you're stopped at a light, where a pedestrian or a motorist would be studiously ignored — there would be a perceived "threat." By the non-cycling world, anyone silly enough to go about on a bicycle is viewed as a harmless eccentric, and therefore "safe" to talk with. Once, on my way from a Manhattan hotel to a show at the Meadowlands Arena in New Jersey, I cycled through Harlem to reach the George Washington Bridge. New Yorkers looked shocked when I told them about it, but I had felt safe on a bicycle, where I might not have in a car or on foot.

David, though, considered cycling more a means to an end. He didn't care what he had to pedal through, or over, it was simply his preferred way of traveling to the places he wished to visit. For me, the rough roads and endless buffeting distracted from what I liked about cycling. I missed being able to sing, or even *wanting* to sing, and I missed the rhythm of steady pedaling, the Zen state of cruising along a flat road, the challenge of a long, slow climb, and the fearless rush of adrenalin that sharpens the senses on a fast descent.

When we finally arrived at Foumban, and David asked me how I'd enjoyed the day's ride, I tried to explain this to him, how I saw cycling as an end-in-itself rather than a means-to-an-end, but I don't think he understood. He turned to Leonard, and asked him the same question. "And how did *you* like it?"

"I liked it okay," said the compliant Leonard.

"Do you mean you liked it as an end-in-itself, or as a means-to-an-end?" inquired David, with an edge of sarcasm. We all laughed, but it bothered me a little that he didn't seem to understand that I wasn't *complaining*, but only comparing the real with the ideal. A common route to misunderstanding.

But then, he'd had a tough day — a tough few weeks. He even confessed to Leonard and me that he was doubting whether he even wanted to *do* these trips anymore. Though he was too tactful and professional to directly blame Elsa, there could be no doubt of the cause. He told us it would be okay if he had an assistant, someone else to ride "sweep" at the back so that he could *lead* the trip, instead of *following* it. I knew David had every right to be in a "bad mood," a rare state for him too. I just didn't want to *share* in it.

So David was down-hearted, Annie was good-hearted, Elsa was hard-hearted, and Leonard — oh Leonard — he had a heart of purest cool. I never heard a bitter word from him about anyone or anything, yet he seemed so self-possessed that you couldn't tell *what* might run beneath those still waters. His impassive features may have reflected a genuine equanimity, or it may have been that his experiences in Vietnam, "working for the government," had left him with a true ambivalence, a love-hatred for mankind which masked as humorous detachment.

And what about me, now that I've dissected everyone else so thoroughly? What about my own "heartedness?" Do I have a good heart — am I good-hearted? Who do you ask? Who can you call? Any four people you asked would likely give you a different answer. No one is the same person to everyone they know.

I guess I *aim* at being a "good guy," though I'd have to admit I don't always manage it. At my best I can be compassionate, thoughtful, and generous, but at my worst I know I have sometimes been mean-spirited, self-centered, and intolerant. I can be moved by the afflictions of a billion strangers, by the blanket of sorrow which sometimes seems to lay over the whole world, but individual complaints often leave me cold, especially with someone I know. 'It's his own fault he hasn't got a decent job,' I think, 'he spent his life just going with the flow.' Or: 'Hey, she *married* the guy!' It's easy to give strangers the benefit of the doubt, to assume that their misfortunes are not their own fault, but when you know someone, the reasons for his or her difficulties can be only too apparent. As someone said, "There are no failures of talent, only failures of character."

But then, my wife accuses me of being too concerned about strangers, like when she vacillates over a menu while the waiter stands at our table expectantly, and I give her a "look." Or when I spend an occasional day answering letters from people I don't even know, instead of spending that time with my family. The appearance of twisted priorities, I suppose, but to me it seems the right way to be in the world — the Golden Rule. I don't like people wasting my time, but I do like it when a person does something unexpectedly nice for me.

But perhaps I am sometimes overly concerned about people who don't really *matter* to me emotionally. For example, I would rather be early for an appointment and have to wait myself than inconvenience anyone else (though I naively expect the same consideration in return).

But at the other extreme, I am jealous of my time and work, and am sometimes short even with my friends when a phone call interrupts me in the middle of something "important" — when it's not *convenient* to speak with them. Again, I justify it to myself, and maybe my friends even understand, but down in that "heart of hearts," I don't feel good about it. I am rarely down-hearted, but when I feel low I sometimes think, in that deep and secret place, that I am not a good person, and if I ever appear that way it's only because I consciously *try* to be. My inner devil tells me that I am only good if I make the *effort* — it doesn't come naturally. That's a sobering thought.

But then, when the darkness passes and I'm back to my normal height of self-esteem, I think, 'Well, is *anyone* really good by *nature?* Doesn't it *have* to be an exercise of will?' Almost always, I guess, though there are a few people who seem to be nice automatically, without ever having to try. But not very many. Maybe three.

At least *wanting* to be good is better than not wanting to, or wishing to appear good. I enjoy the feeling of giving to others without having to *tell* everybody about it. And all those faults — well, I'm working on them, trying to be more tolerant, more appreciative of others. I just need more time.

The Jazz Singer washing my bike.
Foumban.

the paved road

At 4:30 in the morning I was awakened by the *muezzins* wailing from the minarets of Foumban. This eerie call to prayer and the crowing roosters evoked an older, precolonial Africa, though Foumban itself had the Islamic flavor of North Africa: mosques with domes and minarets, and wrought iron star–and–crescent fences among the palms. The region was still nominally ruled by a sultan, and Foumban had been the seat of an ancient empire founded by the Bamum people, who migrated to Cameroon in some unknown past. After driving out the original inhabitants, they had settled the area (an early episode of imperialist oppression).

While touring around Foumban the previous afternoon, I had noticed a larger-than-life bronze statue of the previous sultan, King Njoya, arrayed in the Arabian Nights splendor of spherical headgear and flowing robes. Njoya was one of the most colorful figures in Cameroon history: around 1885, when his father was killed in battle, he succeeded to the throne, at the age of four, with his mother as regent. When the young sultan was old enough to take power himself, he set out to increase the prestige of his kingdom. Njoya was an open-minded ruler — since the Bamum people had no strong religious beliefs of their own, he investigated different religions, even accepted Christianity for a time under the teaching of German missionaries, but eventually settled on Islam. Njoya devised a system of writing, inspired by the Germans and the Arabic script of the Hausa traders, and he also managed to retain his authority through a long period of German, British, and French colonial rule. The French finally deposed him in 1931, after a six-year struggle, and exiled him to Yaoundé, where he died in 1933.

But Njoya's legacy has survived, even apart from the Arabian Nights statue. Because he encouraged and acted as patron to the artists and craftsmen of his kingdom, Foumban continued to be known as an arts center, with two museums of traditional art, and a street devoted to the *ateliers* of modern-day carvers, weavers, and bronze-workers. In Foumban I bought my first souvenir of Cameroon, a small human figure carved from a hippo tooth, said to be a "fetish," to keep away evil spirits. 'Couldn't hurt,' I thought, though as the *muezzins* and the roosters sang me awake that morning, I was hoping my fetish would keep away the evil *roads*.

We set off through the streets of Foumban, circled the market-place, and rolled out of town. The grasses beside the road were gold in the early-morning light, mountains stretched along the horizon in the distance, and the open road beckoned. I accelerated away in a burst of adrenalin, smooth pavement under my wheels, oil on my chain, air in my tires, and a fetish in my panniers.

Glancing back in my mirror, I saw another cyclist coming up fast — white helmet, yellow T-shirt and heavy black panniers. It was David, making a break for it, "ditching" Elsa for the day. When he rode up beside me, the smile in his beard told me he felt like I did. This was going to be a good day, and together we leaned into it and put the miles behind us.

Our pace was slowed only by a return to regular army and po-lice checkpoints — the lack of roadblocks was one advantage I hadn't properly appreciated on the less-traveled dirt of the Ring Road. But by this time we'd evolved a method: as we approached the tell-tale oil drums blocking half the road, we just kept on riding, right around the roadblock, as if they couldn't *possibly* want to stop us. It was a method born of resentment and a certain arrogance, but it worked, as an imperious attitude often does.

At the next checkpoint, however, the "breeze-through" strategy failed; we were called back. A policeman stood in the road, yelled something at us and waved us to the side. He gave us a stern look and demanded our passports. Another officer strolled up and casu-ally started snooping through my panniers. He hadn't spoken a word to me or asked what was in my bags, just started unzipping compartments and pulling out anything that seemed interesting. I hated it. "Looking for something?" I asked, in my most attitudinal French.

"*Non*," he said gruffly, and pulled out my pocket flashlight.

David caught my sarcasm, even if the cop didn't, and leaned over and said quietly, "It's not a good idea to piss them off when there are others coming behind. They might get a harder time because of it."

He was right, and I shut up. The officer rolled the flashlight between his fingers as if appraising its value. With a sidelong glance at me (glaring back silently), he slowly and reluctantly replaced it, and fished deeper. I was seething, as always when someone is rooting around in my stuff. Next he came out with a pair of spare tapes for my recorder, and gave them the same careful scrutiny. Then he held them out to me: *"Qu'est ce que c'est?"*

Between my teeth, I told him, For my *magnetophone*.

'Here comes trouble,' I thought. 'Now he'll think he's caught a spy. Next he'll ask me where the *magnetophone* is.'

But just as he asked that very question, the chief officer interrupted. He'd been leafing through my passport, then held one page up to his face as if to study it carefully. He waved the snooper-trooper away, and demanded, Where is your visa? I took back the passport, and saw that he had been spending all that time scrutinizing an *empty* page — and sideways too. On the very next page I pointed out the stamp, the one that said CAMEROON VISA.

When he'd gone through the same routine with David's passport, making him point out his visa, the head cop finally gave us a sour nod. As we pedaled away, David turned to me. "Aren't you glad they have adult literacy programs?"

"Really," I shook my head slowly, "I can understand why they have to accept illiterate soldiers, but illiterate *policemen* seems a bit much." I laughed at a sudden thought. "How's he going to read you your rights?"

"Your *rights?*" said David pointedly.

• • •

The highway moved up and down just enough to keep it interesting, but we were nearly always wheeling along in high gear, the wonderful end-in-itself kind of cycling I'd been wanting. Answered prayers — or a fully-operating fetish. The landscape reeled by like an ever-changing frieze: mangoes, avocados, casuarinas, giant ferns, and many groves of banana palms. Stranger things grew as well, like a twenty-foot-tall tree whose branches all ended in green bottle-brushes, and several rows of shrubs whose tiny flowers looked exactly like Trix cereal — orange-orange, raspberry-red, lemon-yellow.

In the town of Foumbot we chose an eating-shop for breakfast, then leaned our bicycles against a wall across the street to wait for the others. I climbed on top of the wall and sat there, David sat by the curb, and we watched the town go by. Many of the men wore long white shirts that reached down to their ankles, Muslim style, and I noticed that some of them walked together, hand in hand, or with their little fingers linked. I had often seen the young Maasai warriors in East Africa walking with an arm around each other, and reflected on how refreshing it was to see men whose *machismo* didn't crumble at physical contact with other males. Not the brief bear-hug-and-back-pounding ritual of Europeans, the ceremonial clinch-and-break, or the quick cool handshake of the Brits, but an easy contact — just strolling along the road with hands or fingers joined. Some of them seemed to draw apart when they saw David and me, and I wondered what made them suddenly self-conscious. Perhaps previous white visitors had made fun of them, and showed them the ugliness of sexual insecurity. Or maybe they knew of the western stigma, and didn't want to be thought of as homosexuals. Or maybe they *were* homosexuals? David said no; it was just a comfortable custom among the men here. "Funny thing," he said, "Africans always claim there is no homosexuality in Africa, but I had some friends in the Peace Corps who were gay, and they never had any trouble finding partners!"

Once the others arrived and we'd had our usual omelette, *baguette*, and Nescafé, I headed off alone. I couldn't wait to get back on that *road*. Breezing through checkpoint number four without pause, I went spinning along once more, appreciating the contrast with the previous days, remembering the bicycle bucking under me like a wild horse. With a long, sweeping downhill ahead, I stopped pedaling and enjoyed the free ride, gathering speed as the trees began to blur. But just as I was coasting along the valley floor, I saw another barricade.

This one seemed a little meaner than the others, just a pair of oil drums at the side, a small raffia shelter, and a patched line of rope and strips of rubber laying across the pavement. Two uniformed figures stepped out in front of me, and with a sigh I coasted in.

But something didn't seem right here. One man was too old, spindly, and toothless to be a soldier, while the other was young and squat, with crossed eyes and a vacant grin. Their faded khaki uniforms boasted no badges or decoration, and then I noticed they carried no weapons. But, they also carried no "attitude;" they were friendlier than any *real* soldiers, so I decided to play along for a while.

The old man played "officer," though his French was as halting as my own, and delivered with many grunts and facial contortions. He went through the usual routine: where was I going, where was I from, while the young one looked on expectantly with a gaping grin. They must have thought they'd hooked a big one — a lone white man on a bicycle. When the wobbly old rogue ran out of French, he turned to gestures to describe what he really wanted. He cupped his hand and raised it to his mouth, while the young imbecile nodded his empty head and giggled. They were looking for booze.

"Je n'ai que l'eau," I told them; I have nothing but water. There was more nodding, smiling, grunting, and gesturing, while I pointed to my water bottles, and told them it would be too hot to carry any beer on my bike. They smiled and nodded, uncomprehending. Then the old man made the other time-honored gesture, thumb against index finger, and I shook my head again, smiling. *"Pas de l'argent, pas de la bière."* Sorry guys, no money, no beer. But I shook their hands before I rode away.

Late in the morning the smooth cruising came to an end. The road suddenly turned upward, and *stayed* upward for about four miles. I shifted into a lower gear and bent into the climb, expecting the top of the hill to appear after every winding of the road. Somehow you can tell when the crest of a hill is approaching — by the light, by the amount of sky between the trees. As I stood on the pedals, sweat running into my eyes, I waited for that telltale bit of open sky to appear before me.

A length of dry snakeskin lay crushed on the road. The feathers of a dead whippoorwill stirred in the wind from passing cars and trucks, whose slipstreams also gave me a momentary boost. A military convoy roared by my elbow, four olive-drab trucks carrying thirty or forty soldiers each. As the canvas-covered trucks strained up the endless hill (like me, in low gear) the soldiers turned to stare.

Most of them were stern-faced, though one or two waved and smiled.

By the time the telltale bit of sky told me I'd crested the hill, I was into the traffic and buildings of Bafoussam. I stopped for a warm Coke and some biscuits, and sat down to wait. David came sweltering up just behind, and pulled off to sit beside me. "Well, how'd you like that one?" he said.

"Quite a climb, but even that's okay with me. This whole ride has been great — my kind of cycling."

David told me he was going on into town to check on hotels, and asked me to wait for the others. As I leaned back against the wall, I noticed a big Mercedes sedan parked on a sidestreet across from me. It didn't appear to have been wrecked or burned, but only abandoned and stripped of everything reusable. Cars of that *wabenzi* class were rare in Cameroon, and probably one of the most coveted luxuries in the whole country, and yet it had simply been abandoned.

Elsa too had been abandoned. Leonard came laboring up the hill, the usual waterfall of sweat drenching his clothes, and sat beside me to wring out his shirt and multiple bandanas. As we watched the pool of moisture evaporate, Annie arrived, blowing the limp hair away from her red face. Neither of them had any idea how far behind Elsa was; no one had stayed back with her. When we'd waited a half hour for her and she still hadn't shown, we decided to go on into town and find David.

The streets of Bafoussam were busy, noisy, and stifling, wearing an aspect of dusty neglect. We found the hotel David had mentioned, with him parked outside it, but the place looked especially uninviting. And worse — it was full. We waited there by the street and watched the trucks rumble by for nearly two hours before Elsa appeared, and we moved on to the Hôtel Le Continental.

After two weeks of bucket baths, sponge baths, cold showers, or, like the previous night, going to bed dirty because the water was "seized," I stood in a steamy bathroom and felt the benediction of hot water. The only bad thing was having to make it brief. I could have stayed under that shower for a long time, but there were two others waiting to use it. I didn't want to be remembered as the one who used *all* the hot water.

Music wafted through the open window from a record store across the street, and my ears locked onto something new, a kind of Cameroonian pop music I hadn't heard before. Though still obviously West African in rhythm and sound, it was a little more sophisticated in its arrangements, with dynamics and textures, rather than the usual single-purpose *boom*-ba-*boom*-ba-*boom*. This was not just for dancing; it was nice to *listen* to, with echoes of the smooth "Philly Sound" and hints of Jamaica and Nigeria as well — a fine example of the cross-pollination which has enriched both African and Western music.

It was good music to do laundry by, and soon damp clothes were strung from wall to wall like yachting flags, criss-crossing the room four times. Making my way from one side to the other was like pushing through a soggy jungle.

When the washing was done, I lay back on the foam-slab mattress to read some Aristotle, feeling pink-clean, smooth-shaven and pleasantly drowsy. Happy. Leonard snored from his bed in the corner, while David quietly hung the last T-shirt. The two of them also looked much cleaner, and if not shaven, at least they had clean beards. After a day without Elsa, David seemed fully recovered from his bad mood of the previous day, and looked — happy.

And, with perfect synchronicity, I was reading about that very subject. "Happiness is an activity of the soul in accordance with virtue." Typical of Aristotle, it takes a book to expand on that terse maxim, but the main points eventually came clear to me. Like that old saying, "Happiness is not a station to be arrived at, but a mode of travel." Therefore it follows that happiness is a bicycle.

Once again, I had to remember that *every word counts*. You wouldn't call anyone happy because he experienced a momentary pleasure, or laughed once, or had one hot shower in two weeks. Happiness takes time, in a real sense. It's not the prize you win, but the way you ride the bike. Happiness is a paved road.

And that "virtue" we're supposed to be in accordance with, what do we make of that? Virtue is a funny sort of word, and not a fashionable one. It has a Victorian ring of purse-lipped parsons and aged virginity, and through long abuse has acquired the stain of self-righteous hypocrisy too. No one I know would want to be called *virtuous*. I know I wouldn't. Some translators prefer to substitute "excellence," as a more exact rendering of the Greek *arete*, and omit the "soul" business, so that happiness becomes "an activity in accordance with excellence."

I can live with that. How to define excellence? The proper answer, as to so many other things that *ought* to be self-evident, is: "If you have to ask ..." But I set the book aside to think about it for a minute. I suppose I might define excellence as doing something well enough that other people who do it too admire your work. That can be true of playing the piano, tuning an engine, planting a garden, making tortellini, or just plain *living*. And that would be perfectly in tune with my understanding of Aristotle's meaning — "Happiness is excellent living."

But you know it doesn't end there. For instance, a friend and I once argued for hours over whether excellence is a luxury. I said it was; he said it wasn't. He's not here right now to give *his* side, but I figure nearly everything except vegetables is a luxury. Honesty, good taste, and certainly excellence of all kinds. An excellent house is nice, but a noisy brothel with "seized" water will do. An excellent tortellini is a virtuous thing, but if you're starving you won't quibble if it's not quite *al dente*. You might even eat *fufu*, or rice with junk on it. Excellence is a bicycle — but you can always walk.

● ● ●

These days I can afford to pride myself on a firm integrity, but in other times I have been poor and desperate, and have seen how forgivable, even necessary, stealing can seem. When I was a foolish eighteen-year-old seeking fame and fortune on my own in England, I joined a small-time band. In time, as we rehearsed together and tongues were loosened when we adjourned to the pub, I learned that all of their equipment had been stolen from another band. Even their *van* was stolen. To a small-town Canadian boy this was pretty shocking stuff, but I had to play it cool, just nod and say nothing. I wanted to be worldly, and in any case I wasn't particularly judgmental in those days, except about my parents, so I also didn't flinch when I learned that all this stuff had been stolen by the band's equipment manager, Simon (*equipment manager* indeed!). But Simon was a good guy, friendly to me, and nothing is really a crime to an eighteen-year-old, except being his parents.

During long drives up the M1 to the north of England for small-change gigs, I became friends with Simon, sitting up all night in the shotgun seat beside him and talking, as we watched the dark motorway speed toward us. I liked his northern candor and native warmth, and his extra-legal activities were never mentioned between us. I only heard these things from the guys in the band, who'd also told me that Simon sometimes "knocked over" petrol stations at night.

When those small-change gigs were over, and there was no money and no more work, I became suddenly destitute — lacking the "luxuries" of food and rent. As an immigrant without a work permit, almost an illegal alien, work was hard to get, and so, not knowing where else to turn, I asked Simon if I could accompany him "on a job" sometime. Fortunately for my future, he only shook his head, embarrassed, and slipped me a five-pound note from time to time.

Simon would go on to become a professional "villain" (his word), but he wouldn't drag a small-town Canadian boy into it. Mind you, I didn't quibble about accepting his ill-gotten gains, and my conscience was not stirred by the luckless petrol-station owner any more than it was by the band's stolen van and equipment.

So, I have learned that my precious integrity is no less than a precious *luxury*. I have been fortunate (and stubborn) enough to be able to be honest, to be uncompromising, to pursue excellence. To ride a paved road.

The unpaved road.
Somewhere in northern Cameroon.

people on the bus

Few people in West Africa own private cars; most travel by shared taxi or bus. No visit to Africa is complete without a journey by one of those methods — if you're not in a hurry, and you don't mind being crushed up against your fellow humans for long hours with one buttock on the seat and one suspended in the air.

The southern portion of our Cameroon odyssey was over, and we were catching a bus to the capital city, Yaoundé, then taking a twelve-hour train ride to the north. At 6:30 in the morning we cycled into Bafoussam's crowded bus park, where the Japanese minibuses waited in rows, departing by no schedule, but only when they were full. David was already there, embroiled in an argument with the despatcher and a circle of drivers over the fare for us and the bicycles. Finally he ducked out of the circle like a man emerging from a tent. "All settled," he said with a tight smile, then climbed atop one of the minibuses. Leonard and I passed the bikes and panniers up to him, while the crowd moved over to surround the bus and study the white men and their machines.

I sat on the bus and waited for it to fill up, chewing on a *beignet* and looking out the window. Hawkers approached the bus, hissing to catch our attention, and displayed their wares: toothpaste, wire hangers with pink satin covers, soap, men's underwear, kola nuts, and cheap watches. When a boy hissed and knocked at our window with a tray of toilet paper, Leonard laughed "Hey man, I haven't even finished *eating* yet!"

A man in a long dirty overcoat carried a greasy drum over his shoulder as he strolled aimlessly through the crowd. His hair was long and unkempt, his eyes glazed over, and he didn't actually *play* the drum, just tapped at it nervously with his fingers, as if on a table top. Watching him, it occurred to me how few real vagrants I had seen in Cameroon, so few I could remember each one. There seemed to be no bums, no winos, no armies of the homeless in the streets of Cameroon, and perhaps that was because the ties of family remain so strong in Africa. The reprobates and the unbalanced are kept at home.

Blind and crippled people begged in the streets of the cities, but in this culture begging was seen as a kind of "occupation" for the afflicted, nothing dishonorable about it. And the beggars were often guided by a child; they were cared for, helped. This suggested a parallel as banal as truth often is. Perhaps the splintering family network in the West explains why we seem unable to help the bottom layer of *our* society. Faceless charity cannot reach them, or succor them, and the biggest maladjustment for such people is that no one really cares about them. They are truly lost with their carrier bags, truly alone under their newsprint bedspreads.

I look at their faces in our cities. I feel no disgust, but only pity and wonder. I wonder about their stories. I don't know what it is I seek, really. Maybe some flicker of dignity, or even sorrow. As a child I imagined the bums must know some "secret," must have learned some dark knowledge that caused them to retire from the world into the "hobo jungle" behind the arena in my town. But now I guess they're just confused, maybe wondering why the rest of us *bother*.

Hookers fascinate me in the same way. Working at a recording studio in Toronto, I used to cycle home at midnight through the middle of their territory. I would see them leaning against a bus shelter smoking cigarettes, appraising the passing cars. Some of them seemed so young and frail-looking in their costumes, their heavy makeup, their big hairdos. As I rode by I tried to look at their faces, to see *something* there — someone's daughter, someone's sister — but their masks were tough. I wanted to see some vulnerability, some sense of them as *victims*, but I saw only a cynical, wiser-than-thou stare, like a soldier or a teenage boy. To them, it was just a job.

• • •

The three-hour bus ride seemed much longer. Four of us were crammed into a seat which would have been crowded for three, and we had to stagger our shoulders, one forward, one back. I watched the walls of trees pass by, the highway cutting through the dense rainforest on long, rolling hills. It was beautiful at first, then only monotonous in the cramped bus. The white kilometer markers at the roadside counted down the distance. Discomfort became drowsiness, my eyes grew heavy, but only Leonard could manage to sleep under those conditions. Occasionally the driver lit a cigarette, and I smiled darkly to see Elsa recoil from him as if he'd suddenly contracted leprosy.

Every few miles we were stopped at roadblocks, and stewed in the roadside heat for long minutes while our driver followed one of the soldiers to a more private place — to pay his dash. Sometimes I even saw him take out a few banknotes before he left his seat. Bribery was simply a fact of life for the bus and taxi drivers. You pay or you stay. And not just the drivers either; one time on a bus in the Ivory Coast I saw a woman arguing with a soldier over her papers, but the soldier just ordered her off the bus — *"Descendez"* — shouldered his gun, and turned away. Without even stirring from her seat, the woman called the driver over, handed him some money, and the driver followed the soldier back down the road. A few minutes later we all drove away.

According to the West African lexicon, this was not a bribe, but a fee. In a small town in Ghana, a young bookseller named Fred explained the difference. Fred was about to be married, and his fiancée was studying to be a teacher. Asked what would happen if she were sent to teach in another town after graduation, Fred said that he would have to go see someone and pay some money.

"A *dash*, you mean."

"No no no — you don't understand. It is *not* a dash. Because I want something to be done, I must pay this man to see that it is done."

So then, a dash is a "gift" the bus driver gives to the soldier so that something won't happen to him, while Fred pays a "fee" to see that something *does* happen. Just like the so-called "back door" network in China, or the western exchanging of "under the table" favors in business and politics. It's just that in this respect, Africa is much more *developed*.

Cameroon seemed to be unique among West African countries in the attention the soldiers paid to westerners. Ever since the coup attempt in 1984, they've been convinced we're all spies. In most countries the authorities are content to hassle their own people and leave the tourists alone, but every time that bus was stopped on our way to Yaoundé, they had to see each of our passports, even if the Cameroonians were just given a quick scan.

One time, though, they quietly pulled a guy off the bus and led him away. This was alarming — how little he resisted, and how the other passengers just looked away. I tried to imagine this happening on a North American bus, all the excitement and gossip it would cause among the other passengers. But here people only turned the other way, minded their own business. African countries can hold up the democratic mask, but up close you see the way it really works.

. . .

When we finally arrived at the bus park outside Yaoundé it was midday, and stifling hot. The crowded bus-park reeked of urine. We quickly hauled our bikes down from the roof of the bus, loaded them up and rode away. After weeks of back roads, small towns, and villages, Yaoundé seemed like Manhattan to me. Modern buildings towered above the streets, yet their boldly geometric style made them uniquely African. A gridwork of giant cranes swung above the empty frames of office and apartment blocks.

As we passed the great marketplace, music blared out from stores and cars; people were talking and yelling and selling things. Everything smelled like sewage and exhaust. Traffic was pure chaos, even with policemen "directing" it. Cars snarled down on us from every side; taxis stopped suddenly and cut to the side of the road, and I tried not to panic. In this artificial calm I noticed a few Mercedes sedans among the Peugeots and Japanese taxis, though many of those prestigious *wabenzi* cars bore the scars of frequent accidents, unskilled bodywork, and homemade paint jobs. That and the crumpled taxis suggested that people crashed into each other a lot, and I tried to stay out of their way.

Just after dark we strolled around the corner from the Hôtel Nourrice (meaning *wet-nurse*, oddly). The water, of course, was "seized" — plastic buckets were carried to our rooms from a cistern in the courtyard — but the electricity worked. Sometimes. Life as usual in the capital of Cameroon. The hotel was on a hill above Yaoundé, and the lights of the city sparkled between the dark buildings. Above everything a single huge cloud loomed, lit from within by sudden veins of lightning. Cars seemed to float by on a cloud of dust which filled the headlight beams and ghosted the crowds. The neighborhood accepted us without notice; there were no stares, no comments.

David led us to a corner lined with stalls where fires glowed under iron grilles, and pale light bulbs hung from wires. He stopped at one of the stalls and talked with a fat, perspiring woman who was busily cleaning fish. She looked up from her work to speak to David, but kept slicing with her knife. She smiled hugely and beckoned us to a bench behind her.

An hour later we were stuffed with smoked fish, grilled maize-on-the-cob, barbecued beef, fried plantains, and Fanta. I turned to David. "The best meal I've had in Cameroon." He nodded, and Leonard chipped in a "Yeah man." Annie smiled. Even Elsa seemed happy.

· · ·

In the crowded train station we huddled around our bicycles, stripping them of panniers and pedals to go into the baggage car. A rainshower pelted the forlorn palms for a few minutes, and the throng pressed even tighter under the station portico. No one paid any attention to the garbage fire, a roiling of flames and black smoke between two buildings across the parking lot.

The rain stopped as suddenly as it had begun, and Annie, Elsa, and I stood guard over the bags while David and Leonard pushed the bikes into the building. I saw Elsa aiming her camera at the scalloped roof of the station, and said to her quietly, "Don't do it."

She snapped back, "What do you mean?"

Sweet Elsa. I explained what she ought to have known by that time. "You're not allowed to take pictures of anything governmental, not even train stations. And look at all the cops and soldiers around here." She looked as if she didn't want to believe me, but khaki and camouflage *were* everywhere, and fortunately she put her camera away, shaking her head as if it were *my* fault.

David appeared out of the crowd, pursued by one of the train station hustlers, the two of them carrying on a loud argument in French. Leonard told us this shabbily-dressed teenager had appeared at the baggage car as they were loading the bikes, and had jumped in, unasked and unneeded, to help put them aboard. Now he demanded a thousand francs for his trouble.

As we shuffled our packs through the crowd to the train, the boy jogged sideways beside us, haranguing in bursts of impassioned French. Often the invective flew over our heads, and David and I together couldn't figure out what he was saying, but we got the drift. Finally David offered him two hundred francs, take it or leave it, but the hustler wouldn't do either. He was outraged at David's refusal to go along with the time-honored scam of fleecing travelers.

But David had obviously been through this before, and wasn't ready to give in. The two of them fired blanks at each other right to the door of the carriage. Then the boy stormed off, threatening to take our bicycles off the train. Leonard, the peacemaker, asked if it would be an honorable solution for *him* to pay the boy, but David wisely said that giving in would only make it worse for the next victims.

Once my gear was on board, I shadowed the hustler along the platform, down the length of the train to the baggage cars. Through the open door I saw him hoisting one of the bikes, as if to make good on his threat, so I planted myself in front of the door, summoning some false bravado to go with my real anger. *"Ne touchez pas,"* I said.

I guess I looked bigger than I felt; the boy froze. He put down the bicycle, spread his hands and started into another burst of outrage. Yet he wasn't really expressing anger or hostility; he was almost pleading. The kid honestly believed that he was the one being ripped off here. I couldn't catch all of what he said, but sensed that it didn't really matter; the issues were clear.

"Ne touchez pas," I repeated, *"C'est mon vélo."* It wasn't really my bike, it was Annie's, but I folded my arms across my chest and stared him down. David joined me on the platform and I asked him if we should try to find a gendarme. He told me that wasn't always a good idea — you couldn't tell whose side a policeman would take. Sometimes the White Man was always wrong. Facing two of us now, the boy jumped from the baggage car and stalked down the platform to the station. David and I went back to our carriage, but kept a careful watch on the baggage car.

The boy did return one more time, with a few cronies who acted more curious than threatening, and an older man who seemed to be an official of some kind, though he wore no uniform. David was drawn into another round of bickering, mediated by the older man, and the boy finally accepted David's offer of two hundred francs, though he obviously still felt cheated. At last the train shuddered, then rattled out of the station.

Our first-class compartment was clean and comfortable, two stacked berths on each side. In spite of its gray formica and stainless steel, the compartment possessed the innate coziness of any small, moving capsule — a ship's cabin, a tour bus — and I felt lucky to have it. I knew that on David's previous trip he'd been unable to reserve a compartment, and his group had sat all night on the hard wooden benches in second class.

As the train sped into the sudden darkness I sat reading a two-day-old *International Herald Tribune*, and nibbling at the goodies I had bought at the SCORE supermarket: cookies, raisins, peanuts, and chocolate bars. When the lights went off in our carriage I worked on the crossword puzzle by flashlight, but a commotion at the door made me raise my eyes. An African man was greeting David in the darkness. He worked for the government, some kind of official tourist guide, and David had met him on a previous trip. Behind this man came a German woman, bumping against the doorway with her eyes wide in the light from our flashlights. She seemed hysterical, nearly incoherent, and I thought she must be drunk, or frightened, or both.

She sat down in our compartment, calmed by our lights and our presence, and began to speak in breathless, rambling phrases, occasionally erupting into fits of edgy giggling. Through her accent and her agitation I managed to figure out that her husband was a photographer, and they'd been traveling around southern Cameroon by car. Now, like us, they were on their way north, their Land Cruiser loaded on the back of the train. Apparently she didn't enjoy this kind of traveling, but wanted to be with her husband.

The guide asked us to help get the woman back to their carriage, so Leonard and I led the way down the dark corridor with our flashlights. When we reached the door at the end, and faced the abyss separating the carriages, the German woman was terrified by the noise, the darkness, and the tiny "bridge" she had to cross. Leonard and I placed ourselves at each end of the bridge, while the guide handed her slowly across. I took her hand, feeling it stiff and trembling as I almost lifted her into the corridor on the other side.

At the door of her compartment we were met by the woman's worried husband. He thanked us in a heavy German accent, while his *frau* fell into his arms. She turned and gushed with a gratitude far outweighing our services. As we turned to go I caught Leonard's eye, and he raised an eyebrow.

The train stopped briefly at a few small, unlit stations outside the city, and during one of the stops I saw two coveralled workers pass through our carriage. Leonard and I followed them to see if they were going to fix the lights, and found them at the end of the car, fiddling at a power box. One of them was steadily lighting matches — they had no flashlight. Leonard and I shone our lights on the rows of breakers and fuses, until the men finally located the breakdown. Suddenly the overhead lights came on, and the two men smiled at us. *"Merci. Bonsoir."*

And *bonsoir* it was, for as soon as the lights were fixed everyone seemed to fall asleep — or at least lay very quietly with their eyes closed. I reached up from my lower berth to turn the lights off again, and lay in the dark thinking about Yaoundé, collecting my impressions. Hot, humid, the omnipresent smell of exhaust fumes and urine. Men pissed everywhere on the streets, and I'd even seen a woman hoist her *pagne* and squat on a back street, while her young son waited beside her.

One event stood out in Yaoundé, apart from the excellent streetfood and our hotel being without water for the whole two days we were there. The big event for me was a telephone call home. I'd locked my bike outside the PTT (*Poste, Télégraphe, Téléphone*) building on Yaoundé's main roundabout, then threaded through the beggars and pedlars and went inside to find the telephones. The building was old and dingy, a few people standing lazily along the counter. I don't know what I expected, perhaps a row of telephone booths with an operator to place your call, but I saw nothing that looked promising. 'Maybe another part of the building,' I thought, and walked back outside to look for another entrance. But no, that was it. Finally I asked at the telegraph desk, and was directed to a counter in the corner, where a woman dozed over a single '50s-vintage telephone. I asked her about making a call to Canada, and without a word she passed me a scrap of paper to write down the number. Moments later she motioned for me to sit on the bench beside her, and handed me the receiver.

"I don't understand you," I heard Jackie say, still responding to the operator.

"Hi, it's me," I said, and she laughed with sudden recognition. A delay on the line made our conversation a bit disjointed, but the connection was surprisingly good. She asked me how I was doing, and I told her I was okay. "It's been wild — things are a little primitive here. Had a couple of days when I was pretty sick, and I've been feeling low and homesick sometimes. Not always fun. But it's been, ah, *interesting*. I'm counting down the days until Paris."

She laughed her knowing laugh, "Well, thanks for telling me all the lies, anyway!"

I laughed too, the delay cutting our laughs into one. "I can't talk for very long, it'll be expensive and I haven't got a lot of money right now."

"Okay, well it's good to hear your voice anyway. I've been wondering about you."

"Yeah, I've been thinking about you guys a lot too." Two more weeks until I would see her in Paris, it seemed so far off. And another week after that before I'd see my ten-year-old daughter, Selena. I'd been missing her a lot too.

But that had been my brief contact with that *other* life, the real life. I'd been feeling it strongly, worst when I was ill back in Ndop, but in some ways being in Yaoundé made it more acute. The hints of that other world: a cinema, newspapers, the white Oldsmobile outside the U.S. embassy. Sometimes the longing surfaced on the least profound thoughts — the growing pile of exposed films in my panniers made me think of home, of getting them developed. Or looking at my disintegrating shoes made me think of being able to throw them away. The longing became an ache.

As any traveler knows, a phone call home is no cure for homesickness, or missing someone. It really only makes it worse. But at least you both know the other is still alive. That knowledge was small comfort to me as I lay in my berth on the sleeping train, swaying in the darkness as we sped toward Ngaoundéré.

• • •

Just before dawn I stood in the corridor and watched a new landscape materialize. The air was cool on the high Adamoua Plateau, almost chilling as it rushed in the windows, carrying the smoke from grassfires on the plains. Figures began to emerge from the grass-roofed huts along the tracks.

As we slowed for the station at Ngaoundéré, a woman began screaming desperately in the neighboring compartment. She cried out in great sorrow, keening and sobbing out of control, while a sudden shuffle of people moved up and down the corridor. From one of them we learned that the woman had been robbed; she'd been carrying a lot of money back from Yaoundé, and it had been taken from beneath her head while she slept. I heard the voices of other women trying to comfort her, and men's voices asking her questions, but all she could do was wail.

I understood the ruin this loss could mean for the woman and her family, and was moved to sympathy. I thought of giving her all the Cameroon money I was carrying, forty or fifty dollars, but didn't know how to go about it, how such a gesture would be accepted. In ignorance and self-consciousness, I did nothing. At the station I watched sadly as she was led away in a huddle of flowing robes, bowed and stumbling.

While I stood on the steps of the train waiting for the others to get organized, I felt a bumping beneath my feet, then the train lurched and I had to grab the handrail. It was moving away! Where was it going? I thought this was the end of the line, but who could be sure? David had already jumped down with his bags, and I hesitated while there was still time. I was ready, I could get off and leave the others to their fate, or stay on the train and try to help with whatever happened.

Perhaps the woman's plight had activated my sympathy-responses, for I quickly decided to remain. David could look after himself, but I was the only other one who spoke any French. I stood on the step shaking my head and watching as the train moved in a wide, slow circle, then stopped in the service yards a half-mile away. Already a crew of young boys was moving from car to car, scavenging and cleaning.

I humped all of my bags back to the station, along with one of Elsa's (which she later took back without thanks). At the unhitched baggage car I found David alone amid a crowd of twenty hustling boys, all of them fighting to get hold of our bicycles. Fed up by now, I grabbed two of the bicycles out of their clutches and stalked away up the platform, pushing a bicycle with each hand. Leonard looked surprised at my brusqueness, but he and David followed with the other three bikes. I was beginning to learn that politeness and patience were the weaknesses on which the hustlers fed; if you wanted to escape them you had to simply push right through.

. . .

The little bus had been built to carry eighteen passengers. Thirty-four of us were squeezed aboard the blue and white "Coaster" for the two-hundred-mile ride to Garoua, where we would start cycling again. I perched on the edge of a seat in a most unnatural way, while the rest of our group was scattered among the compressed mass. Leonard nodded in half-sleep in front of me, while at the end of his row a scruffy-looking Australian named Ken delivered a cheerful ongoing commentary to anyone who would listen, or could understand. Ken wore the ragged and slightly unhealthy look of the long-time tropical gypsy. Something about his bearing, his wiry pallor, made him look as if he'd just recovered from some wasting disease. The few whites I'd seen in Yaoundé often wore the same look, French women shopping in the SCORE supermarket, businessmen in the banks. They all looked drained, colorless, even seedy, as conspicuous and ill-kept as the other colonial leftovers, the old buildings.

Ken had been traveling in Asia and Africa for four years, and was so glad to encounter us in this desolate outpost that it seemed he couldn't *prevent* himself from talking. He told traveler's tales of eating monkey and crocodile in Zaïre, of spending days in jail in Gabon for some visa irregularity, and of running from bullets in Uganda. Finally Annie passed him my three-day-old *International Herald Tribune*, and he was quiet for awhile as he devoured every word, from editorials to ads (just as I had). As the crowded little bus rolled on, I watched the yellow grass and thorn trees stretch away under a crystal sky. Now we were in the Sahel, a belt of dry savanna which borders the Sahara.

Suddenly there was a bang and a rhythmic thumping from behind my seat. One of the dual rear tires had obviously blown, but the driver didn't even slow down. I knew one tire wouldn't support all this weight for long, and sure enough, another bang and a loud thumping of tire carcass announced the collapse of the second one.

The heavy bus wove drunkenly from side to side, drawing gasps and cries from the female passengers. Pieces of rubber littered the road behind as the driver finally brought the bus to a stop, then climbed out to have a look. Some of the passengers got off the bus too, and I realized this might take a while. My momentary fear melted to a studied patience. Sitting as I had been, cramped and half-assed, one whole leg had gone numb, so I was grateful for the chance to escape. I was also grateful for our bicycles on the roof, if we *really* had to escape. As I stood and waited while a one-legged man in rags hobbled to the ground, my leg suddenly felt much better.

The crew huddled around the masticated tires. The fat driver chewed his lip while an arrogant young dandy who was a kind of "conductor" jabbered orders to a teenage boy with ruined teeth, who climbed under the bus and started jacking it up. Of course, there was only one spare tire, which might have been of some help if the driver had stopped after the *first* blowout, but now it was useless. I cast another glance at our bicycles on the roof, then settled in the grass on the shady side of the bus. Many of the passengers remained in their seats, waiting stoically, while others milled around outside. The one-legged man hoisted his long tattered shirt, squatted at the roadside and urinated at ground level.

Finally the crew flagged down a truck and managed to borrow a tire. While our driver leaned his considerable bulk on the tire irons, and the younger boy worked under the bus, the *conducteur* kept his chin high and his hands clean, "directing" the operation. David was in there too, doing what he could to help. The midday heat brought a torpor to the scene, and the waiting passengers, even Ken, fell silent. The only sounds were clanging tools and the quiet discussions among the workers.

And so it was almost an anticlimax when the driver waved everyone aboard. No cheers, no smiles, just the *conducteur's* bullying orders and nudges to get in. Like, suddenly we're in a *hurry*? Everyone took their previous places, with a few quiet protests until we all had our allotted few inches of space once more. Two vast women in robes settled their ample hips beside me, their babies still eerily silent; they'd hardly made a sound all morning.

The bus moved off into the dry heat of the day, the breeze bringing little relief. Once again the *conducteur* stood in front of me, just beside Leonard, and continued chatting up the woman beside me, who was invisible beneath brown robes and flowing headscarf. During the stop Leonard had told me this woman's high-pitched babble and giggling was getting on his nerves; he called her "The Chinese Woman." But it was the *conducteur* who bothered me. He had a flat, Nilotic face, with thin lips and the kind of narrow, hard eyes that look only inward, and wore a gray shirt printed with little black horseshoes. Everything about him showed his great self-regard, his supercilious expression, his carriage, his reluctance to get his hands dirty, his behavior to the boy with the broken teeth, and to us passengers. His profession, though, showed the reality. Like the car washer in Foumban, he had disdain for the rest of the world, but he wasn't doing so well himself.

In the heat and discomfort of that endless ride, he continued his jabbering, in love with the sound of his own voice. The self-absorbed monologue was interrupted only by occasional high-pitched responses from "The Chinese Woman." Though his language was unknown to me, the tone was not — the swaggering banter of bars and boardrooms the world over.

The *conducteur* also had the habit of letting his hands wander while he talked. Restless fingers picked at the handlebar bag on my lap, Leonard's bicycle pedals on his lap, and even the knees of my pants. Leonard was dozing again, as only he could, so there was no one to share my annoyance. I glared needles at the *conducteur*, but he was oblivious.

Occasionally we paused at a crossroads to set down or pick up a passenger, and one time the driver pulled off the road at a line of mud–brick kiosks and chophouses and shut down the engine. He told us we should get something to eat, and while we six foreigners huddled around a table with bottles of soda, I saw many of the other passengers laying out their prayer mats and bowing toward Mecca. This was not a "rest stop," but a *prayer* stop, allowing the Muslims to make their afternoon devotions.

During one stop in a small village a young woman stepped aboard. She was in her mid-twenties, and wore a lime-green sleeveless dress, unusually revealing for an African woman, stretched tight across her small breasts and Rubens hips. Her eyes were narrowed over a wide nose and petulant mouth, and her expression was insolent, defiant. She stood in the footwell with her hands raised above her head, bracing herself against the roof of the bus and flashing her furry armpits. I decided she was probably a prostitute. Certainly she was trouble.

The *conducteur* transferred his attention to her, allowing another fortunate female to reflect his glory for awhile. She responded languidly, her body swaying beneath her upraised arms. Then suddenly the whole bus was in an uproar. The boy with the broken teeth said something to her, and she reached out and struck him — hard. As he jumped to hit her back, the *conducteur* pushed him away, the driver shouted back to them, and the passengers erupted into turmoil. A babel of voices shouted around me; nearly everyone contributing, "The Chinese Woman," the two fat ladies, even the one-legged man in front of me, who hadn't said a word all day. The girl in the lime-green dress just stuck out her lower lip and raised her chin a little higher.

The next time the bus stopped it was the boy who was put off, though further along the road, when the prostitute had departed, he somehow rejoined us. He must have hitchhiked up with a faster truck, or perhaps a taxi. And still the *conducteur*, the smooth-talking dandy, went on talking, while I imagined ever more exquisite tortures for him.

But all at once he was forgotten. The bus was in trouble again. It jolted, banged, jolted once more, then began to pour smoke out the sides. Soon it was coasting to the side of the road. This time it was engine failure, and the "Coaster" was finished — it would coast no further. The driver told David not to worry, another engine was on the way (a very likely story) and this illustrated another endearingly maddening African quality.

So often Africans tend to tell people, especially white people, what they think you want to hear. You go into a bar and ask if they have any Coke, and the barman will smile and say "Yes." You ask if it's cold, and he smiles wider, "Yes." Then he brings you a warm Sprite. "Is this all you have?" "Yes." You can't get angry — they truly just want to make you *happy*.

The two soldiers had already flagged down a ride, and some of the other passengers were trying to bargain with passing vehicles. Only thirty miles to Garoua, and we had our bicycles. David climbed up to the roof and passed down the bikes, and the rest of us quickly had them assembled and ready to go. We said goodbye to a sad-looking Ken, and filled our water bottles at the nearby well, me thinking, 'We'll see what happens when *this* hits my system!'

David seemed to share my relief at being an independent traveler once more, and the two of us wheeled on ahead. A Lilac-breasted Roller winged by, sunrise colors of turquoise and mauve and long black tail-streamers rising and dipping in its flight. I cranked the pedals with pumping adrenalin, a sense of release, and a smile on my face.

How different it is to be riding *through* a landscape, rather than just by it. In some ways it makes a strange place less exotic, and yet it becomes infinitely more real. You feel the road under your wheels, the sun and the wind on your body, and there are no walls or windows between your senses and the world. I once noticed this contrast aboard a train in China; I looked out the window at a town and thought how strange and beautiful the houses seemed. The streets looked so truly *foreign*, almost surreal, then I realized with a smile that I had cycled through that very town the day before, and then it had seemed entirely normal and real.

Reality reared its other side — the ugly side — as we rolled into Garoua. The road turned to follow a river where a few men fished in the shallow water. David and I rolled onto the bridge which crossed the river, and halfway across I stopped, admiring the view over the water, the green flats beyond, and the hazy hills in the distance. David stopped beside me, and as I took out my camera I saw him look warily up and down the road. Then he pulled his own camera from the handlebar bag, we each took a picture, and started off again. But a soldier came running from the other end of the bridge, shouting and waving his arms. David breathed a soft "oh-oh" as we stopped and waited for the olive-clad soldier to come up. Out of breath and very angry, he held out his hand and demanded our cameras. *"Où sont vos appareils-photo?"*

Feigning confusion, David handed the soldier his passport (there are times when it is better *not* to speak the language). Following his cue, I presented mine as well. The soldier shook his head, outraged and exasperated with us, and gestured to the other end of the bridge. A little anxious, I pushed my bike beside David to the checkpoint. Photographing anything as strategically sensitive as a bridge was considered an act of espionage, but as we walked David tried to explain to the soldier that we hadn't taken a picture of the bridge, but of the landscape *from* the bridge. Surely that was not *interdit*?

"Tout est interdit," he answered reassuringly. Everything is forbidden.

David, who had played this game before, tried a strategic gambit. He assured the soldier that we'd been told by officials in Yaoundé that it was not *interdit* to take pictures of the scenery, only military things were not allowed. Mention of the capital city, which our soldier had probably never visited, carried the spell of Mecca, in the sense that power was the military religion, and Yaoundé was the heart of this power. Now he seemed a little less sure of himself, and called over another soldier. Fortunately this one was a different sort; his expression was good-natured, and he smiled when he saw my Canadian passport. The two soldiers conversed in a language of their own for a few minutes, and finally the angry soldier stalked away. The good-natured one handed back our passports and waved us on.

After yet another checkpoint, the police this time, we were finally in the streets of Garoua. Like Ngaoundéré, it was a dusty, rundown place of low buildings and corrugated metal. Abandoned cars squatted at the roadside, stripped clean yet unblemished by corrosion in the dry air, and groups of men and children idled their time on the street-corners. As usual, the women were off working somewhere.

I waited for the others in front of a shop, surrounded by curious children in long blouses like nightshirts. By the time David returned from scouting accommodations, the others had caught up and joined me in causing a sensation among the locals, and together we cruised over to the Sare Hotel. As in every place we'd stayed, everyone was obliged to go inside the hotel to register individually, and, as in every place we'd stayed, Annie neglected to bring a pen inside with her — after three weeks of the same routine. When I had filled in my *fiche* I handed her my trusty Bic, and went outside to wait with the bicycles. But when she finally came out, and I held my hand out for the pen, she gave me a blank look. "Hmm?"

Oh Annie. "My pen?" I prompted.

"Oh ... yeah ... heh-heh," and she ran back inside to get it.

My mask must have slipped; my expression must have displayed my annoyance and disbelief a little too transparently, for as Annie handed back my pen she remarked, "Boy, you sure can give a person a *look* when you want to." I had to smile at that — strange how you think you're hiding your feelings by not *saying* anything to someone, when the unguarded face is the most eloquent speaker of all.

Certainly I had divined a lot about the people on the bus just by watching their faces, even though I couldn't understand their speech. After six hours in such close confinement, and nothing else to do but watch the people around me, I really felt as if I knew them, at least as characters. Given time to watch, a quiet observer gains much more than unreliable first impressions; he watches people when they don't think they're being watched. He sees their range of expressions, sometimes put-on, sometimes unmasked. The dynamics of a face can add up to one dominant quality, a true distillate of the mask that is friendly, arrogant, submissive, calculating, bitter, intelligent, or dull-witted. And actions reflect the face.

Does he check his reflection in a passing window? Does she talk much and listen little? The stance, is it natural, or affected? Eyes opaque, guarded, and evasive, or warm and receptive? Head carried high or low? These things tell so much, and after observing a group of strangers for a time I find I am instinctively drawn to some of them, and not to others.

I felt as if I knew those people on the bus, and more, saw in them *other* people I knew. The *conducteur* who aroused such blazing dislike was a type familiar to me. The boy with the broken teeth was a hard worker, kept to himself, and I thought he was probably a good kid. I couldn't imagine why he'd felt compelled to insult the bimbo in the lime-green dress. No doubt she started it. I recognized "The Chinese Woman," hiding her shallow coquetry behind a veil of modesty. The mothers with their stoic acceptance of whatever new hardship came their way, Ken the peripatetic Australian with his cheery, wasting restlessness, the poor woman on the train who had lost her money, even the bimbo's defiant façade of dignity — I knew them all.

I only wished I could stand apart and observe *myself* that way, as another stranger on the bus. That would be a great step along the road of knowing that character I had so much trouble getting outside of, for no matter how well I got to know him from the inside, I could never manage to objectify him completely, could never sit back and evaluate his mask. In some ways it seemed he was more distant to me than any of the other people on the bus.

The "Coaster" — with backup vehicles on roof.
Somewhere between Ngaounderé and Garoua.

the beaten track

Like many West African countries, Cameroon is divided into two distinct zones: a humid region of rainforests and Christianity in the south, and a dry northern area of savanna and Islam. The south is blessed by the ocean winds, the north damned by the ever-encroaching Sahara. The differences between the two are profound, not just in weather, topography, and religion, but in the cultures, the tribes, their dress, even their intoxicants. In the north palm wine gives way to millet beer (except for the teetotalling Muslims).

Political conflicts between north and south are rife in these West African countries, and this has brought civil war in Chad, and repeated coups and uprisings in Nigeria and throughout the chain of tiny countries along the Atlantic coast. Without the colonial imposition of artificial borders, all of these tribes would surely have allied and divided themselves differently. But that is a familiar story throughout Africa.

In Cameroon, the central power from the south posted soldiers to keep *watch* on the hostile north, home of the troublesome former leader, Ahidjo. The nearby borders of Nigeria and Chad, both troubled countries, only increased the tension.

The train from Yaoundé to Ngaoundere had carried us from one "sub-country" to the other, and the bus to Garoua had introduced us to the more sophisticated of its people, those who traveled between cities. Now we would meet the people who seldom left their remote compounds of mud and grass. For this day David's itinerary announced, "We leave the beaten track." While this was true metaphorically, the reality was quite the opposite. For the next few days we would travel roads that were, literally speaking, beaten tracks.

We started out of Garoua on a wide boulevard, which led to the airport and the small road we would take to the north. David warned us to keep our cameras hidden, as security was particularly tight there. A vast area was enclosed by concrete walls and barbed wire, and soldiers in jeeps and motorcycles patrolled the roads around the perimeter, giving us looks as they passed.

Beyond the airport we passed a few ragged cotton fields, then entered a truly desolate land. The rough track was disturbed by little traffic, perhaps one vehicle in an hour, and the flat landscape was interrupted only by sculpted anthills and a barren ridge in the distance, everything vibrating with heat. In places the ground was blackened by grassfires, set before the rains to wash the fertile ash into the earth.

I rode on ahead, steering around the worst ruts and the biggest stones, and bogging down in occasional sandpits. Sometimes I found a firmer track on the narrow goatpaths beside the road, but I saw no goats, and though a few thatched huts appeared among the thorns, I saw no people. The arid heat tended to mute any smells, but the savanna had one subtle fragrance that tingled my nostrils from time to time. Some desert rose perhaps, some perfume of the savanna, wafted through the thin air like incense. The savanna had its music too, the soft lament of the mourning dove, as lonely as the land.

A sudden attack of stomach distress (that well-water the day before) obliged me to lay my bike beside the road and stumble through the thorns. While I answered nature's indelicate call, I heard the sound of tires on gravel, and looked up to see Leonard's bandana-covered head cruise by above the bushes. Absorbed in the process of elimination, I didn't call out to him, but I wondered if he had seen my bicycle laying in the grass, or if he still thought I was ahead of him. As it happened, he *did* miss the bicycle; he *did* think I was still in front of him, and thus he missed our siesta stop in Hama Koussou, one of my most pleasant memories of Cameroon.

The village of Hama Koussou huddled under a cluster of trees, its small houses circular or square, and made of dry mud, laid on a handful at a time. The roofs were neatly thatched into cones and pyramids. We parked our bikes under a big tree in the middle, then sat on a bench in the shade. I leaned back against a rough wall of mud, studded with tiny pink and white stones which sparkled like quartz in the sun.

At first the place seemed deserted, but as we settled ourselves a tall man emerged from the turret-shaped hut beside us. He was dark, mustached, and handsome in a knee-length white shirt and white trousers, and was followed by a pair of small boys, similarly dressed. The man bowed slightly, gave us a smile of welcome, and responded to our greetings in formal, unpractised French. David asked if we might buy some drinks, and the man spoke to the boys. They ran off to fetch a case of Mirinda orange soda, and a rolled–up mat of woven grass, which the man spread for us between the tree and the wall. Then the boys brought a cushion for each of us, four embroidered orange pillows. Charmed and almost embarrassed by the generosity of our reception, we paid for our drinks and thanked the man, but he denied our gratitude in the way of country people everywhere. It seemed to be no more than he would expect if he came to *our* village.

A few of the boys gathered under the tree, glancing at us shyly and talking among themselves. They were pleasant-faced and healthy-looking, skin very dark but with a slight Oriental cast to their eyes. Most wore the long white shirts and trousers, but some had western-style shorts and T-shirts. Our host had taught us the local greeting, *makonya*, and the boys smiled as we struggled with the pronunciation. One silent little girl stood among them, a hand on her hip to hold up an over-large cotton dress, as she stared at us with dark, diffident eyes.

A few chickens scratched in the dirt, and a pair of black-and-brown goats nosed around the houses. One or two mopeds and a few bicycles were the only traffic to disturb this peaceful setting, and what perfect hospitality. We had been welcomed, made comfortable, then left alone.

I took Aristotle from my left pannier and lay back on the mat, resting my head on the pillow and alternately reading and dozing. I waved away a fly now and again, and woke once to brush a lizard from my head, but perfect tranquility reigned in Hama Koussou. Not just timeless, but outside-of-time, a friendly and patient way of life which was all but unchanged from decade to decade. I lay look-ing up into the leaves of the acacia, listening to the quiet buzz of conversation among the villagers on the other side of the tree, and smiled to myself, 'I'm living in a *National Geographic* documentary!'

In mid-afternoon, some unspoken signal brought an end to si-esta-time — for the women anyway. Wives and daughters appeared on the road with their buckets and calabashes, going to fetch water from the well across the road. They wore bright-colored *pagnes* and kerchiefs, with T-shirts or castoff western blouses, and for the first time I realized why this seemed incongruous. Even in Yaoundé, where some women dressed in beautiful *pagnes* and matching headscarves of imported cloth, the upper body was clothed in white silk blouses, and it hadn't seemed right somehow, not "traditional." But now I understood. When the government had decreed that women had to cover their breasts, there *was* no traditional clothing for such a purpose. A few of the women I'd seen along the road from Garoua had walked unselfconsciously topless, as these people had for hundreds of years, but in the village the women seemed, if not more modest, then perhaps more observant of government edicts.

The afternoon hush was broken by the labored chugging of a one-cylinder engine. Following the sound with my eyes, I saw black smoke puffing out of a hole in a nearby hut and peeked through a small window-opening. A wizened, half-naked old man tended a Rube Goldberg machine, and he gave me a toothless smile as I watched the little engine shuddering and bouncing against its moorings. It turned a long canvas belt around a complex set of pulleys to drive a millet-grinder. The women poured calabashes full of dried kernels in one end, and collected the powdered flour from the other — a big improvement on their traditional mortars and pestles.

This machine, the bottles of Mirinda, and our little group were the only signs of the twentieth century in Hama Koussou, and the chugging engine made a good signal for us to get moving. It was now mid-afternoon, the worst of the heat was passed, and we had ten miles still to travel. I didn't know that I was on the way from one of my best experiences in Cameroon, to one of my worst.

An hour and a half later I reached Dembo, and Leonard hailed me from just off the road. I saw him sprawled under a tree, and joined him in the circle of shade. He told me he hadn't noticed the sign for Hama Koussou, or didn't remember agreeing to meet there, but he had been just *fine* for the last three hours, laying under this tree while the local women brought him water. I laughed at the mock-proud toss of his head, and asked him if there was anywhere to buy drinks. He pointed over his head to a cluster of mud-brown buildings.

I left my bicycle with Leonard and walked over, but saw nothing that suggested a shop. Just up the road I spied a group of men climbing down from a truck, so I went to ask one of them. A soldier in olive-drab stood among them, and I decided he might be more likely to speak French, so I would ask him. Bad idea.

I walked up to him and asked, very politely, if he knew where I could buy something to drink. He said nothing, just looked at me sullenly. I started to repeat the question, when he cut me off with a grunt. *"Où allez-vous?"* Startled, I tried to explain where I was going, the nature of our trip, but he interrupted again, *"Donnez-moi vos papiers."* A little alarmed by his belligerence, and by the automatic weapon on his shoulder, I gave him my passport, and while he examined it I gave *him* a closer look. Then I noticed the bad thing — he was very, very drunk. His body wobbled and twitched as he tried to keep his balance, his words were slurred, eyes clouded, and his bloated belly stuck out of his unbuttoned olive-drab shirt. I looked again at the automatic rifle, which Leonard later told me was a 7.62 millimeter, NATO-Class, French-made automatic assault weapon. I noticed its oily sheen, like the beer-sweat on the soldier's face.

Next he demanded my vaccination certificate, something no one in Cameroon had ever asked to see, as he tried to control his obviously numb lips. I tried to control my rising temper, and handed over the yellow booklet. Passing villagers gave the two of us a quick sidelong glance, then moved by hurriedly on the other side of the road, eyes turned away. The wobbly soldier examined the booklet with the careful dignity of the very drunk, then began to shake his head, telling me it was no good. When I argued that all my shots were up to date, he pointed to the cholera shot and the date below it and repeated *"Pas bon. Pas bon."*

Under my breath I muttered, "Bullshit."

I answered his continuing questions through clenched teeth — I knew I had to be cool. A soldier in this remote place was king; he could do as he wanted, drunk, sober, or crazy. My imagination saw that this belligerent drunk with the automatic rifle dangling from his shoulder might be capable of *anything*. He had problems; maybe he was a psychopath. He could even shoot me and claim I'd been at fault. Behind the masks of democracy and freedom, this was nothing more than a Third World police state, and I meant nothing there.

"Attendez là," he ordered gruffly, wait there, and he staggered away with my passport and vaccination booklet, leaving me standing in the road while he disappeared behind a woven-grass wall. What should I do? What *could* I do? I couldn't call a cop; I couldn't

hope for the arrival of the others — that was only liable to make it worse. I could do nothing but control my anger and try to ride out this ridiculous, yet dangerous, situation. The problem might have been defused by a note of the proper denomination, but I couldn't be sure. That too might have made it worse.

He returned a minute later, adjusting his trousers beneath the fat belly, and I realised he'd been "called away" by another symptom of the very drunk: a beer-soaked bladder. The interrogation continued, as he slurred out his questions about my reason for being in Dembo, in Cameroon, and where I thought I was going to stay. I told him we usually stayed in hotels, but he cut me off. *"Pas d'hôtels ici. Pas d'hôtels."* At a loss for an alternative, I remembered David mentioning that we might stay in a school, a "makeshift dormitory," so I tried that. *"Peut-être nous pouvons rester dans une école."*

"Il y a une école, oui," but then he shook his head stubbornly, repeating, *"Mais il n'y a pas d'hôtel."* He was a textbook example of the "mean drunk" everyone has encountered, suspicious, contentious, surly, repetitive, and potentially violent. The main difference was that I had more to fear than a wild, reeling punch — *this* mean drunk was fingering the stock of his loaded and well-oiled 7.62 mm. NATO-Class automatic assault weapon, in a remote village where no one would dare interfere. I was staring evil in the face, and yet he was only another drunken boor, if you took away the gun.

Now he wanted to know my occupation, and automatically I replied "businessman," an answer usually boring enough to discourage further inquiries, while "musician" is always an invitation to more boring questions. But this tireless interrogator wanted to know what *kind* of business, and, groping for something that would be understandable and innocent to him, I came up with my former occupation, "farm equipment." But that too went wrong. Now he thought I was not only a spy, but an illegal merchant as well, here on my bicycle to sell International Harvester tractors to farmers who tilled their crops with cutlasses, and he got even nastier. I'd told him my bicycle was under a tree yonder, with my waiting friend, and finally he demanded to see this friend and sent me to fetch him. He still clutched my vital papers in one hand, and the loaded and well-oiled 7.62 mm. NAT0-Class automatic assault weapon in the other.

Still shaking with rage and anxiety, I stalked over to Leonard's tree, gave him a summary and asked him to come with me. But when Leonard and I pushed our bikes up to the soldier, suddenly his whole manner changed. I saw a dull surprise come over his sagging features, and his bleary eyes widened a fraction when he saw that my friend was *black*. He dropped his belligerent manner at once, took his hand off the gun and reached out to shake Leonard's hand, his head nodding on sleepy springs. He mumbled some French to an uncomprehending Leonard, gave his passport a cursory look, then handed me my own papers. I took them with the mechanical response of a robot, completely stunned, as the soldier stumbled behind the wall again to relieve his insistent bladder. By Leonard's skin my own was saved.

• • •

Leonard's skin was the subject of great interest from the chief of Dembo as well. When the others arrived, David found the chief and arranged to stay in his guest house and have a meal prepared (all for a modest fee, of course) and the chief invited us to sit in a row of lawn chairs beside his chaise longue. He asked about our travels and our homes, and when I said that Leonard was from California, the chief raised his eyebrows. "*Il est Américain?*" he echoed, "*mais il est comme moi,*" pointing to the skin on his arm, "*comme un filbert.*" And the chief laughed a little at his simile.

"What's he say?" Leonard asked.

"He says you look like a nut," I translated loosely.

Leonard nodded slowly at the chief, freezing a quizzical smile. The chief then asked David and me if there were many black people in America, displaying the same surprising unawareness of African history as the family near Kumba. This time we just gave him the facts, didn't even try to explain it. David and I told him there were many black people in America, and left it at that.

The chief reminded me of the later years of Duke Ellington, the same aspect of aristocracy in decline. While he lay back in his chair with his feet up — to reduce the discomfort of his diabetes he said — he told us he was sixty-two, had thirty-eight children, and had been chief of the Dembo area for twenty years. Like the Fons in the Northwest Province, his chiefly duties consisted largely in arbitrating land and domestic disputes for his chiefdom of more than two thousand people.

Some of the chief's children crept up to look at us, though they maintained a respectful distance (from the chief, not from us). Six little princelings clustered under a tree to one side, while six darling princesses huddled on the porch behind us. None came any closer unless they were bidden. The same distance and obeisance were shown by two village elders who called on the chief. The courtiers crept up and sat on the ground, never approaching closer than twenty feet, and spoke to him with their faces averted, never addressing him directly. They conversed as equals — friendly tone, shared smiles — yet the courtiers were bound by strict protocol. And observing that strict protocol, I suffered a flash of mortification.

Without thinking, I had pulled off my shoes and socks to inspect a burning itch on the arches of my feet, some kind of spreading infection, and I began soaking a bandana from my water bottle and rinsing off the raw patches of flesh. The flies were impressed, but I doubted the chief was, and I put on my shoes and socks and tried to look contrite. The chief finished his conversation with the courtiers, and turned back to us. He wished us a good trip, then waved his hand to one of the princelings, who led us away.

The chief's guest quarters were from the same *National Geographic* special as Hama Koussou. A high-walled courtyard enclosed two round huts, thatched in the shape of inverted tops. The open area between the huts was floored in gravel, and roofed over with a network of serpent-shaped sticks supporting grass mats. Two plastic basins of water made a bathroom, and a concrete-lined hole in the ground provided the other necessary amenity. An old sealed-beam unit made a perfect cap over the hole.

With water so scarce in the north, David taught us an economical way of bathing: one small bowl of water to soak the cloth and soap yourself, then another bowl to scrub and rinse with. That way we would each use no more than two soup-bowls, and have clean water left to filter for our water bottles. By the time we had cleaned up and pumped some water through the filters, night was making its swift descent. A kerosene lantern was hung from one of the serpent-shaped sticks, and a wizened old woman brought our supper. We sat on the gravel in the dim light, fingering lumps of *ugali*, a dough-like rice paste, and dipping it into a sauce of meat and okra. The spices burned on my dry, cracked lips, but I'd had little to eat since an omelette in Garoua, at six in the morning.

One of the round thatched huts had been swept out for us to sleep in, and Elsa and Annie spread their sleeping bags on a sagging double bed, the only stick of furniture. The air inside seemed hot and stuffy, and the hard floor uninviting, so I joined David and Leonard on the gravel outside, laying my bed beneath the grass matting. Peace settled over the compound. In this province no vehicles were allowed to travel by night; no electricity meant no blaring TVs or radios, and there were not even any insects buzzing in the trees. Considering our outdoor bivouac, that was a good thing.

It had been almost a textbook day's travel in Cameroon: Omelette and Nescafé near the truck park in Garoua, barbed wire and paranoia around the airport, the perfume of the savanna, the call of the mourning dove, a diarrhea attack in the thorns, the siesta in Hama Koussou, the drunken, white-man-hating soldier with his 7.62 mm. NATO-Class automatic assault weapon. Then everything had changed again. We met Chief Duke Ellington, who was surprised to learn there were lots of *filbert*-colored people in the United States and rented his guest quarters with the thatched huts, the plastic basins of water, and the sealed-beam unit over the shit-hole.

Shaking my head at the whole bizarre continent of Africa, I turned on my little flashlight, leaned it on my shoulder, and picked up *Dear Theo*:

> To think how many people there are who exist without ever having the slightest idea what care is, and who always keep on thinking that everything will turn out for the best, as if there were no people starving or altogether ruined! It grieves me when I am always in a bad fix. What colour is in a picture, enthusiasm is in life; therefore, it is no little thing to try to keep that enthusiasm.

Traffic jam in northern Cameroon.

quixote and quasimodo

The goats scrambled out of my path as I pedaled away from Dembo at sunrise. A pair of doves bathed in the dust of the road ahead, then with a *chuk-chuk* of alarm and a flash of white tail-feathers, flew up into the last of the trees. I was into open country once more, the savanna of dry grass and thorny scrub, everywhere studded with boulders. By 7:30 a hot breeze came rising across the plains, carrying the honeysuckle-like perfume. Charred grass stretched away to a line of jagged hills.

The road continued its alternating torments: treacherous pits of sandy gravel, bone-jarring washboard, and stretches of bare rocks, like a dry river bed, which sent me bouncing from stone to stone. I had one bad moment as I coasted down a hill; my front wheel caught in the gravel and sent me slewing sideways toward a ravine. I jumped off the bike and stood at the brink, heart pounding, and watched a spiral of vultures winding in a high double helix off to the west.

"Rapidité, Securité, Confort" said the signboard on the passing minibus, the first vehicle I'd seen all day. The only travelers I'd met in nearly three hours had been on old bicycles, a moped, and a donkey. For myself, I was not making much *rapidité*, and not traveling with much *confort* either, but I was about to encounter the *securité*.

A whole crowd of police and soldiers appeared at the roadside up ahead, and my nerves began to tense. David had told us this checkpoint in Dourbeye was particularly strict, as it intersected a road coming in from Nigeria, less than ten miles away. A young policeman waved me over, but to my relief he was smiling, polite and *sober*. He even made a little joke, telling me that I would have to go inside and see the officer, but my bike would be safe here — gesturing at the crowd of soldiers and policemen, all bristling with weapons. I no longer shared his confidence in Cameroon's Finest, but appreciated his pleasantness.

A portly functionary in mufti sat behind his desk and looked through my passport. Though my anti-authoritarian guard was still up, he was friendly enough, and since he was from the south, at least he asked his endless questions in English. When he asked where I had received my visa and I told him Ottawa, he was proud to tell me that his brother was the ambassador to Canada. Together we marveled over that, then he sent me out to be "registered" by the young policeman, who added me to a list of foreigners who had passed through Dourbeye. It was not a long list.

The chief of Dembo had provided no breakfast, so I pedaled along the short row of mud-walled buildings in Dourbeye, searching for *beignets*. Stopping in front of a little shop, I leaned my bike against a withered tree and stepped into the shadows. A smiling little man in white robe and headgear sold me a Fanta, and I chose a *baguette* from the sticks of bread stacked like firewood. On the front stoop I sat down with my bottle of warm soda, chewing my *baguette* and nodding to a couple of local men. A young girl strolled up with a basket of *beignets*, held them out to me without a word, and I bought a couple of doughy lumps to supplement my breakfast of dry bread and orange pop.

"*D'où venez-vous?*" asked one of the men idling on the stoop.

I told him I was coming from Dembo today, but was from Canada. The other one, a large warm-featured man, smiled and nodded, "*Ca-na-da!*" and raised his bottle of 33 Export beer in a toast to "*Zhor-zhe Boosh.*" Translated as "George Bush," who had only days before been elected president of the United States, this meant he thought Bush was the new president of Canada too. A more nationalistic Canadian might have been outraged — how Canadians *hate* to be mistaken for Americans! — but I smiled and explained that Canada was a separate country from *les Etats Unis*, and *Zhor-zhe Boosh* wasn't our new president. The man smiled too, but shook his head in dubious wonder; he didn't really believe me. I asked them how far it was to Tchevi, and the two men and the shop-owner fell into a discussion in their own language, seeming to disagree over the correct answer. They finally decided it must be ten kilometers — it would prove to be twenty.

I mounted up again and struggled onward until midday, then stopped at a village well to fill my water bottles. I'd been drinking until I was tired of it, but still felt dehydrated. While I waited for a woman to fill her bucket from the spigot, her little boy looked up at me and burst out crying. I felt terrible, but his mother laughed and patted him tenderly, soothing his fear of the White Man.

Up the road I found a circle of shade under a bushy tree, just in front of the whitewashed walls of a neat compound, and settled myself against the trunk. I unfolded my *pagne* and spread it over my legs to keep the flies off, nibbled on the rest of my breakfast *baguette*, and read a little Aristotle. My eyes grew heavy and I lay back with a bandana over my face to doze for awhile. I awoke to the sound of footsteps, and a young man walked over and squatted before me, saying something I didn't understand. On the mat he placed two brown yams, like baked potatoes, and mimed to me that they were hot. I thanked him in French and English, but he understood neither, so we traded smiles instead. When he was gone I picked up one of the baked yams and took a bite; it was pungent, and turned to paste in my mouth. I finished the first one, each bite washed down with the evil-tasting well water, but I couldn't face the second. Not to be rude, I hid it in my pack and took it with me when I left, then later presented it to an appreciative goat.

My companions had passed their siesta a little behind me, and caught up just as I started off again. We rode together for a time, a rare event these days. The road of white dust, blinding in the afternoon sun, gave way to a rutted, rocky track over steep hills. On one of them, so rough that Annie got off to walk, I followed Leonard up between the rocks. I treated the two of them to another display of "break dancing" when my wheel was knocked sideways, tipping the bike over to land, once again, on top of *me*. After some major cursing, I got up and dusted myself off. Annie and Leonard were impressed by the stunt, as well as my colorful language.

Leonard and I moved ahead of the others, riding together but without talking. It was too hot, the cycling too hard, and the landscape too humbling — all that barren space. Finally we reached an island of green, the village of Tchevi. Its two rows of huts, some round and some square, lined each side of the road, and were roughly plastered of reddish mud, with the cone-shaped roofs neatly thatched in graying straw.

The inevitable barricade appeared, and a small bus was already stopped there, its back door open and the passengers cowering inside. A uniformed officer was checking their papers, and he looked up and waved us to the side of the road. Just beyond the barricade was a junction with another east-west route from Nigeria, so this would be another sensitive checkpoint. Leonard and I straddled our dusty bikes and waited, drinking the last of our water and relaxing in the knowledge that we had reached our destination.

When the gray-shirted policeman finally waved the bus on its way, we had our passports ready. He beckoned to someone, and I looked over as a tall, heavy man in civilian clothes ambled across the road toward us. He greeted Leonard and me in English, telling us that he was an off-duty officer, and was originally from the English-speaking south. So at least Leonard was able to answer for himself as the officer leafed through his passport, then looked up at him with raised eyebrows.

"You are American?"

"Yes."

"*Black* American?"

"Yes."

"You were *born* there?" Once again, an African who was shocked by a black American.

"Yes," nodded Leonard, then changed the subject, and asked him where we might be able to buy a drink. Eyebrows slowly descending, the officer turned and pointed to one of the huts at the junction, where a group of men and boys sat in the shade. Satisfied that we were *probably* not spies, he handed back our passports and waved us on.

We cycled across the dusty roundabout and stopped before the bemused group of Tchevians, all of them in pale Muslim robes, and staring up at us with open curiosity. They spoke no English or French, so we had a difficult time making ourselves understood. Mystified looks and shaking heads greeted my question, *"Est-ce qu'on peut acheter quelque-chose a boire?"* Blank faces turned at an angle, regarding me woodenly.

Then Leonard tried. "Coca-Cola?" "Fanta?" miming a bottle raised to his lips. Still nothing.

"Du soda? Orange en bouteille?"

"Drink? Pop? Sprite?" said Leonard, "Pamplemousse?" At this there was a murmur of understanding, and an old man gestured with his thin arm toward the neighboring hut, muttering something to one of the boys. The boy disappeared into the doorway, then reappeared with a proud smile. He walked up to Leonard with his hands behind his back, and held out the prize to us with a flourish. As we laughed and shook our heads, the boy's hand fell slowly, and there was more mystified talking. It was, after all, what we had asked for — a *pamplemousse*, ripe, yellow, and round.

The English-speaking officer rode up, his great bulk dwarfing a motorbike, and told us he knew where to find drinks. We followed him down the road which came in from Nigeria, and stopped before a high mud wall. He squeezed himself through a gate, then returned with a tiny, wrinkled old woman, and two large bottles of Top orange soda. He loosened the caps for us, and we gratefully tipped the bottles up, swallowing the warm, overly-sweet liquid. Leonard had just paid for the first round, when I pulled out some more francs and asked for another two bottles. The officer sent the old woman off to fetch them, and later Leonard pointed out that our friend had paid her part of the money, then pocketed the rest himself.

When the others arrived, David went off to find a place to stay, and soon we followed him along a narrow dirt track, between earthen walls and thatched dwellings. At the end of the street we halted before an archway, where an ancient man sat dozing against the wall, an enormous cutlass dangling from his waist. Leonard snickered, "Look at this 'sentry,' it would take the old guy half an hour just to *lift* that blade!"

The old man's eyes half opened, and he pulled himself slowly to his feet, straightening one limb at a time. The great cutlass swayed against his unsteady knees as he turned to bid us enter. We left our bicycles under his questionable protection, put on our long trousers and *pagnes*, and ducked through the arch and into the dimness of a large room, the chief's audience chamber. I reminded myself of the proprieties and protocol in the presence of a chief: no shaking hands, no crossing your legs, and no admiring the sores on your feet.

A white-robed figure reclined in a canvas chair, and the five of us smiled and nodded to him, wishing a chorus of *bonsoirs* as we sat in a row of wooden chairs. In his mid-thirties, this was a younger chief than the previous night's host in Dembo. His handsome features had a North African cast, thin lips over white teeth, and a neat beard. His aristocratic head was topped by an embroidered Muslim prayer cap, and even in repose he was obviously tall, his length accentuated by a white robe over light blue synthetic trousers — with a permanent crease.

David and I answered the chief's questions about where we'd been and where we were going, and in eloquent French he told us that his domain included about a thousand people, and that he had been schooled at home in Tchevi, then in Garoua. Like so many other Africans, he was especially interested in Leonard, and it fell to me to tell Leonard's life story one more time. *Oui, il est Américain. Oui, Américain noir.* Yes, he was born in the U.S. No, he didn't know his ethnic group.

While David answered the next question, I noticed the chief's elegant white shoes. They had once been stylish and low-cut in the Italian mode, but now were very old, the leather wrinkled and worn, though obviously often polished by his sleepy old retainer. Most telling of all, they had no laces. As I was daydreaming, spinning an image of the impoverished aristocrat striving to keep up appearances, I felt a sudden pain in my ankle — David was kicking me. Startled, I focused back in, and noticed that the chief was looking at me pointedly. I removed the foot I had unthinkingly placed upon the other knee, which must have been close enough to crossing my legs to be offensive, and muttered an embarrassed *"pardon."*

The chief led us into the courtyard of his compound, which was enclosed by rough walls of hand-laid mud and round huts with pointy thatched roofs. Stooping to pass through one of the doorways, we stepped into the aromatic dimness of a stable, where a squat dwarfish man with wall–eyes and a hunched back tended a pony-sized horse. This sparked another mental image of the tall, white-robed chief astride this diminutive Rocinante, the white shoes dragging on the ground, squired by the wobbly old guard with his enormous cutlass, and the misshapen groom.

The far side of the stable led to another little courtyard and a crude structure opposite: a shelter of hand-shaped gray blocks with a flat roof of corrugated metal. The wall-eyed hunchback brought carpets to lay over the gravel floor, while the chief engaged David in bargaining for our food and lodging. David came away from that discussion shaking his head — apparently our host wanted hotel prices. I smiled and pointed to our quarters. "Just like the itinerary promised: rustic accommodations, a makeshift dormitory."

Over the walls of the compound rose two monumental hills of boulders, like towers which had collapsed into heaps of stone. The sun had fallen below the mound to the west, and the light became soft and lambent. The hunchback brought us two buckets of water, and we took turns washing in a side courtyard, changing, and laying out our beds. As I ministered once more to the raw flesh on the arches of my feet, washing and spreading antibiotic cream on them, I watched David and Leonard trying to get Elsa's camera working. The constant pounding had finally shaken it senseless, and no one could make it work again.

Without looking at me, she remarked, "Well, I guess I'll have to depend on Neil for my photographs. You seem to take the kind of pictures I want anyway."

Startled, I didn't know how to respond to such an oblique request, simply saying a noncommital "Sure."

It was soon dark, and when I was organized for the night, I sat down on my sleeping bag and leaned against the rough wall to read until dinner arrived. The flashlight on my shoulder cast a white circle on the pages of *Dear Theo*. Leonard sat back on his space beside me, half-dozing against the wall. Then just as the hunchback came through the courtyard bearing two large pots of food, Annie sidled over to me. "Um ... I just wondered ... Neil ... like, could I talk to you?"

"Uh, yeah, sure." I closed my book with a mental 'oh-oh.'

She moved from side to side like a child before a crowd, her eyes alternately closing, or looking away, but never meeting mine. "Well ... I was just wondering, like — do I really bug you or something?"

My mind went racing: 'Oh shit. What a jerk I've been. Now she thinks I really hate her.' Leonard shifted uneasily beside me, then rose to his feet and moved around us to walk into the other room for dinner. My responses were confused; initially I suppose I was embarrassed — for her, for Leonard, and for myself. I was genuinely stunned by her question, and mentally flipped through all the times I'd been short with her, or flashed her a "look." I realized I'd given Annie a hard time sometimes about her thoughtlessness, but I didn't want her to think it was more than that, and I was stung by this sudden understanding. Knowing that she evidently cared what I felt about her gave me a pang of guilt and regret.

My confused reactions left me at a loss for the appropriate thing to say. The best I could manage was a mumbled negative, "Ah, no... no," to which she replied, "That's good. I know I can be a pain sometimes." I made a small laugh and shuffled past her into the other room, but I knew I wouldn't be able to leave it at that. 'Later,' I thought, 'I'll talk to her about this later.'

Our meal was a thin stew of bony fish chunks, boiled yams, and a few bottles of Fanta, and had been laid out on the floor of a barren white-washed cell. The single, glaring fluorescent tube was incongruous and, as always, ugly. The lone window-hole admitted no air, so when I had finished eating I strolled out into the courtyard to admire the sharp stars. Mini-Rocinante moved in his stable, stirring the straw on the floor, and the air smelled of baked dust and stones.

Early mornings make for early nights, and before long a row of dark figures lay stretched on their sleeping bags. The carpets over the gravel floor made a tolerably comfortable bed, firm certainly, but at least a little resilient. David remained reading in the cell a while longer, the harsh fluorescent glare spilling through the tiny window, but it was soon extinguished. A few flashlights were the only points of light in the utter darkness, shining down on books, diaries, and postcards. One by one they too went out, until I felt my own drowsiness blurring the words. I closed my book, lay the pocket flash near at hand, and turned on my side.

As on the previous night, we were spared any flying and biting insects, but I soon became aware of a tickling sensation on my legs. The night was too warm to have my sleeping bag fastened, and I had left one side open, and *something* was crawling around on me. Lizard? Scorpion? Snake? I aimed my flashlight down and saw two lines of big ants trailing across my legs, a regular Ant Interstate.

I had endured enough by this time to be monumentally unimpressed. Along with fastidiousness and the niceties of personal hygiene, squeamishness had also departed, and I just brushed the ants away. All through that night, whenever I felt an ant crawling on me, I simply reached down, crushed it between my fingers, and tossed it away into the dark.

• • •

The chief appeared soon after breakfast, tall and elegant in fresh robes, his dark head wrapped in a scarf of small red-and-white checks, and sandals in place of the white shoes. He looked every bit the romantic desert prince, and Leonard wanted to take a photograph. As I translated his request, the chief turned bashful, but agreed with a smile, part shyness and part vanity. His hands moved to the checked scarf on his head and he protested, *"Je n'ai pas de bonnet"* — I have no hat. We smiled at his concern for proper dress, and Leonard asked me to assure him that he looked very elegant. The chief stood stiffly while Leonard took the picture. We pushed our bicycles through the compound and out to the road, waved goodbye to our host and his faithful retainers, then mounted up and pedaled away through the long morning shadows.

Beyond Tchevi the landscape was bleak again: yellow grass, thorn trees, and great formations of tumbled rock under a cloudless sky. The occasional lonely habitations resembled medieval fortresses, walled clusters of round mud huts with thatched turret-tops. Pedaling along, I smiled and waved at the few people I passed, noting that upper-body clothing for women was optional, though mostly the wrinkled old women went topless. One tiny girl stared up from the roadside, her thin body lost inside a faded T-shirt which read "Visit Van City," and a small boy wore a ragged "Dukes Of Hazzard" number. In *The Village Of Waiting*, by a one-time Peace Corps volunteer in Togo named George Packer, I had read of the Africans' humorous response to the clothes they were given by agencies like Goodwill. Calling them "dead yovo clothes," they believed that these donated castoffs came exclusively from dead white people.

The road began to worsen, and I was clenching my teeth and pounding over alternate hazards of corrugated mud, soft grit like kitty litter, rough stones, a dry streamed of loose rocks, a bone-jarring washboard, and back to the rippled mud and sandtraps. The previous night, during a discussion of our favorite subject — the evil roads — Elsa had said she thought the washboard was the worst of all. David thought it was better to speed up over them, and I agreed, with the additional advice that when I went shuddering over the violent ridges, I felt it was helpful to yell out bad words really loud.

It was on my mind to speak with Annie properly, but every time I got beside her the road turned ugly, and I had to negotiate a new hazard. In truth, I didn't quite know what to say, but I wanted to try to explain that I didn't *hate* her, as she seemed to think. Once or twice there was a brief chance, but I hesitated, and it was too late. Finally a short stretch of less-violent road allowed me to ride up alongside her, uncomfortable but determined, and I blurted it out: "Listen, Annie — I'm sorry if I made you feel I didn't like you. I feel bad about that."

"Oh, well ..." She wriggled her shoulders and moved her head from side to side eloquently. "Well, I ..."

"I think it's just that we're such different people, and — I suppose I get impatient. But it's not that I don't like you — I do. Maybe because we're so different. I didn't want you to think that."

"Oh, well ... mmm ... okay. I'm glad it isn't true, anyway ... ah ... heh-heh."

I pedaled ahead a bit on my own, feeling better and hoping she did too.

It's good to let your feelings out, and I found it also worked very well on that perilous road — my bike and I were taking a pounding. Occasionally the road was so narrow and treacherous I was forced to get off and walk, and I hate that. Facing my emotions squarely, I turned the African sky blue with curses, and I discovered that because of this direct release of frustration, the anger lasted only as long as the particular torment — the minefield, sandtrap, or washboard — and I was afterwards purged of any bitterness. I might spend miles and hours growling to myself and swearing out loud, my mind turned sour by the battering, but at the end of the day when I got off my bike, I felt peaceful and entirely calm. There was a kind of therapy in all this. Good thing too.

Between curses I did feel at peace that day, perhaps because some other conflicts than the road had been addressed. The episode with Annie had broken some barriers between us, and some within myself, and the night before Elsa had been forced to ask me for something, copies of my photos. There had been a frosty distance between us for two weeks now, and I felt an ignoble satisfaction that she had been the first to break it, but Elsa asking me for a favor had somehow humbled both of us, and softened my feelings toward her.

It's nice to be given the opportunity to be magnanimous, if you're up to it, and it reminded me of something John Steinbeck wrote, that the nicest thing you can do for someone is let them do something for you.

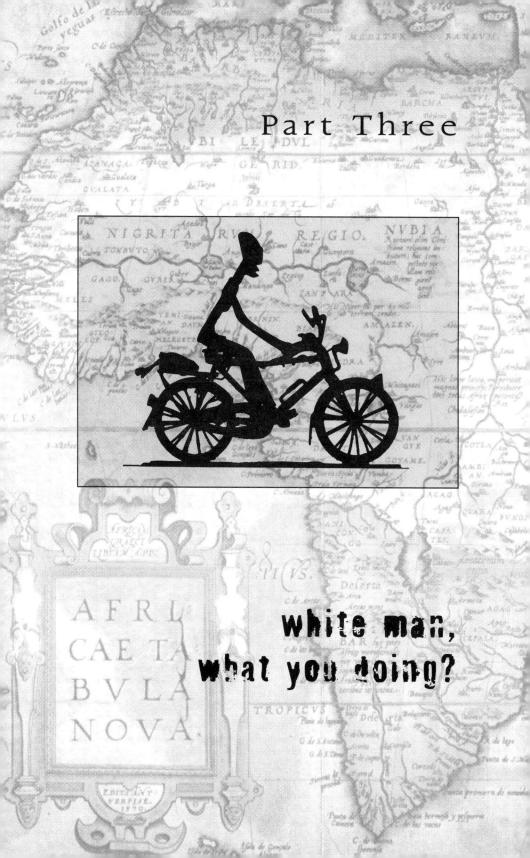

Part Three

white man, what you doing?

Rocinante's stable, left, in Quixote's compound.
Tchevi.

watermelon and satellites

Great columns of stone began to appear above the hills to east and west, and photographs of the area hadn't prepared me for the scale of these formations. One was pyramid–shaped, one a great rounded breast, yet another a spear of swirling rock, as if sculpted by the sea. The tallest one, a great stone phallus, would be the star of them all, Kapsiki. These formations, called inselbergs, were caused by volcanos which had eroded over the eons, leaving behind a vertical core of lava.

Erosion had struck the road too. It disintegrated into a heaving track, then veered left into a trough between tumbled boulders and up through a gauntlet of thorn trees, into the village of Roumsiki. At the top of the hill, mean dwellings crouched on either side of the road, and two boys in their early 'teens came running out at me.

I asked them where I might buy a drink, and they led me across the road, bombarding me with eager questions in French. Where was I going? Where was I coming from? Where was I going to stay? Where was I going to eat? Did I want a guide to Kapsiki? I held my hands up, palms outward, and told them there were more people coming behind me, and I didn't know, and they should just *attendez* — wait.

In the tiny kiosk, a man in pale robes and cap smiled broadly and wished me *"bienvenue,"* then asked the same questions. He closed by offering to cook me a dinner of the local specialty, chicken in peanut sauce. I nodded and smiled, *"Attendez, s'il vous plait. Attendez,"* and bought a bottle of water. I was a little shocked by the price of 800 francs, over three times the price in the south, but when I said the price was too high and tried to offer less, he told me, 'We have to charge 800 francs, because the hotel charges 1,000.' Though I failed to follow his logic, I bought the water and a package of banana-creme biscuits.

The two boys were waiting to lead me back across the road to the pavilion of woven branches where I had parked my bike. I tried to ignore their persistent offers, and pulled a book from my pack to feign deep concentration on the thoughts of Aristotle. I hoped this would serve as a distraction, to them and to me. My fingers tore open the package of banana biscuits, but the dry wafers crumbled like sand in my mouth, every particle of moisture sucked out of them by the desert air. The 'creme' filling had dried into a powder of its chemical constituents. Not only that, there weren't enough of them.

One of the two boys wandered away, and the other closed in, ignoring the Aristotle decoy and my face, which I hoped was as stonily impassive as an inselberg. Jean-Luc, his name was, a handsome boy with intelligent features and a serious, endearing manner. He told me in precise French of other people he'd met from Canada, how they had sent him postcards of the cities and the snow, and how he liked to guide visitors around the village and to Kapsiki. He said the man in the store could make us a very good meal of chicken with the peanut sauce, and we would find it *"une bonne experience."* I nodded and tried to be polite, but really wished he'd just leave me alone. I gave up on the Aristotle gambit, and tried writing in my notebook to create a new diversion.

The other boy reappeared, casually strolling into the courtyard carrying a curious-looking object, a small stringed instrument like a Cubist guitar. This wandering minstrel plucked the strings, without even seeming to look at me, and the dry, pure notes rang out like a harp. Equally casually, Jean-Luc called him over and took the instrument from him. There were five strings, though since they could only be played open, there were also only five notes. But Jean-Luc plucked out a French tune, "Au clair de la lune," and asked me if I knew it. When I nodded, he went on to tell me about the construction of the instrument, carved from wood and covered with antelope skin, and though it was an attractive piece of work, I had my ready excuse: *"Pas d'espace en velo."* No room on the bicycle.

As if on cue, a third boy appeared in the courtyard with a smaller stringed instrument, its bowl-shaped body covered with lizard skin, and a single string which was played with a small bow. Jean-Luc looked a question, as if to say 'maybe *this* will fit on your silly bicycle?' I just shook my head, but then two more boys came out sporting straw hats, obviously new and obviously for sale. By this time the parade of pedlars had become like some bizarre fashion show, each "model" entering with his product and parading it before me. Five or six more boys came strolling in, offering their services as guides, and asking if I wanted a meal of chicken with peanut sauce. Then the proprietor of the little shop was back, the boys herding around him, to remind me that he could cook us a good meal of chicken with peanut sauce. How I wished the others would arrive. It was all I could do to nod and ignore all this high-pressure salesmanship, concentrating on the writing of nothing in particular in my notebook.

I began to sense something strange about all this; it was all so well choreographed. Like Jean-Luc, all of the boys had a carefully-rehearsed routine, and delivered their pitches in refined French, with a studied manner of fetching innocence. I had a mental image of all these Artful Dodgers studying at the feet of their Fagin, the man from the shop, groomed and schooled in their lines and techniques and sent out as bait for the tourists.

At last my companions pedaled up the road, and I called them into the shade of the pavilion. This brought a new flurry of excitement to the Artful Dodgers, and each of them adopted one of the newcomers, following them across the road to the shop while they bought drinks. The boys soon realized that David was the one to speak with, especially in French, and I had told them that he was *le patron*, the boss, so David found himself surrounded by a mob of importuning "agents."

One of the most insistent was an older boy, perhaps eighteen, who was particularly ragged, somehow coarser than the others, and made more pathetic by a stunted, nearly useless left arm. The withered limb was half normal size, bent before him, and ended in a knot of misshapen fingers. He introduced himself as Anatole, and told David that he could lead us to *"un village authentique,"* where we could stay the night, and enjoy a meal of, yes, chicken with peanut sauce. The problem was that the village was a nine-kilometer walk from Roumsiki, and he wanted us to leave our bicycles behind. None of us was very excited about that idea.

David went off to hunt for less remote accommodations, escorted by some of the Dodgers. He visited the government-run *campement*, which charged the equivalent of fifty dollars a night for nothing more luxurious than a hut with a view of Kapsiki, and running water (typically *not* running at the moment). While asking among the locals about more reasonable places, he learned that even if we could stay with someone in the village, we would need a special permit — the method by which the government *campement* protected its monopoly.

On David's return to the pavilion, Anatole closed in again, assuring us that our bicycles would be completely safe in Roumsiki, and that if we went to his authentic village we could meet a *sorcier* (sorceror), and have a wonderful meal of et cetera. Though Anatole tried to put on a smile and make himself personable for us, I noticed that his features in repose bore the scars of his disfigurement, a kind of glum defensiveness, and his speech was coarse, not as smoothly trained as the other boys. His unhappy face deepened into a frown when we told him that we wouldn't go without our bikes.

So the five of us "took a meeting," huddled together on the benches amid a circle of eager entrepreneurs who awaited our decision. David spelled out the options. We could stay at the *campement*, which he was understandably not keen on straining the budget for, or we could rest in Roumsiki for a while, then leave and go on to another village. It was still only noon, and there was plenty of time to reach the next village, Mogodé, though David didn't remember anything about it.

Or, we could go with Anatole to his authentic village. David turned to him and asked if we could possibly ride our bicycles there, and Anatole screwed up his ugly features for a moment, then replied *"Oui, c'est possible."* I felt sympathy for this unfortunate boy, and had to admire his attempt to earn a little money in a highly competitive field. In this pursuit he was handicapped, not so much by the crippled arm, which could arouse pathos in others as it did in me, but it would be his appearance, speech, and manner which would put people off, and these I suppose were the invisible effects of his deformity. I suggested that perhaps we could go to Anatole's village, stay if it seemed good, and if not, we would still have time to move on to Mogodé. After a little more discussion, this plan was agreed on, and when Anatole disappeared to find a bicycle for himself, the rest of the boys divined that we had cast our lot with him, and without a word they were gone.

Anatole led us out of town on a rattling, decrepit old bicycle, a rusty and battered Chinese one-speed which he guided with his good right hand, while he held the other before him as if in a sling. His brakes, I could see, were nearly useless, and when the bike shuddered over more violent bumps, his chain went bouncing right off the chainring, forcing him to stop repeatedly to wrap it back around.

On the rougher stretches of road he sometimes leaned his body forward to rest the stump on the handlebars and help stabilize the bicycle.

We stopped at a lookout point just outside Roumsiki, where the view suddenly opened far and wide to a series of barren light-brown hills, with the enormous gray spear of Kapsiki towering in the middle, and the jagged teeth of other inselbergs on the horizon. While we admired and photographed the view, Anatole was still trying to fix his faithless bicycle, and with a sigh David pulled out his toolkit and adjusted the rear wheel to take out the slack in the chain. As he worked, he turned to me, "Man, once you get started at this, sometimes it never ends. I've spent *hours* in African villages, tightening and adjusting a hundred of these old wrecks." And sure enough, just as he tightened the wheel–nuts, another cyclist came riding up, an old farmer pedaling an equally battered bike, and with the aid of sign language and Anatole's translations into French, the old man made it clear that he too needed mechanical attention. A few turns of a wrench and a little air in the tires sent him on his way, and he smiled and rode off toward the village.

Then it was off the *road* for us, as we followed the unsteady Anatole onto a path which led east across a level plain. At least the surface was no worse than the main road had been — the same hazards of minefield, washboard, and sandtrap. Anatole struggled against the dry streambeds, pitching down into the loose stones with no brakes, then having to climb up the other side, with only one gear, and only one hand. Whatever he expected to make out of this, he was certainly earning it.

Anatole led us along the narrow cart-track for a few miles, over a grassy landscape dominated by the bleak monolith of an inselberg to our left, and low hills ahead and to the right. Anatole wanted us to visit an authentic farm before we went to the authentic village, and led us down a footpath toward three figures. They stood waving and smiling beside a muddy stream: a shy young boy of ten dressed in a coarse tunic, his father, a powerfully-built man in his forties wearing worn-out trousers and shirt, and the grandfather, a spare and silent old man in a loose robe and small cap. Only the father seemed to speak French, but all three welcomed us with smiles as we laid our bikes on the ground and followed them around their little garden. Amid the surrounding arid land, a stand of small trees was a cool oasis along the stream, shading the mixed crops which the family tended. I asked the farmer if the stream continued to run year-round. *"Oui,"* he nodded, but then, with a sad shake of his head, he told me that one year the water had failed.

As we walked back toward their huts, the father began to speak of "something special" he had for us, though the name he gave it was unknown to both David and me. When we arrived in their swept dooryard, he sent the small boy into one of the huts, and the boy emerged carrying an enormous watermelon. Leonard laughed out loud, giving us an old–time caricature, "Well lookee here! A wat-uh-mell-un!"

Anatole told us what a rare luxury it was to the local people, and how much they would pay for one in a village market. But David shook his head, answering that we couldn't carry it with us. Then Leonard spoke up, laughing, "Tell him we'll take it. I'll carry it somehow," so David negotiated the purchase for something below the stated "market price."

Anatole ducked into the hut for a moment, then emerged hastily, bumping his head hard on the low doorway. His usual scowl further twisted by pain, he walked toward us rubbing the top of his head. David called him over so he could take a look at the wound. Seeing a bleeding gash in his mat of wooly hair, David told him he should put something on it, but Anatole only shrugged. Leonard took over as chief medic, and the farmer and his family watched curiously as he washed Anatole's head from his water bottle, then with disinfectant, and finally spread some antibiotic cream on the wound.

While Doctor Leonard performed his ministrations, the farmer turned to me, cocking his head in the late afternoon sun and showing his strong teeth in a smile. In halting French he said, Perhaps you have some medicine for me? Something to give me more energy for my work in the fields?

No, I replied, there's no medicine like that. Only youth. *"Seulement la jeunesse."*

Ah, he said, yes. But I am no longer young.

"Oui," I spread my hands, *"c'est la mode de la vie."* That's the way of life.

He nodded thoughtfully, disappointed, as we remounted our bicycles and made our goodbyes. Anatole assured us that the village was not far away now, pointing to the dark hills in the east, but by the time we'd struggled along for another hour I began to wonder what he meant by "not far." Nine kilometers seemed a modest estimate of the distance, and when we paused for a rest I looked over at Anatole, giving him my best wry look. *"Neuf kilometres?"*

"Oui, c'est neuf kilometres." He glared back at me with a defiant frown, the ever-present chip on his shoulder swelling, and asked me how far I thought it was. But I only shook my head. 'Smartass,' I thought to myself, my feelings torn between sympathy for the apparent cause of his defensiveness, and dislike for its effects.

Leonard was slowed by carrying that watermelon, and it was a while before he arrived, battered and exhausted, with his arms and shoulders aching. He hefted the watermelon, shook his head and announced, "I'm about ready to toss this thing." Two little boys had been following us for a while on a nearby ridge, and Anatole waved them closer, then gestured for Leonard to hand over the watermelon. Without a word, one of the boys hoisted it to his shoulder, and once again we set out for Anatole's retreat.

He told us the village was called Guave, though there was no sign, and the scattered group of walled and thatched compounds appeared on no map. Guave lay cupped in a narrow valley, falling into shadow in the westering sun. The houses blended right into the landscape, because they were *of* the landscape — stones and branches and grass. We were miles from the nearest electricity, or glass window, or automobile. And, I thought as I coasted down a steep tumble of rocks, miles from the nearest doctor.

The only modern convenience in Guave was a well, a source of clean water which was welcome to us, and critical to the village. Before CARE installed that well, the women and children would have had to walk several miles to the muddy stream by the farm we had visited. And I remembered what the farmer had said. One year the stream failed, maybe other years too. As we filled our water bottles, it occurred to me that all the times I had donated to these charities, sometimes specifically for wells in Africa, it had never meant so much as now, when *my* life depended upon it. I mentioned this to David, who replied, "Yes, I guess it's the most important thing people can do here — provide clean drinking water. But, the other side of that, one of the reasons Africa's population is growing so fast is not just because so many children are *born*, but because now so many *survive*."

Anatole led us to our "hotel," a family compound beneath a great round tree. The oval wall surrounding the compound was built of stones, sometimes cemented with mud, and enclosed eight circular huts with thatched cone-heads. Over the entranceway a shelter of woven grass was supported by forked sticks, and beneath it a sinewy, long-limbed old woman, wearing only a loincloth, tended a fire. She nodded shyly in welcome. Behind us the children began to close in from the neighboring compounds. Anatole went inside to announce our arrival, while Leonard paid off the watermelon porters.

The voice of an irate, screeching woman came over the wall, pouring outrage and abuse onto Anatole. It wasn't difficult for us to supply the subtitles, and we looked at each other and smiled. This would be the mistress of the farm, who had been committed by Anatole to be our hostess for the night, and to cook our dinner — the legendary chicken in peanut sauce. While the tirade continued, an old man emerged with a cutlass, smiled wide for us, then turned around the side wall. The squawking of a terrified chicken suddenly added to the screeching of the angry woman. The screeching continued, but the squawking suddenly ceased, and Leonard laughed darkly "There's dinner!"

David laid out some peanuts and guavas on the woven mat by the door, and we sat down to rest and await the end of hostilities. Now that I was able to take notice, I felt the burning of my feet, took off my shoes and peeled the dust-brown socks, now lightly blood-stained, away from the raw skin. Flies immediately began to cluster on the suppurating wounds. I washed my feet with a damp bandana, spread a little antibiotic cream on the angry flesh, and put on clean socks.

The one-sided conversation behind the wall finally subsided, and Anatole appeared in the courtyard once again, stooped but unbowed — this episode hardly even added to the weight of his burdens. He uttered his signature *"Bon,"* which began nearly every statement he made, like an American starting every sentence with "Okay." He pronounced it as a short bubble, then a long "o" sound with a nasal resonance on the end. Leonard had picked up on this already, and whenever Anatole wasn't around, all of us were beginning our sentences with *"Bon."*

"Bon," said Anatole, and announced that it was time for our tour of the village. He started through the fallen maize stalks and the five of us fell in behind him, a long line of little boys in our wake. The valley of Guave lay like a shallow bowl of green in the sea of treeless hills beyond, its floor carpeted with guava trees, mangos, and the strange baobabs. Their eight-foot-thick trunks joined deep

roots which allowed them to survive long periods of drought. Anatole told us that the baobab fruits were used as baby formula by the local women if their breast milk failed, and pointed out another tree from which they made an insect repellent, and another which produced the poison for their arrows.

Poison for their arrows? I translated mentally, and asked Anatole what they used the poison arrows for.

Hunting, he told me.

What can they hunt for around here? I haven't seen any wildlife.

He waved his hand toward the east, vaguely describing an area about ten kilometers away where there were wild animals. A little apprehension replaced my curiosity, but I withheld my questions about what sort of predatory beasts were likely to come hunting around there, and if the Guavians ever used their poison arrows on *people*.

Two more boys came running up, neater looking and better dressed than the village boys, and held out a much-handled old newsletter from the International Bicycle Fund. They told Anatole they'd met the writer two years ago, and had heard in the village he'd been asking about them. David stepped up, and the boys introduced themselves politely as Patrick and Christophe-Colombe. The latter seemed a strange name for a young African boy, but he was the spokesman for the duo. Speaking formal French, his handsome features frowned in concentration on what was evidently a well-trained second language. No doubt he too was one of the Artful Dodgers.

Tension suddenly invaded the reunion, as a bitter conversation arose between Anatole and the newcomers. An argument grew into a rapid-fire exchange of excited French, too much for David or me to keep up with, but it apparently stemmed from competition. Every young male in Roumsiki was a potential guide, and Anatole viewed Patrick and Christophe-Colombe as interlopers. An operatic trio of Anatole's guttural imprecations and the boys' mezzo-soprano defences was finally interrupted by Anatole turning to us, spreading his good arm wide in despair. *"Je suis votre guide,"* pointing to his chest, *"Moi!"*

Yes, said David, you are our guide, but Patrick and Christophe-Colombe are my friends, and they can stay with us if they want. Anatole turned his back in disgust, trudged onward, and the procession fell in behind once again. We marched along the stony path,

David talking with Patrick and Christophe-Colombe about their studies, but before long the line suddenly halted as yet another argument broke out among the three. David and I waved our hands in the air impatiently, demanding to know what was wrong now.

They must go, said Anatole.

What do you mean, they must go? They can stay if they want to, they are friends. Just stop all this right now.

No, they must go. They live in the village and have to walk all the way back before it is dark, so if you have anything to give them you must do it now.

David sighed, then accompanied Patrick and Christophe-Colombe back to the compound so he could give them a few small presents. The rest of us trooped up a stair-like terrace of rock, and entered the courtyard of another homestead. Mud and stone walls enclosed a tight cluster of huts, and goats and chickens scratched in the dry earth. Anatole explained that this was the home of the local *sorcier* — wizard — as well as doctor, blacksmith, leather worker, and part-time farmer, but the *sorcier* was out working in the fields just then. Yet another loin-clothed old woman came out to meet us, and for once, she was even nice to Anatole.

With a *"Bon,"* Anatole led us into one of the round huts, and showed us the forge raised on the middle of the floor. The walls were hung with evidence of all the wizard's trades: odd bits of metal, small carvings, mysterious bundles of fur and feathers, mortars full of powders and herbs, clay urns for water and millet beer, and goatskins hung to cure from the roof poles.

From the wizard's den we climbed along the hillside, and an old man watched us and our procession of boys from over the wall of his compound. Then he suddenly darted out, muttering to everyone and no one, and all the while smiling vacantly. I didn't quite catch Anatole's explanation — this was either a crazy man or the chief of the village. Maybe both. Thin and agile, with a trimmed white beard, a white cap, and a short gray robe, he strode up and down the path beside us, waving his stick and babbling at the boys. He paid no particular attention to us, so I stole a photograph of him. It had been so difficult to take pictures of the people that each one seemed a valuable treasure.

Each of Guave's eight or ten homesteads included a wide shelter covered by mats of woven grass, the riches of the harvest spread upon them: baskets full of different-colored grains, peanuts, or maize, and always two or three large cylinder-shaped stacks of millet, about five feet in diameter, which were protected by conical "hats." These were artfully woven and braided straw sombreros, but sized for a giant, an exaggerated echo of the abominations which tourists returning from Mexico feel compelled to wear as they line up in the Arrivals hall of the airport, when you're tired and hungover and just want to get out of there. I don't know why I thought of that, but that's what they reminded me of.

As I pointed my camera at one of these colorful harvest spreads, catching the Mexican-tourist sombreros in the last rays of sun, an old woman came out and began haranguing poor Anatole. The only word I caught was *allumettes*, and Anatole explained that she wanted some matches because I'd taken a photo of her house. David told her we had no matches, but she wasn't giving up, and wanted *something* for this "imposition." We just shook our heads and walked on, but it struck me that the fifteen or twenty dollars David would pay to the family we were staying with was likely close to a year's income for the citizens of Guave, and everyone wanted a piece of it. David mentioned that he was going to be sure to pay Anatole in front of the family, to make sure they would know how much we were paying, and what their cut should be.

Back at the family compound, we sat down to pull the thorns and prickers from our clothes. The crowd of boys gathered around and began silently picking at our socks, doing us a service that was welcome, and made us smile. We took turns squeezing between the narrow stone walls of the compound to a corner where two buckets of water had been brought for us. Since good water was easily available at the CARE well, I treated myself to *three* bowls — the third one for the luxury of a shave. I was learning the trick of shaving without a mirror, by closing my eyes and *visualizing* my reflection in a mind's eye mirror, then dragging the razor over my face blindly. The scars have mostly healed.

Just at sunset the air filled with hundreds of kites, circling high on the last thermals. Like leaves before the wind, they came spiraling down to disappear into the trees around us, filling them with the invisible flapping of wings. An occasional squawk of argument sent one bird wheeling out in a tight circle, then back into the leaves to seek another roosting place. By the time we had washed and gathered once again on the straw mat, the birds were at rest and darkness had fallen. Anatole, with a final *"Bon,"* had disappeared to visit an uncle who lived nearby.

The family sat in a circle around the fire, beneath the shelter beside us. They ate quietly, ignoring us, as red shadows flickered across their faces. The wrinkled grandparents, the tired-looking husband and wife, and three small children made a living diorama, a timeless vignette of family life as it had passed down for thousands of years. The outside world cast barely a ripple here, the generations succeeding each other around the glow of an open fire. Father and son, mother and child, days without number, world without end, the firelight plays on a circle of faces in the African night.

The mistress of the house, her anger at Anatole reduced to a cool silence, spread our dinner on the mat outside, and we played our flashlight beams over the steaming bowls. The much-vaunted chicken in peanut sauce lived up to its reputation, and was served with cous-cous, which we dipped in a spinach-like sauce, and a dessert of mashed sweet potato. With a great deal of sign language, David managed to borrow a big knife, and Leonard cut into his watermelon with ceremony, as if it were his birthday cake, and passed slices around to each of us. Though the inside was green rather than red, it tasted exactly like the watermelon we knew, and this humble treat was much appreciated. A hint of luxury.

Leonard shared the rest of it with our hosts, and they too appreciated luxury, accepting it gratefully. As far as we could tell anyway; we didn't understand a word they said. But it sounded like gratitude.

Finally, as the *coup de grâce*, the patriarch brought out a half-round gourd — a calabash — full of millet beer, the local intoxicant I had been eager to try. Leonard presided over this ceremony as well, and I held out my folding plastic cup for him to fill. Elsa and Annie took a small taste, while David abstained. He'd tried it before.

The millet beer was a thin, whitish liquid, with a taste that was at once both weak and bitter. Though I'd had visions of getting myself good and drunk one of these nights — "sit down and get fucked-up," as Leonard had put it so eloquently in Bamenda — I found that my enthusiasm for millet beer didn't lead beyond one cupful.

'God,' I thought, 'I'm lost. I don't even like *booze* anymore.'

Shaking my head despondently, I spread my sleeping bag on the sandy terrace and lay back under the stars. After last–minute trips to the bikes, and the bushes, everyone else claimed their spots on the ground beside me, ready for bed. I looked at my watch and laughed. It was a little after 7:00.

With no cities for hundreds of miles, the night was utterly black except for the perfect stars. A few meteors streaked across, to a chorus of "oohs" from the stargazers. Leonard, stretched out on his back beside me, spoke up: "Look at that — a satellite!"

"Where? Where?" I asked, excited and curious, never having seen one before, and afraid it would be gone before I spotted it. I followed the silhouette of his arm against the stars and found the swift–moving dot of light, traversing the sky from north to south with amazing speed, on what Leonard told me was a "polar orbit." Just before the satellite disappeared to the south, another appeared in the reverse direction, and quickly crossed the sheet of stars to the northern horizon.

I don't know by what astronomical calculations, but Leonard figured that at least one of the satellites should be visible again about an hour and a half later, appearing in a different part of the sky as the earth rotated. I struggled to stay awake for it, but it was no good. After all, in another hour and a half it would have been nearly *9:00*, a ridiculous hour to be awake.

As my breathing deepened, I felt the air light in my nostrils and lungs, and thought about the winds blowing clean off the Atlantic for part of the year, then sweeping down over the Sahara during the dry season. 'Yep,' I thought, as my eyelids drew together, 'you probably don't get air much cleaner than this.'

My eyes opened again once or twice during the night, waking from a flow of dreams to shift position on the gravel. One time the moon was just clearing the ridge behind my head, a white hemisphere suspended among the stars. A few hours later I looked up again and the half-moon shone straight above me, bathing the valley in silver light.

When I awoke for the final time the moon was gone, and I lay still in the pre-dawn silence watching the stars go pale. A sleeper stirred beside me, a rustling of material, and the characteristic coughs and sniffs told me David was awake. I looked over at him and caught his eye, offering a weak smile, but we remained silent, watching the light slowly change with dawn.

The inselberg Kapsiki.
Northern Cameroon.

toil and trouble

So I woke up on the ground, ate a stale crust of bread, a few raisins and peanuts, and a wedge of process cheese. Flies circled my face while I ate, and followed me as I rolled up my sleeping bag and loaded the bike, ready to move again. One of the villagers sat on the stone wall and watched me patiently, a thin, rangy man in his mid-thirties. He rocked a silent little girl on his lap, and her stunted right arm curled in front of her, like Anatole's, ending in a knot of twisted fingers. I felt a twinge of sorrow, wondering why there seemed to be so many mutilated people in Cameroon. Birth defects, accidents, fires, improperly treated wounds, diseases — but worse, many West African children had been crippled by sloppy inoculations, the needle striking the sciatic nerve and *paralyzing* the child instead of protecting it.

Any kind of disability would be a terrible handicap in a country where existence was a hand-to-mouth struggle for nearly everyone. Someone like Anatole wouldn't be able to farm, or get a job, and he would probably never have even one wife. Perhaps he was fortunate to have tourism as an option. But what would that sad-faced little girl grow up to?

The father held his crippled child with obvious affection, and gently brushed the flies away from her eyes. He spoke in "Guavese" to Anatole, who translated his question into French. He wanted to know if I had any medicine for him.

I am not a doctor, I answered.

Yes, the other one (David) told him that.

Well, what is wrong with him? Or is it for the little girl?

As Anatole translated my question, the man set his little daughter aside, half-stood, and pointed at his back, his stomach, and his head. Sore back, sore stomach, and headache. Not so serious as the farmer who wanted the Elixir of Youth. Or maybe this was really the same. I told him I had no medicine like that, that it was a matter for a doctor, not a bicyclist. He seemed unsatisfied, disbelieving, and I wondered what kind of white people he had met before, who could perform these wondrous cures. CARE people handing out aspirin, or missionaries handing out miracles? When I toured the mission hospital in Togo, the doctor pointed out huge jars of multivitamins they gave as placebos for such non-specific complaints.

We said goodbye to Anatole and the family, the woman watching carefully as David paid Anatole for the lodging and food. I helped Elsa lift her loaded bicycle over a low stone wall, and turned away just at the moment when she *might* have said "thanks." But she walked her bike down the path without a word. Annie and David pushed away too, while I waited for Leonard, who had just discovered a flat tire. The sidewall was pierced by a long thorn, which he must have picked up on the previous day's ride down the "road" to Guave. That day's *first* disaster was soon repaired, and we followed the others over the rocks and sand. The sun burned down from a blue–white sky, and the barren country of thorns and stunted trees was glorified only by the inselbergs.

After an hour of hard labor, we turned north on the so-called main road — not much different from the trail to Guave, save for the evidence of more traffic: more ruts. I swore out loud at the worst stretches of road, releasing my tension, annoyance, and fear. Leonard laughed at my eloquence, and I called to him, "I hate fear in the morning!" My rear tire was slowly going flat too, but I decided to stop and pump it up when I had to, until a nice shady place came along where I could fix it. On the open road there was no shade, nothing to lean the bike against, and nothing to sit on.

We stopped for *beignets* and soda in Mogodé, a dusty street lined with cone-headed huts and overhung with dusty trees. Naturally a crowd of Mogodites surrounded us, some friendly, others silent and curious. I didn't feel like changing my tire under the watchful eyes of the entire population of Mogodé, so I asked Leonard to stop with me just outside the village. Finding a patch of shade with no one in sight, I stripped off the panniers and released the rear wheel, but while I was laying the spare tube around the rim children began to materialize from the fields and along the road. Soon ten pairs of eyes watched me work. I decided to change the tire as well, and sometimes a new tire is a tight fit. I pulled, pried, and levered at it until anger flared up. Remembering *Zen And The Art Of Motorcycle Maintenance*, I put the wheel down and thought for a minute, then attacked it again. I talked to it, coaxed it, urged it, and cajoled it. Then I finally *swore* it into position. While I was cursing out my wheel, Leonard was watching something on the road.

"What's *this* all about?" he said, pointing at two teenage boys who had just met from opposite directions. One of them was handing a paper bag to the other, who opened it and peered inside. He closed it quickly and placed it between his feet, reached into a pocket and pulled out a fold of money. Then an argument erupted, and suddenly they were shouting and pointing at each other, the first boy grabbing back the paper bag. Threats were made and fists were raised.

A stocky old grandmother came trotting up and began a tirade of abuse and finger-wagging that cowed the boys. They stood circling their toes in the dust and bowing their heads, as the old woman sent them firmly on their way, back the way they'd come. She stood in the road with her hands on her hips, watching them go. Leonard and I looked at each other, wondering what we had just seen. A drug deal gone bad?

A dozen miles, a couple of hours, and many curses later, I saw David stopped at the roadside, and the pale figure of Elsa just disappearing along a tiny road to the left. David had been talking about this place he wanted to visit, a village where "the women wear calabashes on their heads." But, he'd never been there before, knew nothing of the "roads," things were bad enough already, and —

'And just keep your big mouth shut,' I told myself. 'Maybe he's the only one who wants to do this, but complaining isn't going to do a *bit* of good. After all he's had to put up with, it's not so bad that he should want to see one place he hasn't been before. Just shut up.'

We followed what had become a foot-path, pedaling unsteadily over the usual obstacles, squeezing between walls of thorns and dry millet stalks, and occasionally dismounting to push through deep sandpits. Five miles of this took more than an hour, and it was nearly noon. The sun reflected straight up from the dry earth, and the little shade cast by the scattered trees dwindled to a small circle around their trunks. Hungry, tired, hot, and low on water, my mood was not improving. *'Where the* hell *are we going?'*

Finally David pointed to a winding path which led up the side of a small tree-crowned hill, and we got off and walked the heavy bikes to the top. This would be the village of Mabas, according to David, though it consisted of only two compounds, thatched peaks behind walls of piled stones.

A wide patch of shade was cast by an enormous buttress-tree, a gnarled and twisted pair of trunks hung with cable-thick vines. The two dwellings were built on either side of the monumental tree, huddled among a scatter of great boulders. Once again, we were greeted by three generations: a ragged old farmer, his sinewy son, and a laughing boy of eight or nine years. I doubt if any tourists had ever found their way to Mabas before, especially on bicycles, so they regarded us with wonder rather than expectation. They spoke neither French nor English, but the toothless old man finally understood that we were just passing through. With much stuttering and difficulty he managed to tell us *"Je suis guide,"* while pointing at his chest proudly. We laughed at the idea of needing a guide in Mabas (to get from one house to the other?) and the old fellow's brow furrowed.

But there *was* something to see in Mabas, as we learned when we followed the younger man along an indistinct trail — a trail whose usual purpose was indicated by the reek of human feces in the hot, dry air. But that was forgotten as we squeezed between the boulders into the open, and were stopped in our tracks by a spectacular view, spreading far below us in an endless panorama.

"Nigeria," said the farmer, waving his hand across it, "Nigeria." All I could say was "wow!" — looking down from about two thousand feet over a vista of light brown plains, speckled with tiny dots of trees. The land receded into the haze of distance, rugged hills into oblivion, and a steady wind swept the cliff on which we stood. Strange to think we pushed our bikes up a little hill to find ourselves on a two–thousand–foot precipice. I scanned the valley below with my binoculars, picking out dry rivers, roads, and occasional collections of tiny farms.

The smiling little boy danced around us like a goat, leaping easily from rock to rock and chattering away in a high voice. Leonard called him over and handed him the binoculars, but the boy just stared at them. I showed him how to look through them, and he raised the lenses slowly to his eyes. Then with a start, he pulled them away, his mouth open in shock. His high voice bubbled with amazement, and he laughed as he once more aimed the glasses around his "back yard," brought close for the first time.

We retreated from the sun back to the shade of the great tree, spreading ourselves on the flat boulders. David laid out our meager supply of food, a few guavas and peanuts left over from the previous day. Water was equally scarce, and I sipped carefully at my last water bottle while I shelled a handful of peanuts, but it wasn't enough to satisfy either hunger or thirst. I spread my foam pad on the swept gravel, my rolled-up sleeping bag pillowed against a boulder, and I tried to read some Aristotle, maybe doze a little. Elsa accidentally kicked my foot as she walked by, but said nothing.

Mabas seemed such an idyllic spot, and I was momentarily glad we came. But this paradise had its infernal pests too. The squadrons of hovering dragonflies were harmless, but hordes of tiny flies circled my face and crawled on my arms and legs. I spread the *pagne* over my body up to the neck, but the flies still tormented my face, so I finally had to give up, lay down the book, and pull the cloth over me like a shroud.

The wind swept up from Nigeria and sounded in the trees, a susurrance which only seemed to emphasize the silence. I closed my eyes, relaxed my muscles, and felt the underlying weariness. My spirits and resistance were low, and a sudden pang in my stomach heralded an attack of misery. Hungry, thirsty, and homesick, once again I counted the days remaining until Paris.

Mustering a counterattack against the misery, I tried to think of nice things. Having none at hand, I made some up, beginning modestly enough: 'All the water I can drink. Some rice with junk on it. Yeah, and a hot shower. Clean clothes, clean body, comfortable bed. Cold drinks — a milk shake. Wine, champagne — a Scotch on the rocks! A swimming pool. Twenty-four-hour room service!'

As my fantasies became more remote, another pang swept through my mind and body, an overwhelming wave of *want*, a deep longing of vague desire. And I recognized the symptoms: 'A fever of desire,' I called it. But it was really Luxury Fever.

Too restless to sleep, yet prevented by the flies from reading to distract myself from these futile thoughts, I lay there looking up at the light through the weave of the cloth. Forgotten were the aspects of western life I *didn't* miss — the telephone, the counted minutes — and I thought only of the things I once took for granted, the small pleasures. Wander into the kitchen to make a sandwich, or munch a couple of cookies. Grab an apple juice from the fridge on the way by. A reading light behind the bed.

Yeah, home — No checkpoints, no drunken soldiers, no "White Man!" No flies.

I threw back the *pagne*, rose stiffly to my feet and started to repack my things. David opened his eyes and looked up, and I told him: "I'm going to get moving. I'm too hungry and thirsty to relax." Then I smiled, pointing at the heap of peanut shells. "The groundnuts just didn't fill me up."

"Well I'm sorry, but that's what we have," he replied, a bit defensively.

My voice softened, to let him understand I didn't blame *him*. "I know that, but maybe we'll come to a village where we can buy water or food." Water and food seemed to be the magic words for everyone, as suddenly the rest of the group was rising from beneath their shrouds to gather their belongings and trudge toward the bikes. I took out the map and double-checked our route with David, then set out ahead on my own. I carried a vision of a Cameroon Shangri-la: a kiosk which sold drinks and some kind of food.

The road snaked and laddered over the desolate terrain, and I felt myself fading, flagging near the top of the steep climbs, then tumbling down the other side like a skier bouncing from one mogul to the next. Rather than *riding* down the hills, I felt as if I were *falling* down them, and just trying to hang on. It was no good, sloppy and dangerous, and I tried to concentrate and truly control the bike.

Between bumps and curses I recorded an entry:

> I'm feeling kind of low, and right now very thirsty. I've hardly had anything to eat — a small crust of bread this morning and two wedges of process cheese, and then three small beignets in a town, and some peanuts at siesta time. Now that it's probably around three o'clock, I'm really feeling the hunger, and I'm almost out of water.

One swallow of water remained in my bottle, but no matter how thirsty I was I couldn't drink it. It was like a precious reserve, a margin of survival, and a psychological buffer too. If I drank it, I would be *out of water*.

Finally I reached Tourou, our destination, and stopped to ask a boy where I could find something to drink. He didn't understand me in English or French, but he did understand "Coca-Cola?" and guided me off the road and along a rough path, trotting beside me. The market was empty, but the boy pointed to a square earthen building to one side and said "Coca-Cola." I nodded and gave him a weak smile of thanks. Leaning my bike against a wall, I pushed back the curtain over the door and took a step inside. Six male faces looked up at me in surprise, staring curiously, then recovered themselves and bid me welcome with smiles and indecipherable but unmistakable greetings.

A fire glowed in a small room to the side, where a man sweated over a pot of steaming oil, making *beignets*. He looked up when the other men called him over, and I repeated the magic word, "Coca-Cola?" The *beignet*-maker pointed to a pan on the floor, where several soft drink bottles lay "cooling" in water. I opened a Coke and drank it down. Then an Orange Crush. Then a ginger ale. The men sat smiling and shaking their heads at me. Small loaves of bread were stacked on the table, and I bought two of them as well, devouring the first like a starving man, pushing it into my mouth with both hands. Then I moved outside to work on the second, with a *fourth* bottle of soda.

Leonard arrived, directed by the same young guide, and parked his bike beside mine. He ducked through the curtained doorway and started on his first soda, as Annie rode up too, even her perpetual smile looking worn. When David and Elsa finally arrived, poor Elsa was too tired even to be grumpy. She laughed wearily at the madness of it all, and took rare pleasure in a bottle of ginger ale. The usual crowd of ragged boys gathered around our bicycles, and the usual crowd of flies gathered around our faces.

A short time later we were spreading our beds under a shelter of woven mats behind a beer-hall. Fortunately, the bar was closed, perhaps it only opened on weekends or market day, a more likely occasion in Tourou. (When the women wore calabashes on their heads.) Two boys were sent to the well with two clay urns in a wheelbarrow, and we impatiently awaited their return. *Water!* Dehydration had afflicted us all, and we drank the water as fast as it could be filtered, David, Leonard, and I working full-time with the two pumps. Thirst had become a bone-deep craving, and I couldn't drink enough.

Or eat enough. As darkness fell, we sat on the ground in the glow of a kerosene lantern and loaded our bowls with fish stew and boiled yams. The day's hardships seemed to have softened everyone, and the mood was light and friendly. Water and simple food — there seemed nothing to complain about now. When the food was gone, washed down by another liter of water, I was bloated with a surfeit of both, and happy just to move over to my corner of the shelter and lay down.

But after drinking all that water, several times during the night I was obliged to get up and go out back to the "latrine" — my choice of bushes — and water the garden while I looked up at the stars.

. . .

I mentioned that English saying about the only good thing in Scotland being the road leading out of it. You could not say that about Kumba, or Tourou either. At first light we returned to the marketplace, hoping to find some breakfast, and to fulfill the grail of this quest: see the women with calabashes on their heads. But the market was deserted; the only attraction was a group of men leading a complaining bull through the market to a fenced-in corner, the slaughterhouse. Leonard snickered when I cupped my hands and called out to the bull "Run away! Run away! You're going to be *killed!*"

At the earthen hut where we had set new records in soda-pop consumption the previous afternoon, David convinced the busy *beignet*-maker to fry us up some omelettes. We sat at the little table and discussed whether to wait for the calabash-heads to show up. The market didn't get under way until eight o'clock, and it was only a little after six. Elsa decided to leave right after breakfast, while David wanted to wait and see the object of his quest. The rest of us thought we'd wait a *little* while, and see how we felt.

Well, how we felt was hot, restless, tormented by flies, and stared at by the gathering crowds. At least I did. When you go somewhere to look at the people because they're unusual, and find them staring at you because *you're* unusual, it's just too much.

But wait. "Over there — isn't that a woman with — something on her head?" And yes, it was a short, stocky woman wearing an inverted salad bowl, a polished gourd set firmly over her hair like a bicycle helmet. After all we'd been through to get there, and whatever we had to get through to get out, it seemed a little anticlimactic. "Well, okay," I said, "we've seen one now. I'm going to get going," and I took off after Elsa. David looked away, perhaps a little miffed at our lack of cultural enthusiasm.

A milestone at the crossroads arrowed right for Koza, the town where we would rejoin the main road. The sign read "30 KMS," and I headed that way, but at the last house in the village, the road ended. With a muttered *"damn,"* I turned around and pedaled back, scanning the roadside, but there was no other road. I activated my high-tech direction-finder — stopping a man and saying "Koza? Koza?" while I pointed my finger rapidly up the road. He gave me a gap-toothed smile and nodded. Scattered groups of people came up the road on their way to market, leading goats, carrying chickens, baskets of produce, or great bags of grain, and many of the women wore the famous calabashes on their heads. All those people must be coming from *somewhere.*

Back I went. Where the road ended a group of children stared at me as if at a monster from Mars. I tried my direction-finder on them, but they were too stunned; their heads only trembled in fear and disbelief. A footpath led down into the rocks and bushes to one side, and a pair of men emerged from it. I gave them the "Koza?"-and-repeated-pointing routine, and one of them smiled and nodded. Could it be?

'Maybe the path joins up with a road,' I thought, and started down it, steering around the larger stones. Soon the path was nothing *but* larger stones, and I had to get off and wrestle the bike down over the scree. And there came Elsa, pushing her bike *up* the scree.

"There's nothing here but a footpath. It must be the wrong way," she said.

"Well, I've asked everyone I've seen, and they all say it's the road to Koza."

Unsure what to do, we stood beside the path, moving our bikes aside to let more marketers and calabash-heads pass. I spotted a man in green work-clothes and hailed him. *"Bonjour,"* and he answered me in French. I asked about the road, and he told me that it was indeed the only road to Koza, but, he shook his head, it is not in good repair. The road is not ... finished.

Ah yes. *"Merci, m'sieur."* I smiled. We are used to roads like that.

I translated this information for Elsa, and like me she was not daunted by a road that was "not finished." We'd seen a few, and survived them. And he called it a *chemin*, road, and not a *piste*, path. An important semantic distinction, however inaccurate.

The path, for path it was, ran beside a dry stream for a mile or so, and I was able to remount the bicycle and ride, moving ahead of Elsa. Then I was off the bike again, as the path led up the steep cleft of a hill, winding out of sight. The wheels bounced against the rocks and banged the sharp pedals into my shins. I swore grimly, still thinking 'maybe the real road is just on the other side of the hill.'

But on the other side of the hill was another hill, out of the shade and into the already–hot sun. There was no cycling now, just hauling the bike upward, then trying to hold it back going downhill. My right shoe had split across the sole, and I felt every sharp rock I stepped on. The smaller stones found their way inside. A little 'uh-oh' went off in my head; things were not looking good. I hoped it wasn't going to be like that for thirty kilometers. 'Please, not eighteen miles of *this*.'

Thump, bump — pant pant — bang, crash — ouch! Shit.

No more people walked on this "road to Koza," and no more little farms appeared out of the bush. Sweat trickled down my face, and blood trickled down my shin where the pedal had scraped it raw. I worked my way around the shoulder of a hill, then looked back to see someone behind me, a dark-skinned figure in a red tanktop. It was Leonard, and he was actually *riding* his bike, head down as he picked his way along the path. I leaned my bike against one of the many conveniently-located boulders, took a drink of water and waited as he caught up.

I shook my head at him. "Man, I can't believe you're riding on this."

"Me either. It's pretty crazy. I think I'll push for a while," and he laid his bike down and dragged a bandana over his face.

"I'm glad to see you anyway," I said, "I was beginning to think everyone must have turned around, and would be back in Tourou laughing at me."

"No, the others are behind. I just helped Elsa get her bike up one of the hills, and she wasn't laughing." He rubbed his bearded cheek. "I haven't really been laughing either."

"Me either. This is awful. I can't believe David got us into this, without even asking someone about the road, or if there *was* a road."

Leonard was looking away, and he turned to me with visible alarm. "Oh-oh."

"What? What's the matter?"

"Up there, behind those boulders on the hill. You see them?"

My eyes followed his arm to a ridge ahead of us, and I saw a few dark figures — *furry* figures — perched on the rocks. "Looks like baboons," I said.

"*Yeah!* A *lot* of 'em too."

"I don't think they'll bother us."

But Leonard was doubtful: "I don't know."

"No really. I don't think I've ever heard of baboons attacking people, unless they were cornered, or you messed with their babies or something." I took hold of my handlebars and started to push the bike again, but I could sense that Leonard was still shaken. Now he'd made me a little nervous too; maybe there was something about baboons I hadn't heard.

I kept a wary eye on the rock-strewn heights to either side, and saw a dozen or so baboons popping up behind the boulders at random, like shooting-gallery targets. 'Massing an attack,' I thought drily. A solitary woman passed in the other direction, averting her calabash-shaded eyes from me, but she didn't seem to be alarmed by the simian hordes. Then the trail worsened, and claimed my full attention, so I forgot about the baboons.

Now I knew what the man in Tourou had meant when he said the road was "not finished" — it was *literally* not finished. Someone had once tried to make a road there, a long time ago. The shoulder of the hill had been shored up with rock for miles, to make a roadbed of football-sized stones (just the right size for every one of them to catch my wheels and pitch the bike sideways into my leg). The road *would* have been wide enough for vehicles, and was laid out on the steep hills in switchbacks, but the stones were overgrown with weeds and bushes beside a narrow footpath. The "road to Koza" indeed.

At the bottom of a particularly nasty descent, still high above the valley floor, I threw my bike down in disgust, wishing I could just wing it over the side and walk the hell out of there. I'd probably only covered two or three miles, and Koza was *eighteen* miles away.

I remembered Leonard, and looked back for him. He wasn't coming. The baboons? My voice echoed back in the dry air as I called his name. No reply. Leaving my bike where it lay, I walked back up the hill I had just so painfully descended, calling out as I went. No reply. I climbed a little faster, sweating and panting and swearing, half-worried about him, and half-sure that this was all for nothing. As I worked my way around the shoulder of the hill, I saw Leonard pedaling slowly around the previous one. We started back down, Leonard on his bike and trying to thread between the soccer-ball rocks without going over the edge to oblivion, but he soon gave it up. "A person could get hurt around here."

"Yeah, a good reason for walking. If you get hurt, I'm *not* going to carry you out."

"You'd just leave me here, to be eaten alive by baboons?"

"Sure. I'll be outside the *Deux Magots* in Paris, sipping a *Kir Royale.*"

I picked up my bicycle and we turned down the steep path, the bike bouncing through the stones and into me. Thump, bump — *pant pant* — bang, crash — *ouch!* Shit.

"You know," I said to Leonard, "this might be the worst experience of my life."

A short laugh. "Well, I couldn't really say that."

Of course not, I realized — he was in *Vietnam*. This can't really compare to that. I shouldn't feel so sorry for myself. But I did.

We finally reached the bottom, and the trail led us into a valley of high grass and thorns. We managed to ride occasionally, but only for short intervals, until we met a rocky streambed or a patch of deep sand. The thorns bordering the narrow trail tore at my arms and legs, and they were the barbed kind that hook in and *rip*. (East

Africans call them "wait-a-bit" thorns.) Drops of blood on my arms added to the gore of my shins.

Now I was mad, and looking for someone to blame. My thoughts were poisoned by pain and bad temper. Why hadn't David *asked* someone about this "road," instead of committing us to eighteen miles of *this*? Why did he have to see the calabash-heads anyway? No one else cared about it. He didn't even really ask us. Et cetera.

The shade of a spreading tree beckoned, and we stopped to rest. As I leaned my bike against another conveniently-located boulder, I noticed that the front tire (the brand-new Michelin I'd only put on the day before) had been chewed up pretty badly. Chunks of tread had been torn right off, down to the white casing. And, it was going flat.

A slow leak is difficult to find without dipping the tube in water and looking for air bubbles, so I decided to change it. Using the "eloquence method" once again, I levered the tire off and installed a new tube. But as I started to pump it back up again, the tire remained limp. I heard the *whoosh* of air going in, and right back out. Stripping the tire off once more, I found a gash in my brand-new spare tube.

Patch the gash, wrestle the tube back into the tire, and try again. *Whoosh*. The air goes in; the air goes out. One more time; take it apart, find another gash, patch it and put the whole thing together again. And again, *whoosh*. Now I left the tube out while I tested it, patched six holes, and it still wouldn't hold air. I gritted my teeth and closed my eyes for a few seconds, trying not to pick up a convenient rock and start pounding my bike into a twisted wreck.

"Hey Leonard."

"Yo."

"I think this would be a good time for you to tell me a story to make me feel better — about your experiences that were worse than this."

He chuckled, a little embarrassed. "Well, when I worked for the government, you know. When you're out there, and people are trying to kill you just because you're *there*, that's about the worst thing there can be."

"Yup, you're right. I can't begin to imagine it. But I don't really feel better."

"Me either."

My patch kit was empty, and I had to start on Leonard's supply. I'd given up on the defective "brand-new" tube, and gone back to the old one, hoping I'd get lucky and find the tiny hole. I pumped it up and held it to my ear, listening for the inaudible, the trickle of air slowly escaping. I moistened a finger with saliva and spread it over likely-looking areas of the tube, but there were no tell-tale bubbles. I held the limp tube in my hands, and wondered what to do.

Leonard had been moving around a little, perhaps he'd seen some water. I pointed to a watercourse beside us, just out of sight behind the bushes and grass. "Say, there doesn't happen to be a little water in that stream, does there?"

He gave a short embarrassed laugh. "As a matter of fact, yeah, there is. I never thought of it."

I cursed myself for an idiot, and walked over to see a stream running clear over the rocks and sand. Wading straight into it, the water cool inside my shoes, I plunged the tube under. A slow stream of bubbles showed the pinprick hole, and I marked it with a pen.

Just as I stood up, with my feet still in the stream, I was surprised to hear the other three come bouncing down the trail toward us. I'd thought they would surely have turned back.

David spoke with forced jollity, "Hey guys! How's it going?"

I remained silent as I walked back to the tree, but Leonard replied with his quiet irony, "Oh, just wonderful thank you."

I concentrated on putting my front wheel back together. At last it held air.

Elsa was also silent, while Annie, of course, was cheerful. But quietly cheerful.

"How far do you think we've come," murmured Elsa, and David consulted his large-scale map. "About six or seven miles." A chorus of sighs, eleven more to go.

The trail continued through dry streambeds, sandtraps, and thorns. I tried to ride high on the sides, out of the softer earth, but there I was more exposed to the sharp thorns, and lost some more pieces of my arms and legs. I frowned, swore, and kept moving.

Leonard and I stayed together, taking turns leading and following for another hour. We emerged into a wide clearing, where the Cameroon flag drooped over a low schoolhouse. I left Leonard in the shade of a tree while I wheeled up to it. A spectacled young man answered my *"Allo? Bonjour!"* through the door, and came outside. Behind him I saw his students creep to the windows and stare at me. The teacher's French was excellent, and finally, by means of the time-honored method of drawing in the sand, I felt sure I understood his complicated directions.

As I returned to tell Leonard the happy news that maybe we weren't lost forever, David came riding out of the bushes, sweating and panting. "I've been trying to catch you guys. This isn't the right way. A lady back there told us Koza is *that* way." And he pointed back the way we'd just come, and off to the south. "I've sent the girls ahead down a path that leads that way, then came to get you."

I frowned. "Well, I just got directions from the teacher in this school, and he says we can get to Mozogo this way, which is closer than Koza anyway. I think we should carry on along this path."

He glared at me, and I glared back.

"Okay then," David said, "we'll meet in Mozogo."

"Okay then," I replied.

The sorceror's passageway.
Guave.

the lizards are fat at waza

And now we were two. Leonard, bless him, stayed with me, and we continued up the track. The only thing the schoolteacher hadn't told me was how *far* all of those landmarks were, and miles went by as I watched in vain for the place where we were supposed to turn. We threaded along the valley between rocky hills, the sun now directly overhead, and saw only a few farms, walled clusters of cone-heads.

"What if we come out in Nigeria?" said Leonard.

"We'll be in trouble," I replied drily. *Very* drily. I was down to that last mouthful of water again, the one I could never drink, so I was tormented by a desperate thirst — as well as by hunger, misery, heat, and uncertainty. This was getting a bit crazy. We were not on the map, we were *nowhere*, with no food or water, and didn't know where we were going.

The footpath finally led us to a fork, just as the teacher had described. A concrete signpost, like the one in Tourou, marked it with a chiseled arrow pointing one way for Ashigashiya, which my map told me was in Nigeria, where we didn't want to go, and the other way for Koza, where we did — sort of.

The teacher had also said that along this track to Koza we would find a small path to the left, which would take us to Mozogo and save us a few kilometers. Somewhere over there, in the featureless desert of the Chad Basin, was the road we wanted, the *Grande Route* that would take us north to Mora, Waza, and eventually, into Chad. But once again I had no idea how *far* the turn might be, so I hesitated at every little path. On a whim I had packed a diver's wrist-compass, given to me by my brother-in-law, a diving instructor, and now I was glad of it. At least I could tell which direction the paths ran. I strapped it onto my right wrist, opposite the Casio which now said 12:00.

As if we didn't know where the sun was.

Leonard still carried one full water bottle, which he split with me (thereby earning a guaranteed mention in my Will), but even measuring it out carefully, waiting until my mouth was sticking together before I took a small sip of the solar-heated water, it was soon gone as well. Except, of course, for the one precious swallow in reserve.

An old farmer pushed an ancient bicycle out of his compound, the first human we'd seen in many miles. I did the old "direction finder" routine on him, pointing frantically up the track and repeating "Mozogo?" and he nodded. His own pointing finger reached out and around to describe a turn to the left, just as the schoolteacher had said, but there was no way I could think of to ask him how *far* it was to that path. Such are the limitations of sign language. I smiled and thanked him in English and French, neither of which he understood, but I was grateful for his help, and for his sheer *existence* in that desolate place.

After a few more miles, we stopped by a twisted mass of thorns that rose just over our heads, making a small umbrella of patterned shade. Leonard was looking haggard, and slumped over his bike as he asked, "Do you want to rest here for a while?"

Driven by determination, uncertainty, and *fear*, I said, "I'd feel a lot better resting once we know where we *are*. Let's carry on a bit and see if we can't find this path."

He nodded, and we carried on.

One path to the left seemed a little wider than the others, and was marked by wheelruts rather than the footprints of people and livestock — that was something. I checked with the compass, and it ran straight to the east, so we decided we'd try it for a while, and see how it "felt." Across the plain we headed, a pair of automatons pedaling over hard, rippled earth and white dust, past thorns and one or two farms and small dry fields of maize stalks.

A few square buildings appeared on the horizon, and then the track beneath my wheels became a street, leading between rows of earthen houses with metal roofs (that detail alone told me we were in a town rather than a village; villages have thatched roofs, towns have metal). Relieved, but too tired to be joyful, we pedaled into Mozogo, still not absolutely sure that it *was* Mozogo, but it was *somewhere*, and we'd been *nowhere* for nearly eight hours. Better to be lost in the middle of somewhere than the middle of nowhere, I always say. Or I will, from now on.

The unpaved street — but a *street!* — led us to a crossroads, and on one corner was a small shop. Leonard and I dumped our bikes on the ground and started drinking. The first two bottles of Fanta were uncapped and swallowed whole, and then another two, tasting so good and wet and sweet, and everything a person could want. Feeling revived, rehydrated, and reassured by knowing my place in the world, I offered to do a little reconnoitering, see if I could find the well which the shopowner had told me about, and a place where we could wait for the others. That was okay with Leonard, as long as he didn't have to move.

A few people turned to stare as I rode through Mozogo, but the town was largely deserted in the midday heat. I heard a chorus of voices shouting as I passed, but I ignored them at first. I'd grown used to being shouted at by strangers. Then I noticed that they seemed to be shouting my name, and thought they must have another word for "white man" that sounded like it. The voices became louder and more insistent, and there, amid a crowd of children, stood David, Elsa, and Annie, all of them, including the children, calling out my name.

I coasted on for a few seconds in shock. It had been five hours since we'd parted at the schoolhouse, on different paths and aiming for different destinations, and at best I'd hoped we'd meet up again on the main road. And I didn't even know where that *was* yet. The frustration of the whole day dissolved as I turned around and parked my bike, then entered the house where they'd been waiting — also gulping down bottles of soda. We sat on the ground, laughing at this classic Stanley/Livingstone scene. Their path had indeed led to Koza, as ours had led to Mozogo, and both of us had reached Mozogo at nearly the same time. The country had seemed so big, so untracked and desolate, that I had truly wondered if we would *ever* find each other again.

As we sat in the cool dimness of the earth-walled room, David stated our options: we could stay in Mozogo and try to improvise some kind of "rustic accommodations," or we could rest awhile and then go on to Mora, another thirty miles or so, where we could stay in a proper hotel, maybe with running water, beds, a restaurant ...

To my surprise, *Elsa* was in favor of going on, despite all she'd been through, and the rest of us agreed. Annie and I rode back to the crossroads to see what Leonard had to say, and found him slumped against the wall of the little shop, his legs drawn up and his eyes closed. When I told him that everyone else wanted to continue on to Mora, he agreed — in a groaning sort of way.

The others planned to rest until mid-afternoon, to recover from the morning and avoid the heat, but as usual I was restless and wanted to get somewhere, so I set out early. The *Grande Route* from Mozogo up to Mora was not very grand, not even paved, but after the past few days, it was nothing to complain about either. It ran smooth and straight over the flat, featureless terrain of the southern tip of the Chad Basin. I rode for Mora like an eighteen-wheeler, picking the smoothest track between the potholes and washboard and not slowing my pace for anything.

• • •

Westerners who have been long-time residents in West Africa use "WAWA," an acronym for "West Africa Wins Again," to express the occasional frustrations of life there. WAWA, with its appropriate sound of wailing despair, is commonly applied by those who are defeated in their efforts to get something done, approved, fixed, built, moved, bought, or sold with western speed and efficiency.

However, such people view themselves as going *against* West Africa, in a battle of wills, while the nature of our journey was to go *with* West Africa, not to try to make it "just like home." We didn't expect western speed and efficiency, or even plumbing and electricity. We didn't expect much at all, and if you don't expect much, you won't be disappointed. But still, sometimes the place got the better of us.

Two hours later I wheeled into the dusty streets of Mora and up to the hotel David had described to me. *Le Campement de Wandela* was a compound of circular, thatched cabins in a gravel yard, with a few palms and flowering shrubs surrounding the main building, a restaurant. In the late afternoon light I parked my bicycle by the terrace and walked inside, past the empty tables and the "foosball" table, and up to the bar. A woman sat behind it, and looked up at me, expressionless and apparently undisturbed by my dirty, sweaty and disheveled condition. I quickly arranged for our two rooms, and asked her if there was any water.

"Oui," she replied, *"il y en a,"* and I smiled at the vision of getting clean, then sitting down to wait for the others on the terrace

with a nice whiskey — a *large* whiskey. Maybe two. The sober-faced woman led me to a circular hut, and I looked inside. Two beds, a wardrobe, and a *bathroom*, with a toilet, sink and shower. *Yes!* As I unloaded my panniers and hauled them inside, the woman spoke again, then turned away. I didn't quite catch it — it sounded as if she said she was going to get some water.

Thinking I must have misunderstood her, I called her back. *"Excusez, mais je ne comprends pas."* Did you say *bring* me some water? There is a bathroom *here*, and you told me there *was* water.

Yes, there is. I will bring you a bucket of it.

After all we'd been through to get to Mozogo — walking for miles over the hills out of Tourou, then struggling through the sand, lost and thirsty and ripped by thorns — and the only reason we had decided to continue on to Mora had been our certainty that we'd be rewarded for our efforts, that we'd find a proper hotel, one with running water.

But the water wasn't running; it was *walking* toward me, in a bucket, the woman's body curved against its weight. I sighed and took it from her, then opened my panniers mournfully and dug out my soap, cloth, and the soup bowl. West Africa had won again.

. . .

Early the next morning we stopped at another small hotel just outside Mora, hoping to find some breakfast, but it was closed up tight. Elsa wrinkled her nose at the strong urine smell around the walls. The night watchman rose from his nest on the terrace and went to find the cook, and I leaned back against the steps and watched the lizards scampering across the wall, or simply hanging there, defying gravity.

Our omelettes arrived, accompanied by the surprise of toast, jam, and butter (well, margarine). The pre-sweetened coffee was undrinkable, so instead I washed the meal down with a big bottle of warm Top *citron*. It no longer seemed strange to be drinking soda pop at 6:30 in the morning.

Things were going to be better today — *on a paved road!* We hadn't seen a paved road since the ride to Garoua, when the bus had broken down, and after five days of dirt and squalor, forty miles of smooth riding was going to be, as my Dad used to say, "a treat instead of a treatment." My adrenalin went straight to the pedals, shifting up, then onto the big chainring and into top gear, I went racing through the flat savanna of thorns and occasional cotton fields. Small concrete markers appeared at the roadside every ten kilometers, and by timing myself between them I figured I was covering nearly twenty miles-an-hour.

For the first time in many days, my *mind* felt free. I could actually think about things without having to concentrate exclusively on survival, without being totally consumed by the obstacles which threated my position on *top* of the bicycle. I replayed the conversation from the previous night, when Elsa had asked me "So, how did *you* like today's little adventure?"

Not in the best of moods, I had replied, "Well, I thought it was a case of going nowhere, for nothing, with no road out!"

The others had laughed a little, but David had been defensive: "I don't think it was for *nothing*. I thought it was interesting, and the scenery was beautiful."

No one else had said anything, and I'd kept silent, content to let him take it personally. I'd taken it personally too — every torturous mile, every sweltering and thirsty hour, every stone in my shoe, every hole in my tire, every rock that bounced the bike into my bleeding leg, and every thorn that ripped into my skin. I couldn't let him gloss over one of the worst days of my life with words like "beautiful" and "interesting."

But that morning I thought about it some more as I rolled happily along, and wondered why David and I saw that Tourou expedition so differently. I began to tiptoe around an insight: David's mind worked *differently*, that's all. He saw and approached life in a completely alternate way. Wherever he was, that was the right place to be, because he was *there*. And if he wanted to go somewhere else, he *could* always get there from here. David was a *radial* thinker.

And me, I guessed I was a linear thinker. If I stood at Point A and wanted to go to Point Z, there was only one way to get there: the most direct route. The other points along the road, say Point B, or Point M, whatever, they would only be that — points along the road. I might pause to appreciate them, if they weren't too far out of my way, but they would never distract me from the goal: Point Z.

For David, whatever point he was at offered infinite possibilities, infinite alternatives, and the goal of getting to Point Z was entirely secondary, maybe even "beside the point." Each of those intermediary steps was complete unto itself, and if he found himself at Point B, then another complete set of possibilities would appear, none of them less attractive than the straight line toward Point Z. There was no *wrong* way to go, as long as he was *going.*

And *that's* where we were alike, David and I. We both wanted to be *moving*, never mind radial or linear. He had the same restless curiosity, the physical energy, the wide-ranging interests, the opinionated activism. However, we also shared a healthy sense of self-esteem, so that when our wills clashed, like at the schoolhouse on the way from Tourou, neither of us was going to back down from our "vision."

And, I realized, David's way "worked" too. Perhaps it was even better in some ways. Less exigent, less single-minded, less stressful. He *had* achieved some admirable goals in cycling and in life, and I'm sure, like me in my linear way, he had made some of his dreams come true, in his radial way.

And so, as I pushed the pedals steadily and sped down the highway toward Waza, I tried to apply this geometric "mind-map" to other people I knew. If Space was a curve and Time a spiral, maybe people's brains worked that way too. Circular Thinking: those who confine themselves to a narrow sphere of interest, and continually orbit around the same familiar territory. Where "twenty years of experience" is really one year of experience, twenty times over. I knew some of them, and lots of Parallel Thinkers, those who adopt someone else's ideas and follow them blindly. And Parabolic: those whose ideas move in little jumps from time to time, then hibernate between. Zigzag Thinkers, they were many, and the Zero-Thinkers too, those who had stopped thinking entirely around puberty.

Static Thinkers: those who only ever had *one* idea, or one desire — say "making money," or "having fun," and became fixated on that to the exclusion of all else. Even these two examples define diametrically opposite people, but they have this in common: both are intolerant of any other world-view. The mercenary mind thinks everyone else is simply "impractical," but at its most extreme will descend into boring, ulcerated emptiness. The hedonist will accuse us all of "taking things too seriously," while descending into boring, unfulfilled substance abuse.

I like the idea of Concentric Thinking. I have a friend who is an impoverished artist, a painter, musician, writer, activist, and worshipper of the female breast. Mendelson Joe, he calls himself (because that is how the government addresses him), a corpulent, bearded, stubble–headed man perpetually dressed in paint–splattered overalls, his eyes glaring with fierce clarity through black-rimmed glasses. He lives and works in an old shoemaker's shop in an aging part of downtown Toronto, and his storefront studio is piled to the ceiling with a chaos of paintings, papers, and motorcycle. Everything *but* the paintings is spattered with paint. His bed is disguised as a couch, and he hides his bathtub under a pile of junk in the basement, to conceal his unlawful use of a place-of-business as a residence.

Mendelson Joe is opinionated and completely uncompromising, and yet remains funny and stimulating. When you emerge from his studio into the hard winter light you are dizzy and drained by the effort of keeping up with his pragmatic idealism. He is a self-taught *everything*, and has no time for my linear values of learning about things and practising them in order to improve — he just *does* it. He paints, he plays his guitar, he writes letters to friends and newspapers. When he creates something, a painting or a song, he looks at it, sees that it is good, and goes on to something else.

For M. Joe, life isn't a matter of *motion*, but of *being*. He exists, rock-like, in the center of his interests and his as-yet-unrewarded work, just doing what he likes to do. A "dropped pebble," I call him, a Concentric Thinker, as the ripples of his art and opinions radiate out into the world. And he laughs at me.

. . .

A thin overcast whitened the sky, the Harmattan winds bearing the dust of the Sahara. The paved road continued through parched yellow savanna and thorn trees, like the plains of East Africa. The scene lacked only the delicate statuary of the flat-topped acacias which give a mystical cast to the Serengeti. Hornbills, large black and white birds with long ivory-colored bills, flew by in their curious rhythm: a few wingbeats, a dip, a few more wingbeats, another dip. Slow-moving lizards, about ten inches long and bright lime-green and yellow, crossed the road in front of me. They must have been poisonous, and therefore without fear of predators, because I had to steer around them as they moved with the same royal invulnerability displayed by the porcupines in Quebec.

I used to wonder why I saw so many smashed porcupines on the roads of Quebec on my early–morning bike rides, until one day I witnessed the reason. With the sun just rising above the Laurentian pines, I wheeled around a corner and saw a porcupine (from the French — "pig with spines") waddling across the road, its grizzled quills carried flat along its back and sides. A car approached from the other direction, but, fortunately, saw the animal and stopped in front of it. The porcupine didn't change its pace or direction, but as the car turned to go around it, raised its quills and turned its back to the car, rotating to keep the quills pointed straight at the chrome bumper of the giant predator. Then, as the car drove off, the fat pincushion lowered its quills and waddled away into the woods. After thousands of years of perfect defence, the pig-with-spines has yet to learn that it is *not* invulnerable to two tons of speeding steel. The green–and–yellow lizards of Northern Cameroon had the same lesson to learn; the road was regularly splattered with lime–green roadkill.

The land became increasingly desolate, no houses, and often the grass had been burned away to black devastation. The humming of my wheels over the pavement seemed to change its frequency, and I looked down to see that my front tire was bulging against the road. 'Maybe just low on air,' I hoped, but it soon began to feel unmistakably spongy. Another flat. My light mood immediately darkened — was *punctured*, you might say — and I pulled over to change the tube. The others caught up as I worked at the side of the road, and Leonard stayed back with me. I put the wheel back together and we rode another mile, then it went flat again. Bad words were spoken.

By the time we were back on the road, the Harmattan had come up with the heat of the day, and we fought a fierce headwind for the last few miles. Finally a tall rocky hill appeared on our left, the only prominence on the featureless savanna. We had arrived at the *Campement de Waza*, the game park lodge.

David grumbled a bit over the expense — fifty dollars a room — but it was certainly worth it. The round-topped hill was studded with circular white huts under thatched roofs, plumbing that worked, a swimming pool, a bar and restaurant on the terrace, lunch of vegetable soup, tomato and tuna salad, bottled water, and — *mirabile dictu* — ICE CREAM!

My notebook put it best: "hardly to be borne!" After nearly a week without a shower, that alone was worth the price of admission, never mind being able to wash my clothes, enjoy a few lunchtime luxuries, swim in the cool water of the pool and lay in the sun, then take an afternoon nap in a soft bed. At sunset I returned to the terrace for a Scotch on ice, and trained my binoculars on a pair of Crowned Cranes, who fed in the swampy waterhole beside the hill. Even through the glasses they were just slender silhouettes, but I could make out the fanned tiara atop their heads, the source of their name. I took another sip of whiskey and scanned the plains, feeling well rewarded for my sufferings.

Only one thing darkened this idyll, and we discovered the fatal flaw during dinner. We luxuriated over chicken with cream of leek sauce and rice, and drank about ten liters of *eau filtré*, while we discussed the amazing number of lizards which inhabited our rooms, crawling on the walls, the floors, and the screens. We laughed over how *fat* these lizards were, for in other parts of Cameroon the lizards had been lean and sleek. But the ones at Waza were all chubby, even bloated-looking, as they dragged themselves around the rooms. No one could suggest a reason for their obesity, but there was one.

Suddenly we all began to twitch, breathing little curses as we slapped at our arms and legs, then started scratching. *Mosquitoes!* Swarms of them filled the air, even in the dining room, and as we retreated in horror I noticed that the outside of the screen door was covered in a mass of insects. The boggy lake that supported the Crowned Cranes was also a prolific breeding ground for mosquitoes, and when night fell they came looking for blood.

We opened and closed the door of our room as quickly as we could, but the air was already alive with flying things.

"Well, now we know why the lizards are so fat," said Leonard, clawing at his legs, "They're nearly as well-fed as the mosquitoes!"

I started swatting, while Leonard, our electrical engineer, decided to see if the non-functioning air conditioner could be made to work. A few sparks shot out of the motor as he fiddled with a screwdriver, and then it came to life with a roar. It was as ineffectual as all the other air conditioners we'd encountered, but at least the fan stirred the air around.

Just as we were settling into our beds for the night, there was a knock at the door and a voice called out, "Hello? Are you guys awake?" It was Annie.

"Yeah, hello. What's up?" said David.

"Um ... Can you help us?" she called through the door.

"What's the problem?"

"Well, we ... we left our windows open when we were at dinner, and ... and somehow the light was on too ... and well, now our room is full of bugs ... and the air conditioner doesn't work either."

"So what do you want *me* to do?" he asked.

"Well, um ... maybe you could talk to the people here. See, if ... you know ... we could get another room, or something. It's really awful."

With a sigh, David got up again, and he and Leonard went to see what they could do. Fifteen minutes later they were back, Leonard shaking his head. "Man, it's really *bad* over there. *Millions* of bugs, sweltering hot, and poor Elsa's just huddled under a sheet. Not moving, not talking. We couldn't get them another room, or fix the air conditioner, but we got them some bug spray. I think they're in for a miserable night."

I hunted down a few more mosquitoes, smashed them on the wall, cheered the lizards on — "Move your big butts and eat bugs!" — then turned out the light. That night the bugs got fat, the lizards got fatter, and those of us lower down the food chain lost a bit of blood.

· · ·

Had we been the tiniest bit prescient, we might have taken some of those lizards with us the following day, when we traveled on to Ndiguina, which means: "Place where big bugs will eat you all night." I think. Ndiguina was only ten miles from Waza, but the idea was to avoid the extortionate rates of the *Campement* for a second night, and to get a jump on the next day's seventy-mile ride, the longest yet, with possible headwinds and drifting sand.

The day began with a drive through the game park, bouncing over the bush tracks in the box of a Daihatsu truck which David had arranged to hire. I had been looking forward to this game drive for the whole trip, remembering the excitement of animal-spotting from my previous year's visit to East Africa. David had warned me that I might be disappointed at the much smaller scale of Waza, but as I stood in the back of the truck, holding tight to the frame rail behind the cab, I felt the old thrill of the bush.

Through my binoculars I watched giraffes and elephants browse among the groves of red acacia, and giant ostriches stalking the savanna. Warthogs scurried for cover, their tails up like antennae; families of lithe little Thomson's Gazelles bounded away like rabbits, and a few jackals loped off at our approach. The striking Secretary Bird, the only bird of prey which hunts on foot, searched out snakes and rodents in the dry grass, while overhead the hawks and vultures circled on the rising thermals.

As abundant water gives richness to life, so too it brings color, as in the deep tones of the rainforests in southern Cameroon. But in the north, where lack of water drained life from the earth, the landscape became colorless, the grass pale and limp, the trees gray and dessicated. This contrast was evident in people's clothing as well: bright floral prints in the south, plain light-colored robes in the north. Even the sky was drained of blue by the Harmattan dust, so the atmosphere in the game park was wild and bleak. The gray earth was cratered by elephant footprints, giant impressions left in the rainy season and now fossilized in the hard soil like dinosaur tracks.

When we completed our four-hour circuit of the park, I told David that I was certainly not disappointed by all this, but when he was out of earshot, paying off the guide, Elsa complained she thought the drive had been too long. Like a few of the group I'd traveled with in East Africa, the idea of looking at wild animals seemed exciting to Elsa, but the novelty wore off quickly. It never did for me; I loved the expectant watchfulness, standing in the open box of the truck and holding onto a topframe bar against the jolting road, peering intently at the grass and trees. Then the reward — a hint of motion, a solid shape, a glimpse of life in the wild.

· · ·

In the late afternoon we cycled on to Ndiguina, where a brief gauntlet of mud walls interrupted the dead-flat savanna of the Chad Basin. Smiling, ragged children surrounded us as we stopped in the village, and one pleasant-faced little boy kept reciting "Guinness is good for you." He intoned it like a radio announcer, which was probably where he'd learned it, for it was the only English he knew. While the children danced around us happily, staring at us and our bicycles, we smiled and spoke to them in English and French, but they only laughed in response. The little boy repeated his invocation.

And then it got dark, and we discovered that we had no place to stay. David managed to negotiate our most rustic accommodations yet: a mud-plastered shed, perhaps eight feet by twelve. The interior was small, hot, gravel-floored, airless, and very dark. It was also very crowded once we'd squeezed in our bicycles and five bodies. The door and one tiny window were both on the same wall, and covered by white cloth, so that kept out the air. But not the bugs. I tried to read by the kerosene lantern, but had to blow it out when David complained about the smell and Elsa that it was attracting bugs. Then I tried the flashlight on my shoulder, but gave that up when the beam of light filled with flying things.

The swampy lowlands surrounding Ndiguina were perfect mosquito havens, and for once the metaphor "clouds of insects" was entirely apt. I had to bury myself in the sleeping bag and *pagne*, but soon I was sweating and twitching in my shroud. Any patch of exposed flesh became a target, so I couldn't move, and I could barely breathe beneath the *pagne*. Even then, the constant whining of hungry insects around my swaddled head was nearly as maddening as the bites. Somewhere in my panniers I carried some bug repellent, but I knew there was no point covering myself in that greasy, smelly stuff — it never seemed to impress African bugs.

Dripping with sweat, I crept outside and sat against the wall, my *pagne* over my head like a shawl. It felt good to breathe again, and the stars were brilliant in the moonless sky. However, the voracious wildlife soon drove me back inside, under the sticky sleeping bag with the cloth around my head. It was one of the longest nights of my life, and I saw every hour of it go by — waking from a shallow, sweaty doze and pulling the Casio up to my face to push the button and illuminate it: 10:27... 11:16 ... 0:21 ... 1:13 ... 2:34 ... 3:12 ... 4:23

I was on my bike and out of there by 5:30, before the sky was even light, pedaling through the darkness and scratching furiously. My self-pity had turned to sympathy for those who had to *live* in Ndiguina, but all I could think to do was leave a handful of pens in the shed for the children, hoping the "Guinness is good for you" boy would get one.

By the light of the stars and a fingernail moon I could just make out the road. A line of salmon and gray light spread from the east, and gradually the landscape became visible. A few pied crows flew by me in the twilight, and beyond them stretched the savanna, dotted by trees. The sun gilded the top of the reeds and grasses beside the road, and stretches of water reflected the pale sky. These patches of wetland were the remnants of the rainy-season floodplain which extended around Lake Chad, and supported an abundance of birdlife. A sudden rustle in the long grass triggered a rising wave of weavers, thousands of them squeaking upward in a ragged cloud. Their wings were caught in the rising sun like a strobe-flash, holding their flight in slow motion. Egrets and herons lumbered into the air and landed heavily in a shallow pond; a flock of ibis, with their slender down-turned bills, arrowed overhead. Hawks and vultures began their morning reconnaissance, while a flight of black and white storks came to rest among the reeds. The red ball on the horizon rose a little higher, and turned to gold.

A few other people were out already. Men stood in the water up to their waists, bare-chested and muscular as they hauled in nets of small silver fish. Boats drifted through the reeds, fishermen laying their paddles across the gunwales and taking up a bamboo pole. At the roadside villages children sold black curls of smoked fish, and some of them called out *"Nasarra"* as I passed, pronounced with a harsh rolling "r."

Although water was plentiful, little grew except grass and thorn trees, but despite the impoverished soil a few small fields had been cleared, and women walked to them balancing great wooden-handled picks on their heads. Men even helped with the fieldwork, and once I saw an incredible sight — a man and a woman working *together.*

By mid–morning I had covered the sixty miles to Maltam, where we'd agreed to meet, and settled in the shade by a boarded-up shop. This northern neck of Cameroon was barely ten miles wide, and Maltam marked the intersection of the north–south highway with a main route running east-west from Nigeria to Chad. Thus Maltam was merely a few mean shops and chophouses clustered around a base for the military, to keep their eyes, and guns, on this traffic. Soldiers blanketed the area like their army-ant namesakes, pouring in and out of the barracks and descending on everyone who traveled through Maltam. Blue-shirted *gendarmes* wandered among the khaki uniforms like workers among the drones, but I never minded the policemen quite as much as the soldiers. Perhaps because, at least in principle, those uniforms ought to mean different things. In Africa, though, the distinction between police and military was often blurred.

After a while a *gendarme* strolled by my resting place, had a polite look at my passport, then left me alone. I was lucky. Every vehicle was stopped and searched thoroughly, and when David and the others arrived they were held up for half an hour while their possessions were dissected. Annie was obliged to assemble her folding backpack so the soldiers could see what all those aluminum struts were for, and they were strangely curious about Leonard's postcards (of Cameroon!), and wondered where he'd bought his *History of Cameroon* (in Bamenda).

After all that, the mood was low as we gathered at a chophouse and stretched out on the benches beneath a threadbare arbor. We bought a few bottles of soda from a massive lady, then settled into an uneasy quiet, no one suggesting our next move. A Black-faced Vervet monkey, chained to one of the vines, climbed aimlessly up and down David's bike. I tried to coax it into posing on the saddle — for a Bicycle Africa poster, I told David — but it wouldn't sit still. It was restless, tied down, and wanted to be moving. I knew the feeling.

The plan had been to stay in Maltam, but there were too many soldiers, too many trucks, and no real town at all. The thought of another night like Ndiguina was not thrilling to me, and I hoped the others felt the same. Only twenty more miles would put us in Kousseri, a proper town, and right across the river from N'djamena, in Chad, where we would catch our flights out. Out — the power of that word!

Two soldiers sat in the corner working through a row of beer bottles. I'd noticed them staring at us, especially Leonard, and eventually I was drawn into conversation with them. "I am from Canada, my friends are from *les Etats-Unis*. Yes, *him* also. He is from California. Yes, he was born there. Yes, there are many *noirs* in *Amerique*. No, he doesn't know his ethnic group."

The soldiers looked at me in beery wonderment, that a black man wouldn't know his ethnic group, always the most important social division to Africans — one's tribe, one's extended family. One of the abiding problems facing African nationalism is the difficulty in convincing people to pledge their allegiance to their *nation* rather than to their tribe. Nearly thirty years after independence, Cameroon, like all African countries, was still rigidly divided into *peoples*. Tribal conflicts within a country were responsible for most of the violence, the bloody *coups d'état*, and even wholesale genocide, as in Uganda, Burundi, and Rwanda, where tens of thousands were massacred for being in the "wrong" tribe. Then the "wrong" tribe gained power, and massacred tens of thousands of *them*.

On the Togo–Ghana tour David was assisted by an American girl who had been a Peace corps volunteer in neighboring Benin, where one local tribe had enslaved another for centuries — ended only by a Marxist revolution in the 1960s. People of the dominant tribe had told her that white Americans were *right* to look down on black Americans — those former slaves had all come from that *other* tribe, who were only *good* for slaves. People of *their* tribe, they assured her, would never have been taken.

So when I told the soldier in the fat lady's chophouse in Maltam that Leonard didn't know his ethnic group, he burst out in shock, *"Il ne connait pas?"* He doesn't know?

"Non," I said, *"Il ne connait pas,"* and I started to explain that tribal origins weren't so important to North Americans, but then another level of my brain began thinking deeper, of *barrios*, ghettos, and reservations, and I stopped myself. To the soldiers I rationalized weakly "It doesn't mean the same thing," but to myself I thought about it more. In traditional African life, your tribe said *everything* about you, and a stranger would "know" you by those signs, know about your village, your people, and your ways, in the same way an Englishman "knows" a stranger by his accent, or a North American "knows" a stranger by his profession. In Europe "where were you born?"; in America "what do you do?"; in Africa "what is your tribe?"

But for three WASPs, one black American, and David the JAM (Jewish American Masochist, as we christened him one night), the problem was what to do now. "Doesn't look like there's anywhere to stay here," I ventured, and this comment was received with noncommittal mumbles and grunts. Then to David, "Kousseri's only about eighteen miles away; what's it like there?" He said that yes, Kousseri was more of a town, and we could probably do better there than the "rustic accommodations" Maltam was sure to provide, Ndiguina–style.

"So then." I looked around at this apathetic group sprawled across the benches, and asked if anyone wanted to, like, go there. It seemed everyone did, but was somehow reluctant to say so, but eventually we agreed to wait until the midday heat abated, then go for Kousseri. Fine, that's settled, I thought, and fiddled with an unread page of Aristotle until 2:00 came along, time passing as slowly as it had the previous night.

While I stood outside the arbor where the bikes were parked, pushing the *Ethics* back into its slot in my pannier and putting on my gloves and helmet, I heard the fat lady talking to David. She was complaining that I'd taken a picture of her monkey and hadn't paid her. As I pushed my bike toward the road, I heard David say that she'd been there when I took the photo, she should have said something then. When I straddled the bar and shoved onto the highway, slipping my feet into the pedals and rolling away, I heard her complaining voice rising and falling, then fading behind me.

The eighteen miles to Kousseri took me through an uninhabited stretch of the Chad Plain, both sides of the road a flat vista of grass and thorns. Yellow baboons crossed the pavement in twos and threes, scurrying away when a car or truck sped by. The drivers who had finally escaped the soldiers of Maltam, no doubt after the payment of a heavy "dash," seemed especially urgent and reckless, hurtling their ancient cars and overloaded trucks down the highway at white-knuckle speeds (meaning that I had the white knuckles). A sign warned of a unique hazard — a yellow triangle enclosed the silhouette of an elephant, indicating "elephant crossing."

I looked up at an unfamiliar sound, a distant roar in the sky, and saw a big silver jet descending to N'djamena. So close. The previous day I had mentioned to Leonard how long it had been since I'd even heard an airplane, and now the muffled roar of this one struck me with the same sense of unfamiliarity as Ontario licence plates do when I've been away too long.

Either the crazy chief or the chief crazy.
Guave.

african nightmares

Kousseri welcomed me with "open arms" — rifle-toting soldiers at a roadblock. A bus waited beside me, the driver dozing over the wheel while he awaited his release. The sign atop his bus provided us both with an appropriate overview: *Tout passe. La vie continue.* Everything passes. Life goes on. Another bit of "bus wisdom," and its opposite is equally true: Everything goes on. Life passes.

Kousseri was a town of powdery dust and corrugated metal which had grown on the banks of the Logone River, the border with Chad. The river's presence brought color to life again, and I wheeled into town along a road bordered with bushy green trees, past a multi-colored roadside market and a chaotic bus park, then went to find a hotel before the others arrived. Shouts of *"nasaara!"* followed me down the street.

L'Hôtel Kousseri Moderne obliged us to enact a small charade: The manager would not permit two men or two women to share a room, and it was also less expensive for mixed couples, so we switched bicycles and moved into the rooms as two couples and a single, then changed when the manager was out of sight.

After a look at the dining room, we decided to explore other options, but after searching through the dark streets of Kousseri we ended up eating at another hotel anyway — actually *the* other hotel. We hadn't taken our flashlights, thinking Kousseri was a city and would surely have streetlights, but the streets were visible only by feeble starlight, a few lighted windows, or a passing car. We walked uneasily through the soft dust, picking our way between the shadows of houses and fenced yards.

Over a dinner of chicken and fries, David told us about the last time he'd visited Kousseri, when the N'djamena airport, right across the river in Chad, had been bombed by a rebel airstrike. A possible reason for Kousseri's blackout (other than "it has been seized"): When you live next door to a military target, you try not to be mistaken for that target.

L'Hôtel Kousseri Moderne lived up to its name by means of plumbing, electricity, and air conditioning, all more-or-less functioning, though the air conditioner made more noise than coolness. David and I shared a room with only one double bed, but any squeamishness we might once have felt was long dissolved. Two heterosexual adults of the same gender learn to sleep in a straight motionless line on the farthest edge of the bed, and to tune out the other's snoring.

• • •

With only a border to cross — only — we slept late the following morning, though late for us was 6:45. We packed up and rode our bikes to a restaurant near the market and bus park, waving off a few "*nasaara*"s along the way. While we sat over our omelettes and Nescafés, an unusually fashionable young man approached our table, wearing Rayban knockoffs and trendy acid-washed jacket and jeans. Our smiles froze as he pulled a badge from his acid-washed pocket (a fancy-clothed plainclothes cop) and demanded our papers. While he carefully examined each passport and asked us all the usual questions, we mumbled some jokes about "Kousseri Vice" and "the Spycatcher."

Even David, usually so circumspect around authority, became a little belligerent with the sharp-dressed undercover *gendarme's* interrogations. When the cop finally left us, he muttered after him, "No promotion for you today, huh?" The acid-washed back walked on out the door without seeming to flinch, but I'd hate to think a vengeful *gendarme* had any part in what happened later.

While we waited for David at the post office, I noticed a group of children playing across the road, and decided to clear out my remaining stock of Bic retractables. The pens were scratched and worn from bouncing around in my pack, but the bright colors remained, and I had enough for all of the children. I called them over and presented one to each of them, and they went mad with delight, running around screaming with joy, waving the pens in the air, drawing on their arms and legs, and hanging the pens from their collars, their pockets, or their waists, like holsters.

We followed the Logone River to the bridge, passing through a stretch of dusty, windblown, garbage-strewn slums — a hell-hole even worse than Kumba, the original hell-hole. Nameless things smoldered, the stench of excrement stung my nostrils, goats nosed through heaps of refuse spilling across the road, and dirty and abandoned-looking children wailed from tumbledown doorways.

Only the river smiled behind it all, a wide stretch of calm water where women bent over their washing, though even its banks were fouled and rubbish-strewn. When I mentioned that this was the most squalid scene we'd encountered yet, Annie responded, "I don't know, I thought it was kind of nice by the river, all the women doing their laundry along the shore." Not the response you might expect from a modern, liberated woman.

Our *first* three-mile ride to the bridge didn't even get us out of Cameroon. The soldier in charge of the lowered barrier insisted we had to have an *exit* visa. Many countries require you to produce a visa in order to *enter*, but I'd never heard of needing a separate visa to *leave*. David asked the soldier, with surprise in his voice, *"C'est necessaire?"* and the stern soldier answered, with indignation: *"C'est absolument necessaire!"*

Had we been more "sophisticated" travelers, once again we might have smoothed our way by the distribution of a little *largesse*, but we still hadn't learned the African doublespeak: When I say I want *this*, I'm really saying I want *that*. I'm asking for your papers, but I really want some money. David was well aware of this layered mode of communication, but refused to conform to such a system. In Ghana, where the officers came right out and asked you "And what have you brought for *me* today?" David would simply answer: "I'll pretend I didn't hear that." I couldn't blame him for resisting, but a little "dash" might have lubricated the wheels of hassle that day.

However, the rest of us being geometric thinkers facing a different order of reality, we took the soldier at his word and turned around to go back to Kousseri. After much searching and asking, we finally located the *Emigration* office, but my heart sank when I saw the lineup outside — thirty people sitting under the overhanging roof, waiting with that incredible African patience. Biding their time; cooling their heels; waiting. No one moved; no one spoke; they looked as if they might have been sitting there, in suspended animation, for *days*. Boys strolled by offering trays of oranges, peanuts, and cigarettes, and one held up a stack of plastic-wrapped blouses, but no one even looked at them. They hardly even noticed *us* — the most popular crowd-pleasers in all Cameroon — just glanced up for a moment, then returned to that inner place where they could simply *be* until it was time to *do*.

The office door was open, so we went in and stood before a bald man leafing through a stack of papers, and wearing the usual leisure-suit uniform of the functionary. He looked up for a moment, and David explained what we needed. The functionary took our passports, piled them on the desk beside him, told us to wait outside, then went back to his sheaf of papers.

And we waited. For two long hours, like one of those passage-of-time sequences in a movie, where the camera blurs in and out on the characters standing, then sitting, then pacing, then sitting again, we waited. A nervous knot grew in my stomach; we only had one day now. If we missed the next day's flight there wouldn't be another for a whole week.

A middle-aged Frenchman drove up to the *Emigration* office in a Peugeot, handed in his passport, then joined us waiting outside. He was well-suited and prosperous-looking, a businessman or civil servant, and exchanged a few comments with David and me on the frustrations of African bureaucracy. He warned us that Chad would be much worse. He wasn't wrong.

Not one of the locals had approached the office or been summoned. Perhaps they had no papers, or were waiting for some special permit to emerge from the bureaucratic maw, but I felt a little uneasy, not for the first time, that we foreigners were getting some attention at least, while these people just waited, ignored. At the bank back in Bamenda David and I had submitted our traveler's cheques and been told to join the waiting throng in the corner. It had looked as though we were in for a long wait, but in a few minutes our names were called, and we had to push our way through the crowd to get to the front and receive our money. Yet there had been no protests, no dirty looks; it was accepted that the whites would be served first. And this in black Africa, almost thirty years after independence. In many parts of West Africa, if there's no soldier to ride up front in the buses, the white person does. And as George Packer wrote in *The Village Of Waiting*, you can't really protest — not only because you don't. mind escaping a tedious lineup, but because making a scene in the *Emigration* office is not necessarily the way to change social attitudes in a foreign country. But in Kousseri it happened again. When our two hours had ticked by we were called up to receive our passports, newly decorated in red ink, while the locals still sat there, dozing against the wall.

Finally armed with that precious stamp, we followed the depressing river back to the bridge. This time we weren't even stopped on the Cameroon side. A boy came out of the hut, raised the barricade, and we pedaled onto the one-lane bridge over the Logone, our very own Rubicon.

Chad's entry in the *Britannica* yearbook for 1987: "Form of Government: military regime with no political parties or legislative bodies. Civil war has raged more or less constantly since 1969."

And it had been a nasty one. Libya was Chad's unfriendly neighbor to the north, and had involved itself heavily in Chad's affairs, fighting an undeclared war with France for paternal control of the country. The northern rebels were backed by Libyan troops and arms, while the south was backed by France, and as many as five different private armies vied for internal control. Thousands of civilians had been massacred in the capital, N'djamena — the other end of that little bridge we were crossing.

Literacy rate 17%. One doctor per 47,640 people, only *ninety-four* in the whole country. Life expectancy: male 43.4 years, female 46.6. Fewer than half as many people as Cameroon, but more than twice as many soldiers. We were welcomed to Chad by a phalanx of those soldiers, whose automatic weapons directed us to a collection of tin huts squatting in the roadside dust. In one of them our passports were scrutinized, then we were directed to another hut to fill out some forms. Questions in French seemed to come at us from all sides, from soldiers, police, and civil servants, some in uniform and some not, so that we couldn't tell who was "official" and who was just *curious*. David and I did our best to answer them all, including the inevitable questions about Leonard.

Sent on to a third hut, we filled out yet another series of forms, these ones even demanding such sensitive data as our mothers' maiden names. This officer had a smattering of English, which was helpful, though he nervously hovered over every detail on our forms, concerned that everything be properly "in the French language." The first hitch arose when we were asked to provide a photograph to accompany our forms; Elsa had none. The officer was plainly distressed about that, but after much discussion he finally agreed to let her through without it. Another officer accompanied us to our bikes, our panniers were given a perfunctory search, then we found ourselves standing alone by the road. I saw the middle-aged Frenchman we'd met earlier engaged in an arm-waving argument with a functionary, who waved papers at him in return, but no one seemed to be paying any attention to us for the moment.

"You think we can go?" I said to David.

He shook his head. "I doubt it."

We decided to try anyway, and pushed our bikes up to the road, but that was as far as we got. A fat leisure-suit ran out of another hut and hauled us back again. This hut was like a carnival kiosk, with a single raised shutter open to the road. The square window was filled by a crowd of men wearing robes and untidy rag-heads, some of them with tribal scarification marks carved into their cheeks, and the combination of faces and costumes resembled a bizarre puppet show. The fat leisure-suit took his place in their midst, faced us across the counter, and demanded the papers for our bicycles.

The five of us looked at each other. Papers for our bicycles? I tried to explain that these were our own bikes, brought from our homes in the U.S. and Canada, that they would be returning with us, and that there was no such thing as papers for bicycles. Now the functionary became a little agitated, and waved a carnet in front of me — the permit to allow a car to be imported. I pointed out that this carnet was for a *car*, not a bicycle, but he still insisted we had to have one. I explained that I had visited many countries with my bicycle, and crossed many borders, but had never needed any "papers" for it, and again, that there was no such thing. *"Ça n'existe pas."* The knot in my stomach was growing again.

I sensed uncertainty in the functionary's manner, and could tell that he was unsure of his ground. He'd probably never had to deal with bicycle-riding tourists before, but he was determined to cover himself. Perhaps he believed me, but in a rubber-stamp military regime the blame would fall heavily if he was wrong, and he couldn't take that chance.

A muttered conference ensued among the puppets, while David whispered to me that he wished he could take a photograph of this crew. Then Mr. Leisure Suit held out his hand and demanded our passports. The knot tightened. As we passed them over, he told us we would have to accompany him into N'djamena to have this straightened out. He held the trump card — our passports — and there was nothing else we could do.

A dusty blue Peugeot pulled up beside us, and a leisure-suited arm waved us to go. As we pushed off, David suggested we not hurry too much; maybe this guy would lose patience with us and give up. So we all pedaled at Elsa's pace. Through a filter of nervousness and irritation I was vaguely aware of a landscape of brown dust and mud houses baking in the midday heat. People walked slowly along the road beside us, dressed in pale colorless clothes. The Peugeot drove in front for a while, then stopped to wait, and drove on ahead once more. Still we maintained our leisurely pace, all of us silent and uneasy, as we slowly covered the five miles into N'djamena. I memorized the Peugeot's licence number, TCB 2394 P, but as it turned out, everyone had the same idea.

Sparse, drooping trees bordered the streets as we entered the city's outskirts. Small motorcycles and mopeds buzzed by, among a few rundown cars and trucks. The foul-smelling ditches at the roadside were covered with concrete slabs, and everything wore a brown skin of dust. Many of the buildings were bombed-out, their lower floors vacant caves, and nearly all of the walls were bullet-spattered. Just as it had been difficult to picture that cluster of huts at the bridge as an international border, it was difficult to picture N'djamena as a nation's capital.

David pulled up at the roadside and pointed across the street. "There's the U.S. Embassy, do you think I should go in?" Yes, we agreed, good idea, let's get some help if we can. David left his bike with us and went into the gatehouse of the embassy. The high walls, iron gates, and armed guards were a dark contrast to the quiet openness of the American embassy in Yaoundé. Leonard pointed out that the Chad soldiers guarding the entrance carried Soviet automatic weapons.

The Peugeot stopped in front of us, and the functionary's arm reached out the window and waved us on. I shook my head repeatedly, until finally he got out of the car and walked back to me. He said that we should just follow him to the *Douanes* office and get this taken care of, but again I shook my head. I told him we'd check with the embassy first, and continued the argument begun at the puppet-kiosk. Heartened by the American presence, I was irate and more confident, and went into a flight of French I wouldn't have thought myself capable of, telling him to give our passports back and leave us alone, there was no such thing as a carnet for bicycles — *ça n'existe pas!* — all delivered with a perfect Gallic sweep of my arms. My shining hour *en français*, after years of effort, even had its effect on the functionary. He was visibly nervous now, sweat breaking on his wrinkled forehead as he pointed to his watch and half-heartedly tried to wave us on. Again I frowned and shook my head, and he went back to his car and drove away, still holding the winning hand — our passports.

David returned and told us the embassy staff were at lunch, but we felt we'd made our statement to the functionary at least, and set off to find the office of the *Douanes*. Outside the humble tin–roofed building we searched among the many dusty blue Peugeots until we found the one — TCB 2394 P — then went to find our man.

Accompanied by a tall, dignified superior, the functionary was more nervous than we were now, sweat pouring down his face as he tried to explain the situation to his boss. Unperturbed, the tall man asked us a few questions about our journey, then looked at our bikes and asked if we were carrying any *armes*. I saw Leonard conceal a smile as I assured the man that our packs contained no bombs or automatic weapons, and, satisfied, he handed back our passports and turned away. The functionary followed a step behind him, walking quickly to match his boss's long stride, still afraid he was going to be blamed for *something*.

We headed across town to find the Hotel Hirondelle, which was listed in *Africa On A Shoestring* as N'djamena's "only cheap hotel." Some claim to fame. As we searched through a network of narrow, reeking dirt streets behind the market, I finally began to overdose on squalor. I knew there was a French Novotel in town, and as we stood before the seedy, collapsing structure of the Hirondelle, breathing the stench of excrement and garbage and surrounded by a mob of ragged and dirty children, I quietly suggested that I'd be glad to pay for my own room if anyone else wanted to treat themselves to the Novotel. No one spoke up, and I wasn't yet desperate enough to go off on my own, so into the Hirondelle we went.

The whole ground floor was taken up by a dingy bar, furnished with benches and wobbly tables. The "rooms" were on the roof, five or six concrete cubes and a shared "bathroom" — a filthy sink draining onto the floor and a toilet encrusted with I-don't-want-to-know. It was my turn for the single room, and I scraped open the door to a cell of turquoise plaster riddled with cracks and soiled by years of grime, a slab of sponge on the bed covered by a stained cloth, and a rusty ceiling fan. Unaccountably, the fan actually worked. The Hirondelle, N'djamena's "only cheap hotel," was the lowest point we'd reached in our rustic accommodations, but hopefully it was the last one. And at least they had cold drinks.

We learned the banks were only open from 7:00 until 11:00 in the morning, so we couldn't exchange any money. David had a little Chad currency, but the rest of us were now paupers. The airline offices maintained similarly strange hours, but re-opened at 4:00 in the afternoon, so David and I set out to confirm everyone's flights for the next day. Two young men opened the UTA office nearly on time, and I was relieved to learn that I still had a seat on the plane, as did Leonard and Elsa. David and Annie were flying out on Air Afrique to Mali, Annie to meet a friend and travel in that country, while David would cycle down to Abidjan to meet his next tour group.

Remembering the morning's hassle over exit visas, I asked the UTA man if we needed anything like that to leave Chad. *"Oui,"* he said, we needed a stamp from the *Gendarmerie*. But then he shook his head, saying that he didn't think we could get it in time. Again I felt a sinking heart and rising fear. Only one flight a week, we *must not* miss it! So off we sped to the *Gendarmerie*.

Along the way I noticed that N'djamena was not only a military capital, it was a military city. The majority of its citizens seemed to be dressed in olive drab and camouflage, and carried weapons as they filed in and out of the huge barracks. Jeeps and army trucks made up most of the traffic among the bombed-out buildings and bullet-sprayed walls. N'djamena's atmosphere was tense and uneasy, and so was I.

In the large compound which housed the police and immigration offices, we were shuffled around until at last we were directed to a blue leisure-suited man who reclined in a canvas chair, relaxing in the shade outside his office. He took our passports, glanced through them, then stood and led the way to another office, marked *Immigration Et Emigration*, but it was closed. Then he announced he would keep our passports, and we could return the following morning and reclaim them with the necessary stamp. David and I were doubtful, and argued that we would need them with us to deal with banks, hotels, the U.S. Embassy, and — thinking of our experiences in Cameroon — what about the soldiers and police wanting to see our papers? He shrugged off our protests, insisting we would have *"pas de problèmes"* with the soldiers and police, and that it was better if he kept the passports. The nightmare was growing, and I was becoming frantic. I held my hand out to him, insisting, as politely as I could, that he give us the passports, but, just as politely, he refused.

When he turned to leave, we followed like children, pushing our bikes and refusing to go without our passports. *"S'il vous plait, m'sieur,"* I entreated as we walked along, but he only held them closer to his chest. He stopped before another functionary, and again we insisted on our need for the passports. The other man conceded that we would need our passports to check into a hotel, and, hoping that might sway the situation, we didn't mention that we had already been accepted at "N'djamena's only cheap hotel."

We followed on, across the road to a military compound, where a crowd of soldiers lounged under the trees, drinking and laughing. He led us to the office of the *Bureau des Etrangers*, the Office of Foreigners, where another functionary sat behind a desk piled in forms with photographs stapled to them, like the ones we'd filled out at the border. This leisure-suit insisted that we would also have to see *him* before we could leave the country, and fill out another set of these forms, with our entire histories down to our mothers' maiden names, plus present him with another photograph. Unbelievable. At least, though, we managed to reclaim our passports, and raced straight back to the U.S. Embassy. Help!

David went through the gate of the embassy while I waited outside with the bikes, feeling scared. So much uncertainty and hassle, strangers walking away with our passports, the threat of not being able to make the next day's flight, the terror of spending a week in N'djamena waiting for another one — all of it was adding up to a genuine physical *malaise*, and I felt shaky and unwell. I sat on the curb, staring at the ground, and felt the icy tingling of fever play on my nerves and blur my vision.

David emerged at last, having learned nothing except that the attaché would look into it for us and let us know in the morning. I stood up with difficulty, feeling weak, dizzy, and nauseous, and mounted my bicycle. In one of those feverish hallucinations, I felt as if I were twenty feet above the ground, but I managed to pedal unsteadily back to the Hirondelle. Even *that* mean sanctuary was welcome, and I collapsed onto the foam slab of my bed. But then suddenly I was up again, stumbling across the roof to the "bathroom."

My body exploded violently, vomit and diarrhea one after the other, and then again. I shuddered and retched painfully, shaking my head between bouts like a punch-drunk fighter. Weak and shivering, I crept back to my room and sprawled across the bed again, groaning in despair, then a few minutes later had to make another run across the roof.

A powerful thirst arose in the wake of the repeated purges, and I had soon drunk the rest of my clean water, then spent the last few Chad francs I'd borrowed from David on two bottles of soda. When I went down to the bar to get them, the colors and lights seemed to blare at me, while sounds were muffled and brassy. My head throbbed and my legs were weak as I mounted the stairs to my roof–top cell. Then I felt my insides rising up, and ran to the toilet yet again. Unable even to get over the target, I had to "shoot" from a distance, though I couldn't believe there was anything left to come out. There seemed to be plenty. After the cramping agony of dry heaves, I stumbled, bent over, back to the cell and collapsed once again. I didn't even bother with clothes any more, just lay beneath my *pagne* and wrapped it around my waist when I had to go.

I lost all sense of time in this abject misery, and wished now that I'd just gone ahead on my own and checked into the Novotel. My despair left me without hope, and now I was afraid I'd be trapped in N'djamena for some indeterminate time — maybe even more than a week — to recover from this illness. If that happened, I decided, I was going to move to a real hotel, and suffer in some semblance of human dignity, if not luxury.

David knocked on my door when everyone was leaving for dinner, but I couldn't face the thought of food, and just asked him to bring me something to drink. He felt my forehead and pronounced it hot and feverish — no surprise to me — and asked if I wanted him to see about a doctor. "Not yet," I said, and after they left I dozed for awhile, lost in dark dreams until a knock on the door brought me to dizzy consciousness.

It was David again, back from dinner and calling to see how I was. Annie and Leonard were there too, and they'd brought me a wonderful gift: a blender-type concoction made of orange juice, cream, and ice called a *frappé*. It was just what the doctor would have ordered, had there been a doctor, and I drank it down. My thirst was uncanny, far greater than I had known when we'd been lost between Tourou and Mozogo, and as the night wore on my throat was dry and aching, mouth foul-tasting and gummy.

I heard music and voices from the downstairs bar, and schemed how I might buy another soda. I had some American cash, and my hopes elevated for a moment thinking I could change some of it. But I sighed with the futility of that idea, knowing they'd have no idea of the rate. I dug in my wallet and found some stamps — maybe I could trade them for a drink? But no, they were from Cameroon, no use in Chad. There was only the water from that disgusting sink, probably straight from the Logone River, and though my desperate thirst was tempted, my uneasy stomach was not.

That night was even longer than Ndiguina had been, as I sweated and writhed through brief stretches of oblivion, alternating with dashes across the roof, then back to lay in the darkness, tortured by thirst and painful cramps. The bar went silent after a time, and the three fan-blades circled slowly in the sweltering air, like the restless spinning of feverish thoughts.

Curious eyes in Hama Koussou.

parisian dreams

As the slow fade from darkness to light began, the eerie wail of the *muezzins* sounded from the the twin minarets of a great mosque. From high above N'djamena, the call to prayer went out over the corrugated-metal rooftops. A gray light began to creep across my ceiling; stains and cracks came into focus on the wall; the turquoise fan kept whirling. I heard brooms and buckets downstairs, an early-morning cleanup crew in the bar, and, desperately thirsty, I began to scheme for a bottle of orange soda. I stood up experimentally, to see how I felt — not too bad, weak but not dizzy — and walked downstairs.

One of the sweepers opened the cooler and handed me a Fanta, and I told him I'd pay for it later. He didn't seem to care, and a few minutes later I was back with the empty bottle to ask for another. When I heard the other cyclists stirring I borrowed some Chad francs from David to pay my "bar bill," and as we carried our bags down and loaded the bikes, everyone was quiet, sharing my worry of what this day would bring.

The first thing we needed was money. We knew that if we *were* allowed to leave, there'd be a departure tax to pay. When the bank was open we lined up at the foreign exchange counter, waiting for *it* to open; the other tellers were already busy in their glass cages. When our teller finally showed up, he couldn't get the door open. Everyone in the bank tried to open it; one by one they came to the door and tried each of their keys, while we watched with impatient disbelief. Finally someone did get it open, but by then the *teller* had disappeared, perhaps gone home to get his keys.

We had no time for WAWA that day; it was down to a matter of hours, and we still had to run the gauntlet of police and immigration, not to mention any last-minute surprises at the airport. While we waited, I looked at the counter on the other side of the glass and saw a key resting innocently between the rows of rubber stamps.

When I pointed it out to the neighboring teller, he shook his head and pointed to his money box, indicating that now they were searching for the key to the foreign exchange cashbox. Finally David gave up and went down the street to another bank with some of our American money, and came riding back with his thumb raised — success.

We raced off to the embassy to see if the attaché had learned anything helpful. The rest of us waited with the bikes while David went inside, but the attaché's answer was inconclusive. He didn't *think* we needed any special permits; he *thought* we just had to go to the airport. Not very reassuring, but we decided to run with it — fingers crossed and adrenalin flowing. Outside the airport a roadblock of heavily-armed soldiers stopped us with a gruff "*Où allez-vous?*" but when I explained that we were catching a flight, they let us pass. Dozens of armed soldiers guarded the terminal as well, and they immediately began ordering us around: You can't bring bicycles in here; you must park them on the other side of building.

But we're flying out with them.

You must take them outside.

But ...

We started disassembling the bikes. Then another soldier came along and ordered us *inside*, to the area of the terminal we'd been headed for in the first place. Idle soldiers stood around and watched us take the bikes apart and pack them up. Two friendly locals, made conspicuous by *not* wearing uniforms, approached me and began asking for something, but I couldn't understand what they wanted. By their energetic miming and sound effects I finally understood — they wanted *tire patches*. Mine had all been used up during that frenzied ride out of Tourou, but I sent them to Leonard, who gave them the few he had left.

Obstacle one: we checked in for the flight. Obstacle two: our bikes were taken by the baggage handlers. Obstacle three: Passport control. We paid our departure tax, the passports were stamped, and there was no mention of exit visas.

What??!! After all that panic, all those people hassling us the previous afternoon, the guy running off with our passports — all of it had been *meaningless*? I couldn't believe it. I was glad, but I couldn't believe it.

Obstacle four: Security. The metal detector beeped as I walked through the doorframe. I took the coins out of my pocket. *Beep.* I took off my belt. *Beep.* My watch. *Beep.* Even my "Beyond War" button. *Beep.* Finally they ran the hand-held detector over me. Nothing, until they got to my shoes. *Beep.* The metal soles in my cycling shoes. I took them off and walked through the archway.

Obstacle five: The shakedown. Two plain-clothed guys pointed me into a curtained alcove, and began a strange interrogation, all about *money.* Did I have any French francs? *Non.* Was I sure? *Oui.* The clumsy interrogation went around and around the same subject, until I finally decided this was a good time not to speak French, and just stared at them dumbly until they gave up.

David and Annie still had a couple of hours to wait for their Air Afrique flight, so I said goodbye to them across the barrier. After all this time, it was a strange farewell; we'd shared a month of adventures and hardships, but we'd been companions without really being friends. Unlike other partings I've faced at journey's end, with former strangers now become true *friends*, this time there was no emotion, no embraces. Just a business-like handshake with David, and Annie's always warm smile. Good luck on your travels etc.

Leonard and I sat in the plastic seats in the departure lounge, breathing a little easier now. "Looks like we might actually make it," I said, but he shook his head. "I want to hear that landing gear retract!"

We heard Elsa's voice rising from the curtained alcove. "I don't *understand* you!" and Leonard turned to me and smiled. Then she came striding out, frowning, and sat beside us. Through the window we watched four fighter jets descend and land. French *Mirages*, Leonard told us. They were all painted in desert camouflage, and carried a battery of heavy missiles underneath the fuselage.

Then the big silver and blue DC-10 was on the ground, and we were walking across the tarmac to identify our luggage, for security reasons. I am haunted by that scene forever, because only a few months later a bomb exploded on that very flight, maybe even that very plane, thirty thousand feet above the desert in Niger. All 171 people on board were killed, though again, little was heard in the western media.

The engines whined, then roared, and the huge plane taxied down the runway and lifted into the air. A vibrating whirr shook the floor beneath my feet, and the landing gear retracted with a solid, satisfying *thunk.*

. . .

Paris by night. The taxi glides through the glittering, crowded, opulent, beautiful City of Light. No other city affects me like Paris, and Paris has never affected me as now. I've never been happier to get *anywhere* in my life, even home. Aristotle says "Every rational activity aims at some end or good" — cycling in Cameroon had not been entirely rational, but Paris is the end, and it is good. My eyes flicker hungrily over everything: so many cars, so many buildings, so many lights. Shop windows full of things people can buy, streets full of people who can buy them. What an appetite I have! And my appetite is not for food, but for this unrestrained, bustling *life.*

Across the Seine, rippling lights on the dark water. The loom of Notre Dame. Through the narrow streets of the Ile de la Cité, the river again, and into St. Germain. Cars and lights and buildings and shop windows. Then the Rue des Beaux-Arts, and the little hotel. The porter takes my bicycle away — I won't see it for a week and I don't want to. The tiny elevator whisks me upward, then I'm walking faster, around the circular atrium to the room. Then she's in my arms and I squeeze until she laughs. "You made it."

I sit on a chair among the luxuriant furnishings and plush curtains, shaking my head at everything. "I made it."

Every luxury is a precious blessing to me, and I take *nothing* for granted. Hot baths, clean sheets, napkins and silverware, reading lights, newspapers, bookstores, oysters, sidewalk cafés, art galleries and museums. I turn my head to watch elegant cars whisper by, taxis with only one or two passengers, buses crowded but not crammed. I look at the faces, pleased with their confidence, their purposefulness, their pride. No one stares at me; no one calls names after me. No roadblocks or security checks. I can take a photograph of *anything* I want to, even walk down the street talking into my tape recorder if I feel like it. This is *freedom!* This is life.

I stare eagerly into the shop windows, wanting to buy some meaningless trifle. Even the cheap souvenir shops on the Rue de Rivoli seem wonderful to me; I feel the urge to buy some tacky plastic Eiffel Tower or Sorbonne T-shirt — just because I *can*. And all the "c" words: cornflakes, cognac, capuccino, chocolate, champagne — all the small luxuries seem so wondrous, to think about as much as to consume. Not food for the stomach, but food for the *spirit*.

And all of these responses add up to the one big "c" word: civilization. Our Western world is so easy to criticize, our fixation on so-called materialism so easily satirized, but those same critics always have their own material fixations, however they clothe them in spiritual raiment. "Beware the streak of crass Western materialism in development," said the pope. If *spiritualism* rules the richest corporation in the world, and builds the very-material cathedrals which dominate our towns from Rome to Kumbo, what of the people whose money pays for these monuments? Food and shelter are certainly material things, and most of the faithful addressed by the Pope during his African visit were farmers prying their yams from the parched earth — if the rains allowed them to grow anything at all. Tell *them* about materialism.

Spirits in the material world, indeed we are. Our bodies, the imperfect vehicles of movement and action, are material. The tools of the artist, musical instruments, paint and canvas, pen and paper, these are material things, but they are only raw materials waiting to be imbued with the spirit's visions. Like all things, they are no better and no worse than what is done with them. To a farmer in Northern Cameroon, a Stradivarius might represent a good stock of kindling, for a fire to be lighted with pages torn from the *Ethics*. A piece of painted canvas might help to patch the roof, regardless of the "Vincent" scrawled in the corner.

> Oh, Theo, why should I change myself? I used to be very passive and soft-hearted, and quiet; I am so no more, but it is true I am no longer a child. These days are full of anguish that can neither be diverted nor stilled. I tell you, if one wants to be active, one must not be afraid of failures, one must not be afraid of making mistakes. Many people think they will become good by doing no harm; that's a lie, and you yourself used to call it a lie. It leads to stagnation, to mediocrity.
>
> You will say that I have no success. I don't care; to conquer or be conquered, in any case one is in emotion and action — and those are nearer being the same thing than appears. Just dash something down if you see a blank canvas staring at you with a certain imbecility. You do not know how para-

lyzing it is, that staring of a blank canvas which says to the painter: You don't know anything. Many painters are afraid of the blank canvas, but the blank canvas is afraid of the real passionate painter who dares.

Life too always turns towards a man an infinitely vacant, discouraging, hopeless blank side on which nothing is written. But however vacant and vain and dead life may present itself, the man of faith, of energy, of warmth, who knows something, does not let himself be led astray. He steps in, and acts, and builds up — *ruins*, they call it. Let them talk, those cold theologians!

Yes Vincent. Like the sign on the Cameroon bus: "Let Them Say." We will take our material world and scratch the marks of our spirits upon it. We will take the masks that people put on us — the masks of White Man, Infidel, or Failure — and under those masks we will wear yet another, one of our own design. We will ride out into the world wearing those masks, knowing that when we reach our secret destinations, alone with Life, we can take them off.

Have a drink. Get naked and party.

Here's to rational activity and the blank canvas.

Here's to us all.

Look Out! Elephant Crossing . . .

Checking the map with the Chief of Tchevi.

602